GOING TO KINDERGARTEN

A Year with an Outstanding Teacher

Donald J. Richgels

A ScarecrowEducation Book

The Scarecrow Press, Inc.
Lanham, Maryland, and Oxford
2003

A SCARECROWEDUCATION BOOK

Published in the United States of America
by Scarecrow Press, Inc.
A Member of the Rowman & Littlefield Publishing Group
4720 Boston Way, Lanham, Maryland 20706
www.scarecroweducation.com

PO Box 317
Oxford
OX2 9RU, UK

British Library Cataloguing in Publication Information Available

Library of Congress Cataloging-in-Publication Data

Richgels, Donald J., 1949–
Going to kindergarten : a year with an outstanding teacher / Donald J. Richgels.
p. cm.
"A ScarecrowEducation book."
Includes bibliographical references
ISBN 0-8108-4532-6 (hardcover : alk. paper)—ISBN 0-8108-4533-4 (pbk. : alk. paper)
1. Kindergarten—Case studies. 2. Kindergarten teachers—Case studies. 1. Title.
LB1169 .R48 2003
372.21 '8—dc21

2002011392

∞™ The paper used in this publication meets the minimum requirements of American National Standard for Information Sciences—Permanence of Paper for Printed Library Materials, ANSI/NISO Z39.48-1992.
Manufactured in the United States of America.

[redacted]

To my parents, Daniel and Rita Richgels

CONTENTS

FIGURE LIST

PREFACE

The observations reported here were made during one school year, when I attended kindergarten for 164 of the 175 school days. I assisted the teacher, Mrs. Poremba, on many occasions and conversed regularly with the students, but the greatest amount of my time was spent making field notes. I gathered samples of the students' writing, including all their sign-in sheets and Words for Today sheets and most of their journal writing, Writing Center writing, incidental writing (as in play centers), and special occasion writing (such as their making signs to advocate environmental awareness). Much of their reading and being read to was recorded.

Two audio tape recorders were operating most of the time, one with a remote microphone that hung from the ceiling and one with an internal microphone. Sometimes, one was used as back-up to the other, as when I recorded whole-class activities. At other times, the two devices were placed to record the talk of two different small groups or pairs. I videotaped forty-three hours of classroom activities.

From almost the first day, the kindergartners were unaffected by my placing an audio tape recorder in their midst, my constant note taking, and my frequent videotaping. On rare occasions, students intentionally spoke into a microphone, remarked that I was videotaping, or expressed curiosity about what I was writing, but even then they quickly reverted to their usual state of being oblivious to my recording or note taking. More common was their approaching me with a question or including me in conversation even while I had the video camera on my shoulder! I was accepted by the students as another teacher in their classroom.

I dated all artifacts, word processed all field notes (from seven spiral-bound notebooks of handwritten notes), and transcribed selected audiotapes and videotapes. The word processed notes allowed for cross referencing and easy searching for specific events, repeated routines, and specific students' appearances in the database. I did all audio- and videotape transcribing myself. Most students' voices became familiar to me. Still, some voices are more distinctive than others; their contributions to classroom talk were more easily identified by name. Whenever I was unsure of a speaker's identity, I identified that child only as a kindergartner.

The students' parents gave me permission to use their children's names. To establish some measure of anonymity, I have eliminated mentions of students' last names (except in chapter 1, where Derek, from the previous year's class, is given a fictitious last name) and of the calendar years in which the study occurred.

As with any narrative, this one is selective. I had to decide what I would be able to share of my 164-day experience. Even now I have not listened to all the audiotapes; selections that appear here are based on what emerged from early analyses as important classroom routines. I also wanted to represent unique events and to include all the students. There was never a subset of kindergartners who were to be focus subjects. I believe that my account captures important particulars, as well as the general feel, of life in Mrs. Poremba's kindergarten. No doubt, there are important omissions. Responsibility for those and for any errors is mine.

Donald J. Richgels

ACKNOWLEDGMENTS

First thanks are due to Nicole, Elizabeth, Zack, Deborah, Jeff, Eric C., Eric D., Jason, Lauren, Sarah, Kaitlynn, Tara J., Tara G., Erin, Ian, Elise, Nathan, Ben, Alyssa, Freddy, Mayra, Meagan, and Steven, who shared their kindergarten year with me.

I cannot adequately thank Mrs. Poremba and Mrs. Roloff. They were completely welcoming. Not once did I feel that their behavior or words were different from what they would have been without my presence. To invite me, as Mrs. Poremba did, to be present virtually all the time testified to a self-confidence and generosity, without which this project would have been impossible. I feel extremely fortunate and grateful for that. I appreciate, as well, Mrs. Poremba's writing the reflections that end chapters 3 through 9.

I am grateful to the kindergartners' parents for their generosity and trust (a byproduct of their trust in Mrs. Poremba). They were kind to me in many ways beyond giving me permission to study their children's kindergarten; when they visited the classroom, they were always completely accepting of my presence and friendly to me.

The principal and staff at Mrs. Poremba's school were so welcoming and helpful! I was greeted warmly each morning, unremarked when leading a group of kindergartners through the halls, and given generous access to the copy machine!

My work was supported by research grants from the College of Education at Northern Illinois University and by a sabbatical from Northern Illinois University. The editorial and production staffs at Scarecrow Press have turned my narrative into this book; I especially appreciate the contributions of Cindy Tursman, Amos Guinan, Debra Schepp, Leslie Evans, and Beth Easter. My colleague, Carl Tomlinson, encouraged me through years of data collection, data analysis, and writing. My family, Mary, Ted, and Carrie, supported my work in countless ways, not least of which was their listening to my frequent dinner table talk about—as they came to call them—those wonderful kindergartners.

Thank you, all.

1

TELL ME WHAT YOUR THINKING IS ABOUT THAT.

This is the story of going to kindergarten as I wish it could be for all children. Kindergarten is a unique year, a special opportunity in the lives of our children. Every parent of a child of six years or older knows the momentous, scary, exciting, full-of-possibilities, sad, happy moment of leaving a son or daughter in the care of the child's kindergarten teacher. Regardless of how much nursery school or day care or Head Start a child has had before kindergarten, this is different.

IT'S SCARY.

It is the beginning of mandatory education, of formal education, of turning over control of one's child's life to strangers. As one parent I know put it, "Short of enrolling Stephanie in a private school, which I can't afford, or doing homeschooling, which I could never handle, I have no choice about how this huge undertaking is going to go. I can't just take her out if I don't like it. She has to go; I have to leave her there. She has to do what they say. I have to go along with it. It's scary."

I teach college students to be teachers. When I talk to them about their roles and responsibilities, I give them the flip side of this parent's lament. "You are taking on a position not greatly esteemed or rewarded by our society but one of great power. You will be one of the most important people in the still young lives of your children. For nine months, one-eighth of the life of a kindergartner, you will be in charge of much of what the children do from day to day. You must not abuse that power; you should use that power carefully and wisely to support your students' best and fullest growth, their emotional, physical, social, and intellectual growth." This side of the coin is also scary.

I have a simple wish for all kindergartners and their parents. May the person taking on the scarily powerful role of kindergarten teacher in their lives, into whose care both parent and child are usually not freely giving themselves, be like Mrs. Poremba. The purpose of this book is to explain and demonstrate this simple wish. It takes explaining and demonstrating, because as simple as it is to state this wish, it is one that hides profound truths, truths about the nature of childhood, the course of growth, and the processes of learning and teaching.

WHAT MAKES A GOOD TEACHER?

Friends who know that I was once a first-grade teacher and that I now teach prospective and current preschool, kindergarten, and elementary school teachers, often ask me—especially when their children are beginning their formal schooling or when their children have a poor teacher— "What makes a good teacher?" I ask myself that same question as I begin each semester in my role as preparer of a new crop of teachers, all of whom I want to be good teachers.

It's easy to make a list of ingredients: understanding of children; caring about children; knowledge of what must be taught; skill at communicating; skill at managing large numbers of children and the intricate demands of the school district's scheduling and subject matter expectations; patience; optimism; empathy; ability to encourage, cajole, inspire; and immunity to embarrassment. This thing about embarrassment is captured in what my daughter's acting teacher described as the actor's necessary "willingness to play the fool." Teachers must sometimes be good actors, willing to assume roles that might embarrass them in life outside the classroom.

It's easy to make a list of the ingredients that make a good teacher, but when I first encountered Mrs. Poremba, I knew she was the best teacher I had ever known and that I didn't precisely know why. I knew that if I could come to know why and if I could share that knowledge with my students, I would be doing a great service to them and their future students. This book is the story of my attempt to gain that knowledge and to share it with those who care about what happens to the five and six year olds to whom we say, "Now you must begin your formal education. Starting now, you must turn yourselves over to us, your teachers."

My first encounter with Mrs. Poremba was over a several-month period when she and her students' parents made her students available to me as subjects in a study I was conducting of kindergartners' spelling and word-reading abilities. I spent a few days in her classroom so that her students and I could get to know one another. Then I spent many short periods in her classroom waiting for the least inconvenient times to take individual students to a testing room where I asked them to spell and read simple words as part of my research project. What I saw in Mrs. Poremba's classroom greatly impressed me. Here, students were learning every day: learning about dinosaurs and chickens and rocks, about how to get along with one another, about what reading and writing are and what they are used for and how to do them; learning how to sing and paint and draw; learning how to use numbers for important everyday tasks such as counting the number of days since the school year had started. Mrs. Poremba told me early on that her first goal is that every student enjoy school and leave for home each day looking forward to coming back to kindergarten the next day. Everyday I saw evidence of her achieving that goal. Her students were totally at ease with being kindergartners, confident about their abilities, and happy to be in school.

CAN A DINOSAUR JUMP?

One activity that impressed me during my first days in Mrs. Poremba's class was the Sign-In Routine. The first thing students did each day was to go to their assigned places at one of several long tables at one end of the room and write their names on a sign-in sheet at that table. They received practice writing their names as part of this procedure, which was also functional—the sign-in sheets served for attendance taking. But there was more. At the top of each day's sign-in sheet, Mrs. Poremba wrote a question for students to answer in writing next to their names. I will write more about the Sign-In Routine in chapter 4. For now, I want to tell about what happened on February 24 of my second year with Mrs. Poremba, when I was visiting her class weekly and tape recording interactions such as the following one. On this day the question at the top of the sign-in sheet was *Can a dinosaur jump?* (see figure 1.1).

Typically, as children signed in, they relied on one another, taught one another, questioned one another, and explained to one another the nature of their tasks and their attempts at performing the tasks. They worked in small groups, usually with their table mates but also with others nearby. For example, Bill said, "I know what the sentence says, Josh."

"What?" asked Josh.

"'Do dinosaurs jump?'"

"No—It says, '*Can* a dinosaur jump?'"

The kindergartners also worked individually; they put their signatures on the sheet and wrote personal answers to the sign-in question. These efforts served as the basis for personal interactions with Mrs. Poremba

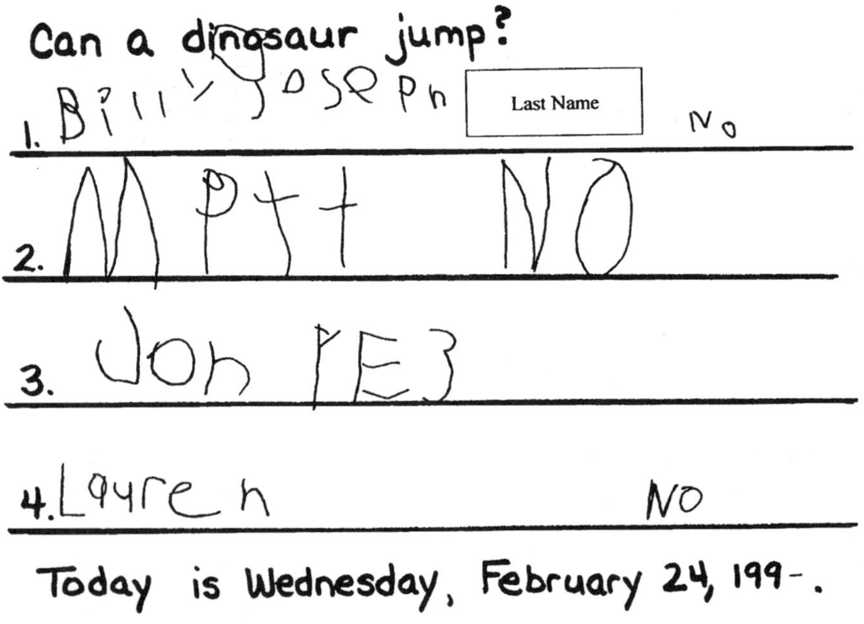

Figure 1.1. Can a Dinosaur Jump?

and for whole-class discussions of the children's reading and writing work and of the topic of the sign-in question.

On this same February day, Mrs. Poremba commented as she picked up sign-in sheets and dismissed children from this activity, "Matt can go. Oh, Matt's [not the same Matt in figure 1.1] seen some jumping dinosaurs in books. Good for you. Ian says, 'No.' Lauren, you want to finish signing in? Derek Sanders. Derek, great that you are writing your last name. Good for you. Derek says, 'No.'"

KINDERGARTEN RESEARCH

Later, she encouraged the children to consult their classroom collection of dinosaur books for evidence in support of their answers to the sign-in question: "Some of you said 'Yes,' and some of you said 'No.' What could we do to find out more information about that?"

Children answered, "Look in a book," and soon they were doing what Mrs. Poremba called "kindergarten research"—"when you're trying to get more information, you need to learn something, and you decide to do things like look in books to find answers."

A few volunteers soon inspired a whole class of researchers: "We need to know if dinosaurs can jump. We need to get some ideas about that. If you're interested—oh, lots of people are interested. Bill, go on over and get some research going. Samantha, go right ahead. Kristen, go right ahead. Christina, Dana, go right ahead. Ian, go right ahead. Go right ahead, Melissa. Okay, we've got a lot of scientists over there who are going to do some research."

When Bill found some pictorial evidence, he declared, "I found one jumping!" When Samantha found similar evidence, Mrs. Poremba, anticipating a whole-class sharing session, said, "Very interesting. You might want to save this for us, Samantha. Would you just hang on to that picture? Because we need to talk about that."

Later, during that sharing session, Mrs. Poremba called on Samantha: "Samantha, want to come on up? Samantha—okay, Samantha, can you tell me your thinking about this picture?"

"Um, I think this one's jumping," said Samantha.

Bill, too, was invited to share his evidence and his thinking with the whole class. "Bill, tell me what your thinking is about that," said Mrs. Poremba.

Displaying the picture he found, Bill said, "His whole body is up in the air instead of on the ground."

This sort of evidence did not impress Mike. "They can't be jumping, I don't think. Because, like one foot's up and the other foot's down."

But Matt and Dan had an answer for this: "Well, Mike . . . *about* to jump."

Mrs. Poremba acknowledged this thinking: "Matt and Dan think they are getting, they are just about ready to jump."

Melissa said about her picture, "I think that one's jumping because its tail goes back."

Derek thought that the dinosaurs in these pictures "could be jumping . . . possible . . . or could not be, too. Could just be walking or running."

Finally, when Mrs. Poremba tried for closure, the class's decision was based on everyone's ideas. "Now if you saw on your sign-in sheet *Can a dinosaur jump?*, now that you've done some research and you've gotten some ideas, how would you answer that question now?"

Still, some children answered yes and some no. Mrs. Poremba observed that "some of you appear to have changed your mind" and suggested, "maybe you need to do a little bit more research. So we have some people who aren't convinced yet."

When one child offered, "The big dinosaurs, um, *they* can't jump," Bill voiced the final consensus: "Some can jump, and some can't jump."

TRUST

Mrs. Poremba's trust in her students is absolute. She has no doubt that they know something about a unit topic such as dinosaurs, a poem newly displayed on an easel, or a problem suddenly presented in the block corner, whether how to build a ramp there or how to determine who gets to play there.

These five and six year olds know *something*. It may not be all they need to know. In fact, it usually isn't. That's why they are in school and why they have a teacher—because they need to learn more about reading poems, more about such kindergarten study topics as chick development, more about how to build block structures, and more about how to get along with and even be friends with classmates. But what they will learn must be built on what they already know, and Mrs. Poremba's understanding of children includes the insight that what they already know may not be immediately recognizable by others, especially adults.

Children's understandings are frequently different from ours. There is a benefit for Mrs. Poremba as well as for her students in her response to this difference. Besides letting her students know that she acknowledges the legitimacy of their understandings, Mrs. Poremba, by her patience and trust, gives herself the time to discover what those understandings are. Only then can she build on them with her teaching.

ONE HUNDRED AND FOUR DAYS

Reading and writing about dinosaurs weren't the only venues for exploration and shared learning in Mrs. Poremba's classroom. Two weeks before the *Can a dinosaur jump?* episode, I witnessed a remarkable, spontaneous discussion of numbers. I will write more about number and calendar routines in chapter 6. For now, I want to tell just a bit of what happened on that February 11th.

Part of the routine for starting the day was keeping track of how many days of school there had been so far. Each day the children added another drinking straw to a set of three cups attached to a bulletin board. The rightmost cup was the yellow *ones* cup, the middle one was the blue *tens* cup, and the leftmost one was the red *hundreds* cup. When ten straws accumulated in the *ones* cup, Mrs. Poremba would put a rubber band around them and move this bundle of ten to the *tens* cup.

This was the 104th day of kindergarten. So four days earlier had been a momentous day. On that one hundredth day of kindergarten, the ten straws in the *ones* cup became a bundle of ten, and that bundle was the tenth bundle of ten in the *tens* cup. So those ten bundles of ten were bound together as "one great big bundle of one hundred" and moved to the *hundreds* cup.

Today, there was that great big bundle of one hundred straws filling the *hundreds* cup, on which was displayed a card with the numeral *1*. There was an empty *tens* cup, now showing the numeral *0*. And from yesterday, there were three loose straws in the *ones* cup, which showed the numeral *3*. So these numerals made the number *103*, for 103 days of kindergarten through yesterday (see figure 1.2).

Mrs. Poremba called on Mike to "give a straw cup report." He said, "The *1* stands for one big bundle, the *0* stands for zero straws, and the *3* stands for three loose straws."

"Tell me about that *0* again. What do we usually put in here, Mike?"

Mike didn't answer.

"Do you remember anything about what we usually put in here?"

"Bundles."

"Bundles. How many are usually in that bundle?"

"Ten," answered Bill.

"Oh, good, I'm glad you're thinking about that." Mrs. Poremba took the great big bundle of one hundred from its cup, and said, "Now let's talk about that one, great big, huge bundle of—"

"Ten," answered the kindergartners, accustomed all these many days since the tenth day of school, to saying "ten" after the words *bundle of.* Until four days ago on the one hundredth day, the only kind of bundle they had ever considered was an ordinary bundle of ten, never a great big bundle of one hundred.

"How many?"

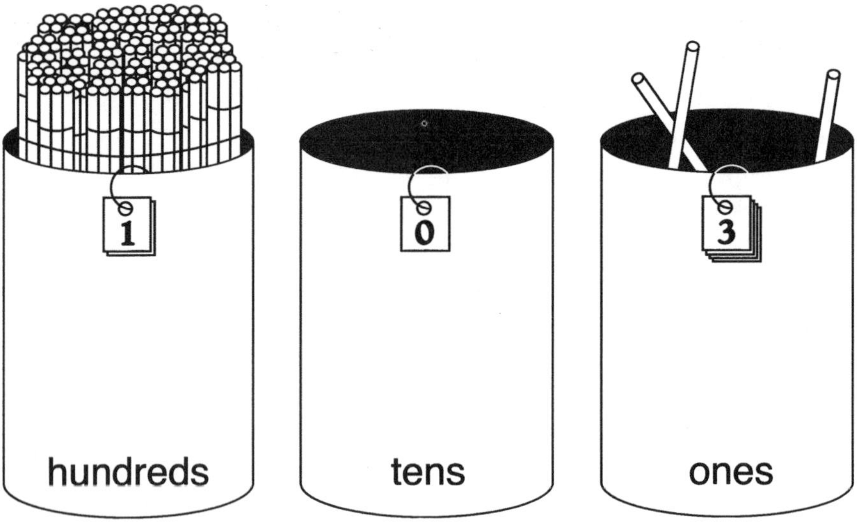

Figure 1.2. Straw cups for 103 days of school

"One hundred," said a few kindergartners, not sounding very sure of themselves.

"Maybe we need a refresher on this," said Mrs. Poremba. She removed the rubber band holding together the great big bundle of ten bundles of ten, and she invited the class to join her in counting by tens as she set each bundle of ten in her lap.

"Ten, twenty, thirty, forty, fifty, sixty, seventy, eighty, ninety, one hundred!" they said, nodding their heads with each number.

"So I'm going to take all of those bundles of ten, and I'm not going to have them be bundles of ten anymore, because I'm going to wrap them all the way around with another rubber band that holds all those bundles of ten together. So ten bundles are being put together to make one—"

And the kindergartners joined her, "—great big, huge bundle of—"

Mrs. Poremba stopped. The kindergartners stopped. And then, showing that this demonstration hadn't worked, two kindergartners said: "Ten." "Ten."

"One hundred," Mrs. Poremba quickly asserted. But she was not worried. "The more we do it, the easier it will get," she predicted.

It may have been difficult for these children, only four days into their new century of school days, to call that great big bundle a hundred, but some of them were thinking about the problems inherent in this process.

"Teacher!" Bill said. "When we get to, um—nine hundred, we're still going to be using the blue cup."

But the blue cup is the *tens* cup, not the *hundreds* cup. "Hmmm," responded Mrs. Poremba. "Anybody else have some ideas about those cups? That was interesting, Bill. Amanda?"

"But when we get nine hundred, then—" Amanda began.

"Past nine hundred!" interjected Bill.

"We're not going to be past nine hundred," asserted Melissa.

"Why, Melissa?" asked Mrs. Poremba.

"Because we can't. Because then everybody will be grown up in this school. They'll be too old to go in kindergarten."

Derek had his hand up. He shook his head in response to Melissa's explanation. Then he blurted out, "It only goes up to—there's only nine in one row of numbers."

ONE HUNDRED AND SEVENTY-EIGHT DAYS

"Okay," responded Mrs. Poremba in a quiet thoughtful voice. "I want to go back to what Melissa said." She took a small erasable board and erasable marker from beside her chair. "I'm going to write a number down on this board. And this number is going to show you how many days we'll be in kindergarten. The number I'm going to write is the *last* day of kindergarten." She wrote **178** in big numerals on the board, holding it in her lap so that the class could watch her write.

"One," said one kindergartner, in a very quiet, tentative voice as Mrs. Poremba wrote the **1**. "Seven," said this kindergartner as she wrote the **7**.

"Seventy-eight!" shouted another kindergartner as Mrs. Poremba finished the **8**. "Seventy-eight!" repeated many kindergartners.

"Seventy-eight days of—" said a kindergartner.

"Think about it," urged Mrs. Poremba.

"Because it has a one-seven-eight," said Dana who was still standing next to Mrs. Poremba. And she pointed to the three digits in order.

"No. I don't think all those days could fit in those cups!" responded a classmate. "No."

"No, they have to, because—" said another kindergartner.

But other kindergartners interrupted with more thoughts: "Seventy-eight." "Seventy hundred?" "Seven hundred? Seven hundred days?"

"Keep thinking," prodded Mrs. Poremba, looking over the top of the erasable board in her lap, her eyes and mouth set in thoughtful but expectant lines.

"Seventeen hundred."

"No. No," said Derek.

"Derek doesn't think so," commented Mrs. Poremba. "Kristen, what do you think it might be?"

"Um, I think it's—" Kristen said.

"Seventy-eight," coached a classmate.

"—seventy-eight," finished Kristen.

"Well, you know about the seventy-eight part, don't you,?" said Mrs. Poremba, pointing to the last two digits. "What about that *1* though?" she asked, pointing to the *1*. And then Dana tapped the *1* for added emphasis.

"One hundred and seven! One hundred and seven, eight!" declared Bill.

Mrs. Poremba smiled.

"No! No! No! No!" protested Derek, waving his arm.

"Is it one, seventy-eight?" asked Dana, again pointing to each digit in order.

"No! I know!" declared Derek.

"You know what—we're getting, we're doing—" Mrs. Poremba began, about to wrap things up.

But Derek couldn't contain himself any longer: "Eight. Seven and eight days of kindergarten!"

"One seventy-eight, I did," repeated Dana.

"Bill, what did you say?" asked Mrs. Poremba, wanting to return to Bill's earlier comment, the only one to include the words *one hundred*.

But Samantha interjected, "One hundred and seventy-eight."

WHERE'S THE ZERO?

"Samantha, what did you say?"

Mrs. Poremba nodded as Samantha repeated, "One hundred and seventy-eight."

"Now let's see if that fits. She said, 'One hundred,'" quoted Mrs. Poremba, pointing to the *1*, "'and seventy,'" pointing to the *7*, "'eight,'" pointing to the *8*. "What do you think?"

"Where's the zero?" asked Melissa, who is used to zeros in all the *one hundred* numbers the class has had so far: *100*, *101*, *102*, and *103*. She repeated this question three more times as her classmates continued to speculate about Mrs. Poremba's repeating of Samantha's "One hundred and seventy-eight."

Mrs. Poremba shrugged. "What do you think?"

Dana repeated her "One seventy-eight," and that was what her classmates most frequently took up. Maybe not calling that *1* "one hundred," even in the face of Samantha's and Mrs. Poremba's example, seemed best to these kindergartners, considering the lack of zeroes. Certainly no one had picked up on Samantha's answer, and when Bill responded to Melissa, he used Dana's, not Samantha's, formula. "One seventy-eight doesn't have a zero," he declared.

"Melissa, Bill said one hundred and seventy-eight doesn't have a zero," Mrs. Poremba said, inserting the word *hundred* into Bill's explanation.

"It doesn't. Bill's right," confirmed Samantha.

"I think it's one seventy-eight. Because it has a *1* and a *7* and *8*," explained Dana yet again.

"No. It can't be seventy hundred," declared Derek. "Because in a hundred and every other number that's like a hundred, it only goes up to nine."

Mrs. Poremba gave Derek a long, thoughtful look. "What did you mean, Derek? Tell me more about that."

"I mean it only goes, a hundred and two, a hundred and three, a hundred and four, a hundred and five, a hundred and six, a hundred and—" replied Derek, his body rocking forward and back with each number.

"Seven," filled in a classmate.

"—a hundred and seven, a hundred and eight, a hundred and nine!" finished Derek.

"Then what happens?" asked Mrs. Poremba.

"It goes higher than a hundred and nine," suggested Meredith.

"And then it goes like a million or something like that," answered Derek.

"Well, Meredith says it goes higher than a hundred and nine," said Mrs. Poremba.

"My mom told me that," explained Meredith.

"Your mom told you that? We'll talk more about that number as it comes, but you had a very interesting discussion."

Matt raised his hand. "Matt did you have one more thing to say about that number?" asked Mrs. Poremba.

"I think we're going to leave when that cup is all filled up and the [ones] cup is all filled up."

"Hmmm," responded Mrs. Poremba.

"That, and that, and that," said Dana, taking up Matt's idea, but including all three cups in her pointing.

"You think so?" asked Mrs. Poremba.

"But I think it's one seventy-eight," said Dana, pointing yet again at the *1*, the *7*, and then the *8* on the erasable board still in Mrs. Poremba's lap.

"That's never going to be filled up," objected Derek, perhaps reflecting on his having seen the *ones* cup emptied every time all school year that it got to the point of having ten loose straws.

"Dana, I think you might be right," replied Mrs. Poremba.

Dana giggled with delight and added, "Because it has a *1* and *7* and *8*," again pointing to each digit as she named it.

Mrs. Poremba said, "Okay. We'll do a lot more talking—Josh, what do you think? Are you clear on this? What did you think?"

"That it's one seventy-eight," answered Josh.

"One seventy-eight? One meaning 'one hundred?'" replied Mrs. Poremba. And she pointed to the digits and said, "One hundred and seventy-eight? That's actually what the number is. One hundred and seventy-eight. And we have a lot more days to talk about numbers that get this high, because that's a pretty big number."

"Teacher, you know what?" asked Mike.

"That's what I said," added Samantha.

"Yeah, that's a big one," answered Mrs. Poremba.

"Teacher," persisted Mike. "You know what?"

"Mike?"

"Um, you can't fit any more big bundles in the red cup, 'cause one bundle only fits in there."

"It would break. It would break apart," added a classmate.

"Mmmm. Good point, Mike. Mike says we can't fit any more big bundles of a hundred in that red cup. It's too filled."

"We won't. We won't anyway," asserted Samantha.

ONE BIG BUNDLE OF TEN

Mrs. Poremba then proceeded with the straw cup routine, where this discussion had begun. Dana added a straw to the *ones* cup and changed the number displayed on it to a *4*. The class read the *1* on the *hundreds* cup, the *0* on the *tens* cup, and the *4* on the *ones* cup as "one hundred and four." Then Mrs. Poremba asked what number to write on the number line which is stretched across the top of the bulletin board and on which the number for "days at school so far" is added each day. "How about if we get to our number line? We need some help up here. Christina, you want to give it a try? Listen to what Christina says and see if she agrees with your thinking."

Christina directed Mrs. Poremba: "A *1*."

"What's that *1* for? Go ahead."

"One big bundle of ten," answered Christina.

Mrs. Poremba's marker stopped.

"A *1* for one big bundle of one hundred," Christina corrected herself, and Mrs. Poremba wrote a *1*. "A zero for zero bundles, and a *4* for four loose straws," continued Christina, and Mrs. Poremba finished writing the number.

"Anybody remember that *1*?" asked Mrs. Poremba. "Is it for one, great, big, *huge* bundle of a—"

"—hundred!" finished several kindergartners together.

"Okay, where are we?" asked Mrs. Poremba about their list of things to do to start the day.

But Ronnie called out one more question about numbers: "What if we counted all the straws that we have up there?"

"All of these right here?" asked Mrs. Poremba pointing at all three straw cups, with their 104 straws.

Ronnie got up, "No. Even—" He walked to the front and took the big bundle of one hundred from its cup. "Even these bundles separated," he said as he indicated the ten bundles of ten gathered together in the big bundle of one hundred. "And these bundles separated," he continued, indicating the individual straws in each bundle of ten, all of which he had seen accumulating all school year, bundled into tens every tenth day of school and into a big bundle of ten only four school days ago.

Mrs. Poremba took the big bundle of one hundred from Ronnie and held it up before the class so that they could see the ends of all the straws. "I wonder how many we'd have if we counted all of these separated?"

"Woah!" exclaimed several children.

"A really lot!" said another kindergartner.

"And these, too," added Ronnie taking the four loose straws from the *ones* cup.

"Well, let's just think about that," said Mrs. Poremba returning the loose straws to the *ones* cup and directing the class's attention to the big bundle of one hundred. "Does anyone have an idea how many we would have if we separated these?"

"A hundred," said one kindergartner matter of factly.

"We'd have a hundred," confirmed Mrs. Poremba, nodding her head. "Remember when we made each of the bundles?"

Ronnie announced, "I can count to one hundred and seventy-five hundred!"

"I believe you!" answered Mrs. Poremba. And to the class, "That was a good discussion. Boy, you got my brain going today!"

KINDERGARTEN TALK

Perhaps most noticeable, certainly most charming, about this "good discussion" is these kindergartners' wide ranging, free wheeling exploratory talk. What would happen when there got to be nine big bundles of one hundred? How many big bundles could the *hundreds* cup hold? Would more than one big bundle be needed to record days in this year of school? What happened to the zeros in *178*? What comes after *109*? These kindergartners not only posed these questions, they freely speculated together about the answers.

But more to my purpose in sharing this "good discussion" is what it reveals about Mrs. Poremba. I have seen other kindergarten teachers do the straw cup routine. Celebrations of the one hundredth day of school are nearly as common in kindergartens nowadays as celebrations of Halloween or Valentine's Day. But I have never seen a teacher deal with the straw cup routine as Mrs. Poremba did on this 104th day of school.

The conventional wisdom is that the daily, concrete experience of dealing with these straws and bundles will inculcate an understanding of place value in our base-ten number system. But this good discussion clearly shows that children internalize such experience in different ways—different from one child to another and different from what we adults, with our mature understanding, expect. Every day for 103 days of kindergarten, these children had participated in the straw cup routine. Most had a good understanding of *tens*. Some, like Samantha, understood *hundreds*, but most seemed to be working on that. Many of them at the beginning of this good discussion wanted to call that big bundle of one hundred a bundle of ten. At the end, Christina still fell into that habit. And Ronnie either wanted to demonstrate his counting prowess or just didn't trust all this hundred talk without separately counting every straw in the big bundle of one hundred.

A teacher can hope to guide children through their experiences and toward mature understandings only by taking their lead ("leading from behind" is an educational cliche, but Mrs. Poremba really did that when she followed up on Bill's and Melissa's exchange about a theoretical 900th day of school), by letting them talk, by using what their talk reveals, and by providing supportive talk that nudges them to the next levels of understanding. Mrs. Poremba did this.

I can list the qualities of a good teacher that Mrs. Poremba revealed by her part in this good discussion:

- Faith in her children's thinking and communicating abilities.
- Patience with her students' working through their own questions and answers.
- Vision to see what those questions and answers reveal about her kindergartners' evolving understandings.
- Acceptance of her students' developing, not fully evolved, understandings.
- Confidence that although her students' developing understandings are not the same as mature understandings, they will eventually lead to mature understandings.
- Readiness to model thinking processes, elaborate on students' statements, and prod students toward next steps in their evolving understandings.
- Willingness to back off, never pushing, when students reveal that they are not yet ready for those next steps.

I would rather, however, that you see for yourself these qualities in action all year long in Mrs. Poremba's kindergarten. That is what I was able to do during one of the most enjoyable and inspiring years of my career as a student and a teacher. Rather than leaving you with a list, handing you a formula, I wish to tell the story of my going to kindergarten. My first experience of Mrs. Poremba's teaching was when I took students out of her room for my research about spelling and word reading. The next year, I visited Mrs. Poremba's kindergarten once a week. Fortunately, those weekly visits enabled me to be present for the *Can a dinosaurs jump?* episode and the 104 straws discussion. But I couldn't help wondering what I was missing during the other four school days each week. And so I asked for, and Mrs. Poremba readily agreed to, my visiting every day the year after that. This book is the story of that year.

2

THE FIRST DAY OF KINDERGARTEN

It is the first day of kindergarten, Monday, August 30.

"We have a few early customers," declares Mrs. Poremba. She invites Steven and his mother to come in and tour the classroom. Steven is a big, quiet boy, with dark red hair, an open round face, and curious eyes.

THE CLASSROOM

The classroom is a typically large kindergarten room (see figure 2.1). When you enter from the school's interior hallway, there is an alley with wood cubbies on each side and an outside door straight ahead. The cubbies have hooks for hanging coats and book bags, eye-level shelves for other belongings, and foot-level shelves for boots. The students will call these lockers though they have no doors. The left row of lockers is against the left wall of the classroom. The right row is freestanding, about five feet tall; it divides the locker area from the rest of the classroom, except for space to walk around it on both ends. The back of this freestanding row of lockers, the side facing the rest of the room, is covered with one continuous bulletin board, on which are the calendar and other displays that will be used throughout the year in opening-of-the-day routines (see figure 2.2). The

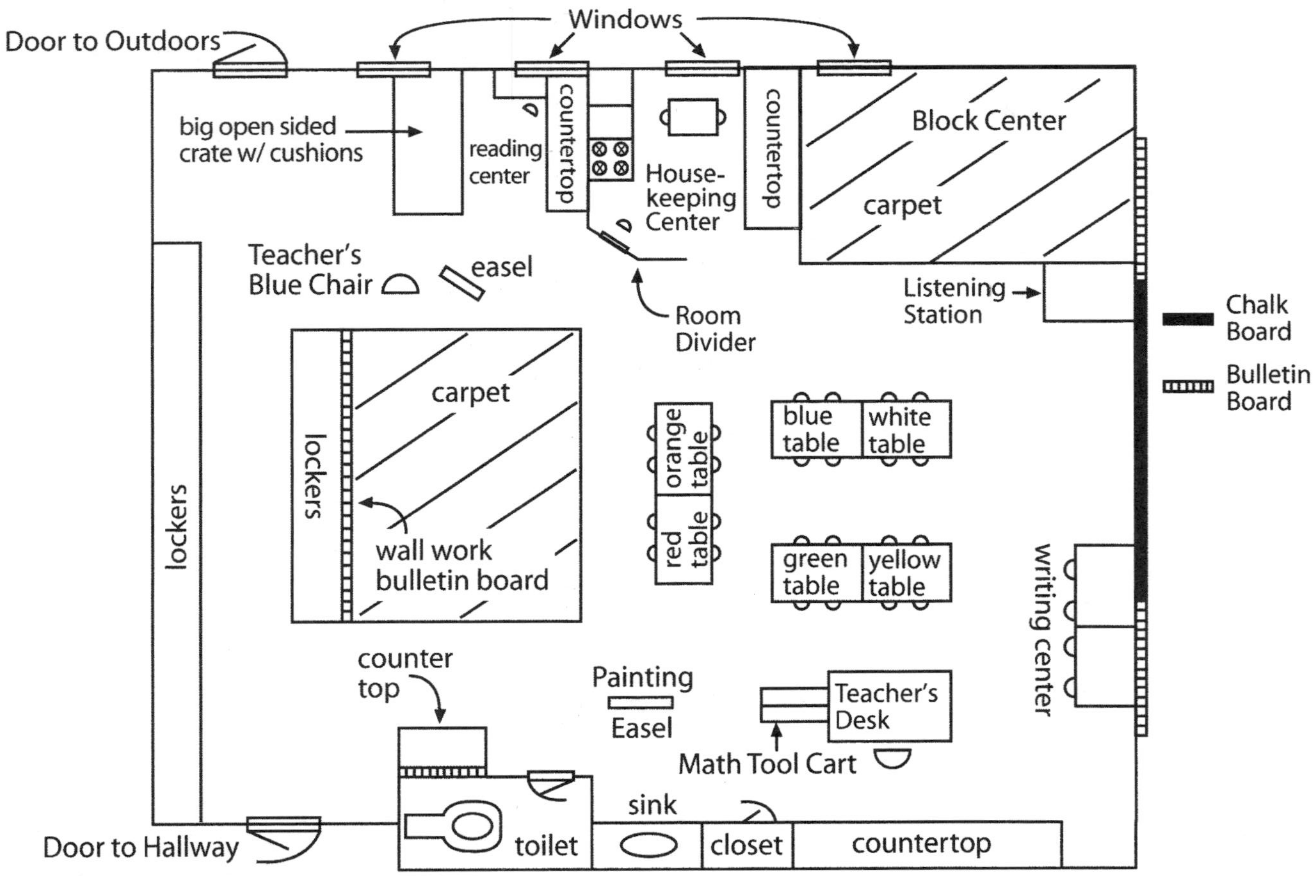

Figure 2.1. Classroom Map

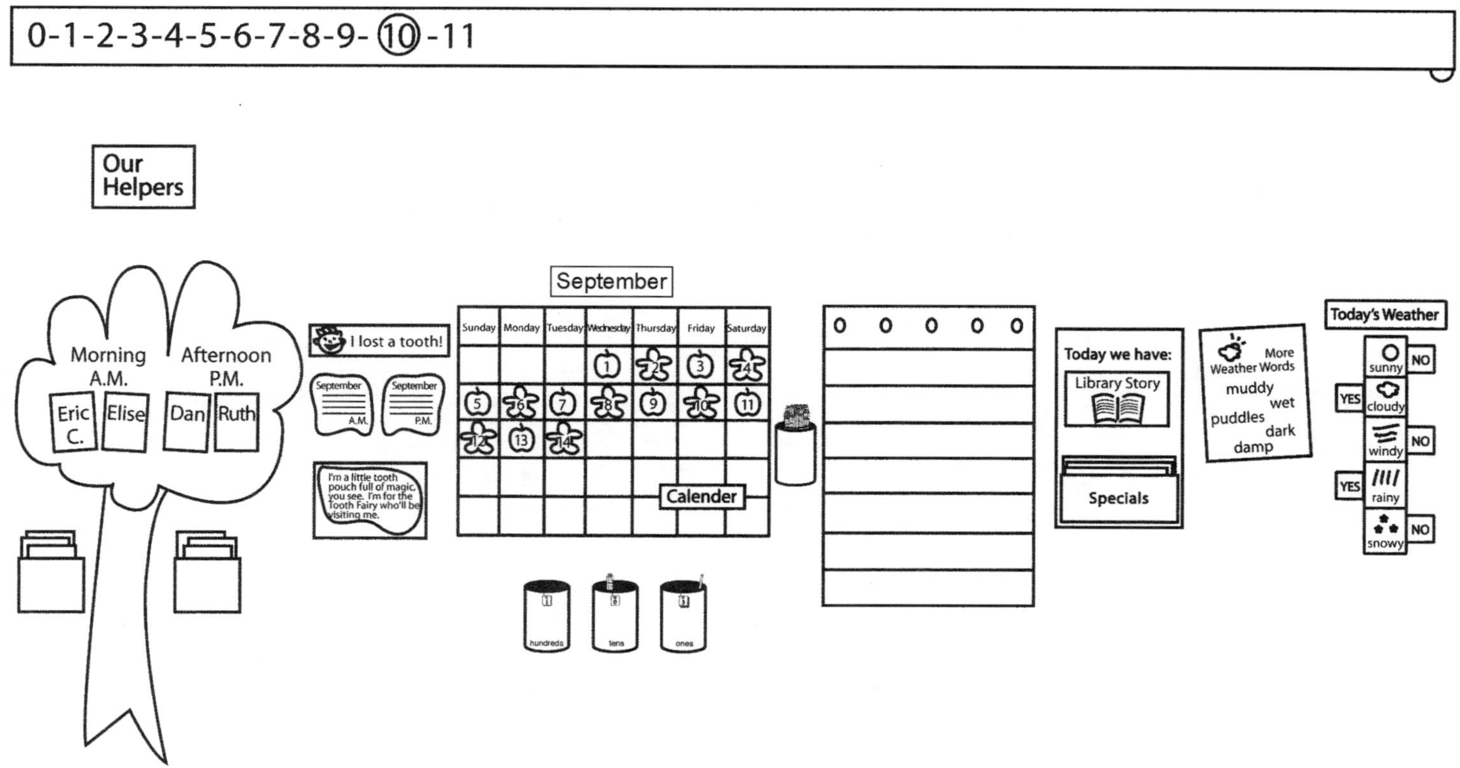
0-1-2-3-4-5-6-7-8-9-10-11
Our Helpers
Morning A.M.
Eric C.
Elise
Afternoon P.M.
Dan
Ruth
I lost a tooth!
September A.M.
September P.M.
I'm a little tooth pouch full of magic, you see. I'm for the Tooth Fairy who'll be visiting me.
September
Sunday
Monday
Tuesday
Wednesday
Thursday
Friday
Saturday
1
2
3
4
5
6
7
8
9
10
11
12
13
14
Calender
hundreds
tens
ones
Today we have:
Library Story
Specials
More Weather Words
muddy
wet
puddles
dark
damp
Today's Weather
sunny
cloudy
windy
rainy
snowy
YES
NO

Figure 2.2. Wall Work Bulletin Board

kindergartners will refer to these activities on this wall-sized bulletin board as "wall work."

With this wall work bulletin board to your left, the rest of the room stretches to the right, a wall with windows straight ahead, a wall of chalkboards framed by bulletin boards at the far-right end of the room, and a low cupboard running most of the length of the wall behind you, with a sink and the door to the toilet room also behind you, bringing us back to the corner of the room with the hallway door. The space between the wall work bulletin board and the chalkboard wall is about evenly divided between a carpeted area big enough for the whole class to gather, seated on the floor, and a tiled area holding six large tables, with chairs. These tables are arranged in a *U* shape, two tables each for the bottom and the arms of the *U*, but with walk-through spaces between the bottom and the arms of the *U*. The bottom of the *U* is toward the carpeted area, the open end of the *U* toward the chalkboard.

In the carpeted area are an easel for displaying big books and other texts, such as poems written on lined poster paper, and Mrs. Poremba's blue-painted wooden arm chair. Around the edge of the room are a Reading Center, with bookcases and a huge wooden crate open on two sides with cushions on its floor, on which kindergartners will lie down while reading; the Housekeeping Center, with kitchen props and make-believe costumes; another carpeted area in the far-right corner of the room, stocked with both wooden and pasteboard blocks (it will be called the Block Center or the Gold Carpet Area, after the color of the carpeting there); a Writing Center in the near-right corner, consisting of two side-by-side tables stocked with writing materials, two electric typewriters, and pigeonhole mailboxes for all the kindergartners; Mrs. Poremba's desk; a Math Tool Cart, whose shelves contain clear plastic bins of small plastic interlocking blocks and other math manipulatives; and a Painting Center, with back-to-back easels stocked with large tablets of newsprint, jars of tempera paint, and brushes. Posters cover available wall space, and almost every permanent object is labeled, for example, *Math Tool Cart*, *clock*, *easel*, *paper towels*.

EXPLORING

Jeff is second to arrive. He's tall, with thick, sandy-colored hair in a Prince Valiant cut. He has a confident, almost aggressive walk; he's comfortable in any space, perhaps not enough aware of other people's space. He knows Steven.

Mrs. Poremba acknowledges this. "It's nice to have a friend the very first day," she says.

As if demonstrating this, two more buddies arrive together. They are nearly the same height, both are blond, both carry book bags, and both are named Eric (I will distinguish them with their last name initials, though they were not addressed that way in Mrs. Poremba's kindergarten). Eric C. is the quieter of the two. Already he is a studious observer. Eric D. has an erect posture and open features in a square face that seems a match for his loud, husky voice. It is a voice that will soon lead the way in many a classroom discussion. Eric and Eric are next-door neighbors and attended the same preschool. They cross the room together and peek into the toilet room. They speak quietly to one another.

When Elise arrives, she joins the Erics. All three know one another. Elise has a round face; shoulder length, light brown hair; sparkling eyes; and a thin, upturned smile, the kind a child draws.

With her very first directive of the school year, Mrs. Poremba gives children choices. "If you'd like, you can look around and see which locker you'd like. You can pick any one you want," she announces. "Did you find a locker, Jeff? How about if you get your name tag and we'll put it on?"

Ian arrives, a tall, thin boy with crew-cut blond hair, small mouth, and arched eyebrows to fit his wide open eyes. Mrs. Poremba lets Ian know that she already knows him. "You must be Ian," she says. She directs him to his first job, at the same time letting him know that she considers that he knows what to do: "I see you're ready to pick out your locker."

Some parents are taking pictures; one is making a videotape. Grown-ups outnumber the kindergartners today. In addition to the parents, Mrs. Poremba, and me, there is Mrs. Poremba's full-time classroom aide, Mrs. Roloff. Her main responsibility is to help with this school's inclusion program. One student—and later in the year, a second student—is placed in Mrs. Poremba's room rather than in a special-education classroom. With Mrs. Roloff's help, this student is able to learn among typical kindergartners. Also as part of the inclusion program, Mrs. Poremba is advised by a special-education teacher and a speech teacher who visit her classroom regularly. Mrs. Roloff also helps with all the other children in Mrs. Poremba's room.

Steven's mom coaches him at the table on which name collars are spread: "You know how to spell your name, so you should be able to pick it out."

"*S-T-E-V-E-N*," spells Steven, and he finds his collar. It is a one-by-one-and-a-half-feet rectangle of orange felt with a hole in the center. When Steven puts his head through the hole, half of the rectangle drapes over his chest and the other half comes to the middle of his back. His name is written with black marker on both the front and back along with a *KP* that stands for "Kindergarten, Poremba."

Eric and Eric find a huge floor puzzle and begin putting it together on the carpeted area. "I like the way you're working on that," says Mrs. Poremba as she brings Elise over to join them. Then Tara G. also joins them (there are two Taras in Mrs. Poremba's class, so I will distinguish them, as with the two Erics, with their last name initials, though they were not addressed that way in Mrs. Poremba's kindergarten). She is a talkative, confident girl, with wide set dark eyes, dark hair, and a wide mouth that spreads into a ready smile.

Ian breaks away from his mother to examine a flannel board set up on one of the countertops. Before it is a tray of letters and shapes. Mrs. Poremba confirms the difficulty of the job Ian has chosen and lets him know that in this room children's knowledge is valued. "Sometimes it takes children to help me figure out the best way to put this one together," she says as she and Ian work on the flannel board together for a short time. As soon as she leaves him, he rejoins his mother.

Nathan is a big boy, with straight, blond hair, a round face, and usually a serious look that is betrayed by a twinkle in his eyes. He approaches me with a big smile on his face. I introduce myself and say I will be helping out in Mrs. Poremba's room this year. Nathan nods, smiles again, and says, "Oh."

"Do you like to be called 'Nathan' or 'Nate?'" I ask.

"Nathan," he replies.

Elizabeth is a small girl with short, dark hair and bangs. She seems hesitant about kindergarten, her eyes darting about the room. At the table with the name collars, she points to Erin's.

"Close!" says Mrs. Roloff. "It starts with an *E* just like this. Can you find your name? And it's long. Can you see it?"

Now Elizabeth points to her name and puts on her collar.

Other children arrive, choose lockers, find their name collars, and begin selecting activities around the room. This is half of Mrs. Poremba's morning kindergarten class. Only on this first day of school, they will go home at midmorning and be followed by the other half.

"This is a really big puzzle. Can you tell what it's going to be?" Mrs. Poremba asks Eric and Eric.

"Big Bird!" they answer and show their puzzle to two girls who are working a smaller puzzle nearby.

"When you're finished with the puzzle you have now, please put it away and come over by the blue chair," Mrs. Poremba says.

TALKING TO PARENTS

When the kindergartners have gathered at her blue chair, Mrs. Poremba says, in a soft voice, "Good morning. I want to teach you something right away today. I'll teach the way to say 'Good morning' in sign language. Just like this. Good—" Mrs. Poremba places the fingertips of her right hand at her lips and then moves that hand from her mouth to a palm-up position before her body. "—morning!" She rests her left hand in the crook of her right elbow, with her left arm horizontal before her body, and she raises her open right hand, with palm toward her body, to an upright position, like the sun rising over the horizon. "Can you try that with me?" She demonstrates again and a few kindergartners imitate her. "We'll work on that some more, but that was great."

Mrs. Poremba introduces Mrs. Roloff and leaves the children with her to play with math cubes. These are one-inch plastic cubes in many colors that snap together. The children begin making towers of these cubes while Mrs. Poremba talks to the parents at the other end of the room.

In this short time with her students' parents, Mrs. Poremba identifies herself with progressive ideas, establishes her credentials, enlists parents as partners in her teaching their children, and demonstrates her understanding of child development. She describes her education and experience. She has a bachelor's degree and a master's degree in early childhood education. She has taught kindergarten for nine years, five before her two children were born and four after they began school, leading up to this, her second year at this elementary school. "I'm thrilled to be at [this] school. This is a great place to be. I love working with the staff. We have a very supportive principal. And we have a lot of real progressive ideas going on here . . . and I'm proud to be part of that."

Mrs. Poremba tells about her weekly newsletter and other ways she will maintain school–home communications. She asks the parents to read an article she gives them, "Reading Begins with Scribbling" (Fields and Hillstead 1986). "It talks a lot about the reading–writing connection. Some of you were able to be here Tuesday evening for our Parent Night, and I talked a little bit about the connection between reading and writing and how we are going to be supporting children's literacy development in kindergarten this year. This will give you some more of a philosophical research base of information that will help you to know where I'm coming from, that these are not just ideas that I dream out of the sky. The ideas that I'm using in my classroom are supported by current, respected research. And I want you to read this so you know more. One of my goals this year is to educate parents as much as possible. I want you to know and understand why I'm doing what I'm doing in the classroom. And this will be a good start. It really opens up a lot of things to think about and how you can support literacy development—even in your own home, because believe it or not, it's happening already. And this will just help to point out some of the wonderful things that your kids are already doing, helping them to develop into literate persons."

Mrs. Poremba encourages parents to use her weekly newsletter to keep up with classroom events. "That will highlight everything we've done that week. So when your children come home from school and are tired and say they haven't done anything, just refer to the newsletter, and that will give you some ideas to start conversation. I want to explain that to you, because over the years I've come to understand why young children say, when they walk in the door, 'I didn't do anything today.' It's because they live for the moment, and that's the nature of the young child. And what happened two hours ago or an hour ago is not necessarily pertinent to what's happening that moment. And I've experienced that with my own sons. They'd come home and I'd ask the question, 'How was your day?' They'd say, 'It was great!' 'What did you do?' 'Nothing' or 'I can't remember' or something like that. Very frustrating for a teacher, believe me! But later on, as they made a connection with something that was happening at home to what happened at school, it would come out."

Mrs. Poremba tells a story about her son. One evening, in his bath, he suddenly remembered what he had learned in school that day about the properties of water, though he had reported upon arriving home from school that very day that he had learned nothing. "So he was living for the moment, and at that moment, that particular bit of learning was important to him. And that's very much the way it is for young children, even more so for kindergartners. They live for the moment." And so Mrs. Poremba advises, "Use the newsletter to start conversations."

Then Mrs. Poremba introduces me and invites parents to volunteer to help out in the classroom for whatever lengths of time they'd like and as often as they can. I go with the parents to the school library to talk about my research program.

MATH CUBES: COLORS, PATTERNS, LENGTHS, AND "I'M SORRY."

When Mrs. Poremba rejoins the students, they are excited about the strings they have made by joining math cubes together. They have been talking and cooperating with one another. They talk to her, excited to share what they have done, and she responds, emphasizing color names and the word *pattern*. Patterning is an important part of the math program for kindergarten.

"Oh! Look at the patterns!" she exclaims. "Oh, you must really like green and yellow! I wonder whose is taller, Ian's or Tara's? I wonder how we could figure that out."

"His is tallest," says Eric D.

"How do you know?"

"'Cause. It looks taller."

"Mine's taller?" asks Ian.

"No. Mine," says Jeff.

"Eric, put yours like this," Eric D. directs. "His is about this tall," Eric D. demonstrates against Eric C.'s body. Soon several children are measuring their cube towers against their bodies.

"Mine's up to my thigh—a little taller," says Tara G.

"Mine's taller than me! Except if I stand up," declares Jeff.

When he stands, Mrs. Poremba comments, "It goes right up to your name there."

"I need a blue. I need dark blue," declares one kindergartner.

"It's fun to play with these, isn't it?" observes Mrs. Poremba.

"I wish my mom would buy these."

"You really like [math] cubes."

"You can make a stick," notes Jeff. He swings his stick of cubes at Erin's.

"Hey! He broke mine!" Erin tells on Jeff.

"You know, I think it was an accident," responds Mrs. Poremba. "You know, Jeff, when something like that happens, you can just look at Erin and say, 'Oh, I'm sorry, Erin. I didn't mean to do that.' Maybe she needs to know that it was an accident."

A NEW WORD AND A PRACTICAL REASON FOR MATCHING NUMBERS

Now Mrs. Poremba directs the children's separating and putting away the math cubes. She emphasizes the word *separate*, and she demonstrates using the labels on the containers and shelves for putting things away in their designated places.

Already on this first day, she uses explicit language about behavior, language that lets children know what she wants and how they can show her that they are doing what she expects. "I need all of my kindergartners to stop, with your hands nice and still, and look right at your teacher. I need to see two eyes from everybody." She calls on some children by name, asking to see their eyes, and she repeats for everyone, "I need to look out and see everybody's eyes."

Then she is ready to talk about separating. "I'm going to teach you about a very, very important word right now. It's the word *separated*. I'm going to show you what *separated* means. I'm going to take this [math] cube tower, and I'm going to separate it—by taking the cubes apart so they're not hooked together any more." She begins demonstrating. "That's called separating."

Immediately, there is a flurry of separating, accompanied by Mrs. Poremba's naming what they are doing. "Wow, there's a lot of separating going on." When one kindergartner presents a filled container and wants to know what to do with her remaining cubes, Mrs. Poremba reflects the problem back to the children. "Well, I wonder what we can do if one tub gets filled up too much. What could you do?"

"Put 'em in the other one that's not filled up," suggests Tara G.

Soon the strings of cubes are deconstructed, and the cubes are in their containers.

Mrs. Poremba goes to the Math Tool Cart, on which are stored containers filled with many math manipulatives. "You know, I need some help. I need kindergartners to bring the [math] cube tubs over here. And I'm going to show you where they go when we're all finished with them."

The containers and the shelves on the cart have matching labels.

Mrs. Poremba explains, "This is the special place on the gray cart where the [math] cubes go. Now, this [math] cube tub has a number on it right here."

"Five," says one kindergartner.

"Does anyone know what that number is?"

"Five," answer several kindergartners.

"The number 5. Alyssa, could you come over here? Do you see a 5 down here?"

Alyssa's blond curls frame a wide face. "Yes," she answers, quietly, but confidently.

"Where?"

Alyssa points.

"There it is. So I'm going to take the [math] cube tub with the 5 and I'm going to put it right by that 5. See how they match?"

Mrs. Poremba has given her kindergartners an opportunity to show her whether or not they can identify numbers. Some can; some can't. She and the students who do know number names have modeled number naming for those who are learning. More important, Mrs. Poremba has given all her kindergartners a way to respond to numbers even if they can't identify them—they need only match similar looking numbers. And most important, she has provided a functional use of numbers. Her students will want to play with the math manipulatives on the math cart, for already they've learned how much fun the math cubes can be. They have also learned that it is their responsibility to put away what they have used. They will not need to circle matching numbers on a mathematics workbook page for visual discrimination training; they will be matching numbers every time they put away their math tools.

Soon the tubs are put away in their designated places. Mrs. Poremba uses the rest of this half-morning of kindergarten to show the children the cups for placing drinking straws to keep track of the number of school days, to read a poem that is on the easel, and to read a big easel-sized book about school buses. Then it is time for the children to go home.

THE SECOND GROUP OF MORNING KINDERGARTNERS

Soon the second half of the morning kindergarten class begins arriving, accompanied by their parents. Freddy's red hair is short and is greased to stand up in a spike cut. He goes immediately to the Housekeeping Center.

Zack's eyes sparkle beneath the bill of a yellow and purple cap. The cap has a Foreign-Legion-like drape that covers the back of Zack's neck. His broad smile and open stance confirm the cap's suggestion that Zack is ready for the adventure of starting kindergarten. He removes the cap to reveal a shock of unruly, nearly white, blond hair.

"Hi, I'm Mrs. Poremba. What's your name?" says Mrs. Poremba, offering Zack her hand.

Zack replies with his name and a big smile.

"You need to look around at what I did to get the room ready," suggests Mrs. Poremba. Zack needs no further prompting. He joins Freddy at the Housekeeping Center, where he picks up a clipboard and writes on it.

Jason's blond, short-cut, curly hair tops a tall forehead and a serious face. He stays close to his mother as they tour the room.

Meagan is a small, pretty, doll-like girl with fine features and light brown hair cut to just above her shoulders and in bangs. Her mother stops in their walk about the room to point out the *paper towels* label on the towel dispenser at the sink. At the Color Cats bulletin board, she quizzes Meagan about the color words that label cats cut from differently colored pieces of construction paper. Meagan answers too quietly for anyone but her mother to hear. Next, her mother points to the upper- and lowercase alphabet on cards across the top of the chalkboard. "You already know those, don't you?" she says.

The room is filling up with milling kindergartners and their parents. Tara J. and Kaitlynn are a contrast in appearance and style. Both are handling this first day at kindergarten with confidence and ease, but while Tara's is a quiet confidence, Kaitlynn's is expressed in voice and motion. Tara has long, straight, brown hair, knowing eyes, and a small mouth that seems always poised on the verge of a smile. Like Jeff in the first group of today's kindergartners, Kaitlynn conquers any space. Her long, blond hair is pulled back from an animated face. Her appearance is that of the young Haley Mills. Her voice can be heard above all others as she meets the challenge of her kindergarten morning at full throttle.

Kaitlynn presents Mrs. Poremba with a bouquet of yellow pink-tinged roses, yellow daisies, and small, star-shaped blue flowers.

"Oh, my goodness, these are beautiful!" remarks Mrs. Poremba as she accepts Kaitlynn's bouquet.

"Thank you," answers Kaitlynn.

"I'm Mrs. Poremba."

"Say your name," prompts Kaitlynn's mother.

Kaitlynn answers with her first, middle, and last names.

"How did you know I like flowers? I'll have the prettiest desk in the school."

As they go to the cupboard together to locate a vase, Kaitlynn names the flowers in the bouquet.

NAMES

At the name collar table, Tara J. and Freddy point to their names, but they don't pick the collars up. "How do you know that's yours?" asks Mrs. Poremba.

"'Cause I know how to spell my name," answers Freddy.

Sarah's short, brown hair frames a round face and delicate features. She hesitates at the table with the name collars. "Is your name over here?" her mother asks.

"Do you see yours, Sarah?" asks Mrs. Poremba. "Is that it?" she says about Tara's collar.

Sarah shakes her head.

"It's close. It has *A*s like your name. Your name needs an *S*."

Sarah finds her name and puts on her collar.

Most of the children are at either the Reading Center or the Housekeeping Center. No one in this group chooses puzzle work. In the Housekeeping Center, Tara J. writes on a clipboard and Kaitlynn recites her phone number in response to her mother's quizzing. Then she talks on the telephone there.

In the back corner, by the outside door, Jason, Freddy, and Mrs. Poremba are huddled over the boys' cupped hands. They cross the room to show Freddy's mother the crickets they have trapped, and then Mrs. Poremba leads the boys outside where they release the insects in the bushes that border the building.

I HAVE TO GO TO THE BATHROOM.

After Mrs. Poremba talks to this group's parents and I take them to the school library to talk about my research program, she joins the kindergartners and Mrs. Roloff.

"Woah! It's way across it!" exclaims Kaitlynn about this group's math cube snake, which stretches the length of the carpet in the whole-group area.

"Holy cow! Look at that!" says Mrs. Poremba. "Boy, you guys did great. You all worked together. Well, kindergartners, I need everybody to stop—"

"I have to go to the bathroom," says Jason.

"Go right ahead, Jason. There's a light switch right inside. Do you see it?"

"It's right over here," directs another kindergartner.

"That's right. We have a special bathroom right inside our door. The light switch is right here, Jason. And the fan is going to go on. So you're going to hear a sound when the light goes on. It's just the fan. Can you hear the fan? Okay. Now, close the door." Now, Mrs. Poremba speaks softly to the rest of the kindergartners, "When Jason is finished, he's going to go over to the sink and wash his hands."

She returns to the carpeted area. "Okay, I need your eyes right up here."

"I can build while I'm looking at you," says a kindergartner, still busy with the math cubes.

"I want to look out and see everybody's eyes." The toilet flushes loudly. "Thank you for flushing the toilet, Jason. I'm glad you remembered to do—Jason, could you go over to our sink and wash your hands, please? I wonder if you can find the soap. Mrs. Roloff will come and help you."

After these kindergartners put away their math cubes, they gather by the calendar bulletin board. "My goodness! Look-at—these kindergartners know how to put their bottom right on the carpet. And they're folding their legs up so people don't trip on their feet! Boy, is that nice to see! Mrs. Roloff, we have some terrific kindergartners!" ("Look-at" is pronounced "LOOK-ut" and is used when pointing, as a shortened form of "Look at this" or "Look at that.")

Jason has a wallet in which are pictures of his family. Of all the kindergartners in this group, he seems most to need the reassurance of this connection with his home life.

"That is a really nice wallet. Thank you for sh—Oh, look at those pictures!"

Jason's classmates gather around him.

"Thank you, Jason! Beautiful wallet. When you're all finished looking, you can come back and sit down."

Sarah presents Mrs. Poremba a note. "For me?" asks Mrs. Poremba. She reads, "'To Mrs. Poremba. Love, Sarah.' Thank you, Sarah. That's very nice."

ONE DAY OF KINDERGARTEN

When the group is again sitting before the calendar, Mrs. Poremba asks, "Well, kindergartners, today is the very first day of kindergarten. Anybody know the number that means first?"

"One," answer several kindergartners.

"Yeah. It's the very first number you say, is the number *1*." Mrs. Poremba introduces the straw cups. She places one straw in the *ones* cup for this first day of school and flips the *1* card into position on the front of the cup. "One straw," she says, "and there's the number *1* for one day of kindergarten. Every day, we'll count the days we've been in school. I wonder how many days we'll be in school tomorrow?"

"Two"—"Two," answer two kindergartners.

"Two! Today was one, tomorrow will be—"

"Two!" finish Mrs. Poremba and several kindergartners.

"My, you are smart! You are so smart!" Next Mrs. Poremba invites the kindergartners to the other end of the carpeted area by the easel. "I'll meet you over by the blue chair over here." Mrs. Poremba sits in the blue wooden arm chair by the easel, and the kindergartners sit on the rug around her.

READING A POEM TOGETHER

Mrs. Poremba orients her students to the meanings that will be found in the poem on the easel and to the source of those meanings, the words of which the poem is composed. It is a simple, six-line poem about finding a shady place to sit out the heat of an August day. The last three lines are very simple, just a triple repetition of *And sit*. This is an effective poetic device for young children and an aid to their reading and remembering (Cullinan, Scala, and Schroder 1995). Mrs. Poremba has drawn a picture beneath the poem. It shows a girl sitting in the shade of a tree. And she has written the poem's lines in alternating colors to make it easier to look at and talk about the poem one line at a time.

Words is a new word to many kindergartners. They will need to know that writing is comprised of units called *words* and that knowing what those words are is what unlocks the meanings in a text. "Okay, I want to read you a poem about this hot day we're having today! Ho! Is it hot! Can you make sure that you are sitting in a place where you can see our words?" Mrs. Poremba introduces a technique that she and her kindergartners will use with many texts throughout the year. It is called finger point reading (Morris 1983; Uhry 1999). It requires the kindergartners to attend to print when reading or hearing someone else read a text, and it helps them to see that words are important units in a text.

"I'm going to read the words, and I'm going to touch the words with my ruler. Jason, could you put your bottom all the way down, sweetie? There you go—then it helps friends behind you to be able to see. It goes like this, Zachary: She reads the title and the first line, but she stops before the last word of that line.

"—hot" "—hot," finish two kindergartners.

"—hot," echoes Mrs. Poremba. "Good reading! She does the same with the second line, but now one tiny kindergarten voice shadows hers.

"—spot," say Mrs. Poremba and several kindergartners together to finish the second line. And then with one kindergartner's voice still following her, Mrs. Poremba reads the rest of the poem.

Mrs. Poremba lets her students know how a picture can help them determine what a text is about. She points to the drawing beneath the poem. "Look at that little girl! What is she doing?"

"Shady spot!" answers one kindergartner.

"Sitting in a tree," says another.

Mrs. Poremba uses these kindergartners' answers. "She found a shady spot, didn't she? And she's sitting there. I'm going to read the poem again. Can you help me this time, if you think you remember some of the words?"

This time many more kindergartners read along with Mrs. Poremba and supply the last word in each line when she pauses for it. "Good reading!" she says. "I like the way you're watching the words." Next, Mrs. Poremba reads only the *And* of the first *And sit*; as she points with her ruler, several kindergartners read the remainder of the last three repetitive lines of the poem.

"You did it! Wow!" Mrs. Poremba promises more work with this poem the next day. "But right now I want to read you a book."

READING AND COUNTING TOGETHER FROM A BIG BOOK

Mrs. Poremba reads a big book, which she displays on the easel as she reads. A big book is a publisher's special edition of a children's book printed in larger-than-normal size. This one is *School Bus* by Donald Crews (1990). This book will help prepare the children for their first day of school bus riding tomorrow. But Mrs. Poremba also uses this reading as an opportunity immediately to reinforce what she has just taught about picture clues and word reading. As she places the book on the easel, with its cover picture of a big school bus and its title in big letters, *SCHOOL BUS*, Mrs. Poremba asks, "I wonder what this book is about?!"

"Buses!" declares Freddy.

"How do you know that, Freddy?"

"Because I can see the bus."

"The picture helped you to know that this book was about buses. Anybody else have another idea?"

"Bus."

"Bus."

"It says, 'Bus.'" says Jason.

"You mean the words up here? Jason, you're right," says Mrs. Poremba. "The words up here help us to know what the book is about. It says, 'School—'"

"'—Bus,'" read Mrs. Poremba and a few kindergartners together.

Mrs. Poremba continues reading. The class joins her for some repeated, predictable words as she points to the words while reading them. They count thirty-two buses on one page! Mrs. Poremba decides to write that number on a small, erasable-marker board. "I'm going to write that number down. Anybody know how to write a *32*?"

"No"—"No," answer several kindergartners.

"Watch this," says Mrs. Poremba. But two kindergartners do have some ideas about this, and Mrs. Poremba will affirm what both have to say, even though only one has the whole idea.

"*I* do," says one kindergartner.

"How do you do it?"

"By a two," interjects Jason.

"First you do a *3* and then you do a *2*!" says the first kindergartner.

"That's right. There's the thirty—" Mrs. Poremba writes 3, "—two," and she writes 2. "And, Jason, you knew there was a *2* in it, didn't you?"

The kindergartners make connections with their own experiences, including their upcoming school bus rides. Almost all of them will ride buses to and from school every day.

"You know what? I know what's on the back of them. Emergency door!" says Freddy in response to one of the pictures.

When Mrs. Poremba reads, "'Large and small,'" responses include: "I'm going on a large one"—"Me, too"—"Yeah, so am I!"

When Freddy says, "I don't know which bus I'm riding!" Mrs. Poremba assures him, "You might ride the small one. Tomorrow, Freddy, I'll ask you, 'Freddy, did you ride the large bus or the small one?' You can tell me tomorrow!"

They explore word meanings. When Mrs. Poremba reads about empty buses, she asks, "*Empty*—what does that mean—*empty*?"

"No kids in them!" declares Zack.

When Mrs. Poremba points out a red light that means stop, the children immediately know what to read for a green light on another page. "Look at the light."

"Green—go," say the children together.

"Yeah! There's the word *Go* down there. Good for you!"

One kindergartner makes a connection with her experience of buses: "The buses have stop signs on them!"

"They sure do. Tomorrow when you're riding the bus, or when you are going to get on the bus, you can take a peek at that sign."

When the book shows a bus full of children arriving at school, Mrs. Poremba reads the text, "'Here we are!'" And she asks, "Where are they?"

"At school," answer the children in unison.

Mrs. Poremba directs the children's attention to a relevant part of the illustration on this page, "Oh, that's what that sign says, 'School.'"

When an illustration shows empty buses lined up outside the school, Freddy suggests repeating an earlier activity: "Let's count!"

"Count the empty buses?" asks Mrs. Poremba.

"One, two, three, four, five, six," count the children and Mrs. Poremba together.

When Mrs. Poremba then proceeds to ask where the children are, a kindergartner wants a more complete repetition of the earlier activity. "Write the number!"

"Oh, good idea. How many did we say?"

"Five," answers one kindergartner.

"Six!" answer several others.

Mrs. Poremba counts again. Then as she demonstrates writing 6, she says, "I think I'll put the *6* over here. We don't want to get it mixed up with our *32*."

"Let's count 'em!" demands Freddy when the next page shows six school buses, now full of children after school.

"You like to count, don't you?"

Everyone counts: "One, two, three, four, five, six!"

"We've already got it up there don't we?"

"Mmm hmm. So we don't need to write it!" says Freddy.

Now Freddy has an ally. When the next page shows many buses crossing town, Jason says, "Let's count 'em again."

"Let's count 'em," agrees Freddy.

"Okay," assents Mrs. Poremba.

This time the count is nine.

"I'm putting the *9* way over here so we don't get it mixed up with our *32* and our *6*."

"Looks like you only have room for one more number," observes Zack. But there will be two more numbers, so Mrs. Poremba writes them small in order to fit them on the board.

When the next page shows only two buses arriving at children's homes, Freddy says, "Two, let's write *2* down!"

"How about if I make a little *2* down there?"

And the last page shows sixteen buses at their parking lot. Everyone counts to sixteen.

"Ooo. I'll write that right over here."

"A little one," Zack reminds.

"A little *16*," agrees Mrs. Poremba.

GOING HOME

It's time for the kindergartners to exchange name collars for book bags at their lockers and line up for the end of the day. "It's time for us to go out to the playground to learn where our bus will bring us tomorrow morning. Let's go pick up mom, too. Okay?"

When Jason is with his mom at the curb outside the school, ready to go home, Mrs. Poremba crouches down to his eye level. "You had a great day today, Jason!" she says. "You found the first cricket of the year!"

Jason has seemed unsure about kindergarten, but he's not so anxious to leave his first day of kindergarten behind that he'd give up an opportunity to tell another animal discovery story. He tells Mrs. Poremba about seeing a squirrel earlier. And then he's ready to go. "Good-bye," he says to Mrs. Poremba.

3

DAY 154

Let's skip ahead to the 154th day of school, Monday, May 9. As we follow today's activities, it is helpful to notice two catalysts and two sources of structure. Mrs. Poremba facilitates today's planned activities by displaying new materials and old and new texts, but students influence today's *un*planned curriculum by bringing objects and ideas from home. Two sources of structure and context for much of today's teaching and learning are the many routines that have evolved over the past eight months (Richgels 1995) and a science unit that is in its fifth week.

ARRIVALS

Mrs. Poremba's class has spent four weeks studying about chickens and hatching. In their classroom is an incubator containing eighteen chick eggs, expected to hatch tomorrow, their twenty-first day of incubation.

As the children enter the classroom, they find chick paraphernalia displayed on two large tables. There are a brooder box, a food dish, a water bottle, a container of mash, and a heat lamp, each labeled (the last with the word *light*). Also at these tables are informational resources about chick hatching that the children have seen and used before: two posters (one prepared by Mrs. Poremba and titled *A baby chick grows!*

and the other a commercial poster titled *How a Chick Hatches*) and three informational picture books. The books are clothespinned open to pictures of chick development and hatching.

Freddy is one of the first kindergartners to arrive today. He brings a special object, his own incubator. Compared to the incubator for the chicks, with its plastic and metal and electronic parts, Freddy's is primitive. It is a small pasteboard box, lined with cotton balls and warmed by a heat lamp clipped to its side. Resting among the cotton balls is one small blue robin egg that Freddy and his mother found near their house. Freddy's mother reported to Mrs. Poremba that at home, Freddy would turn the robin egg from time to time. "Mrs. Poremba says you have to turn it," he told his mother.

Kaitlynn has been away for a whole week on a family vacation to Georgia. "Hi, Kaitlynn, welcome back," says Freddy.

"Kaitlynn, you're back!" says Mrs. Poremba. "Oh, we missed you so much! Oh, I'm so glad you're back! How are you?"

"Good."

"Oh, I'm so glad!"

Kaitlynn has a plastic bag of very small seashells.

Mrs. Poremba says, "You have a lot to tell us at Headline News, don't you? Oh, I can hardly wait to hear!"

"My god! These are small shells!" exclaims Freddy.

"Kaitlynn bought them in Georgia," explains Tara G.

"Lots of things to look at today, aren't there, Erin?" asks Mrs. Poremba.

"Yeah."

CHECK-IN AND SIGN-IN ROUTINES

As the children arrive, they engage in the check-in and sign-in routines. They put their book bags away in their lockers, move cards bearing their names from a pocket chart (known as the *Friends Board*) to an envelope clipped below it, and pick up pencils and sign-in sheets and attach the sheets to clipboards. The sign-in sheet is an eight-and-one-half-by-eleven-inch sheet of paper with horizontal lines spaced about an inch apart. The first four lines have preprinted prompts: *Name* at the beginning of the first line; *Number chart*, a small rectangle, and a small oval on the second line, with space next to each shape for writing; a small triangle and a small diamond on the third line; and *Today is* at the beginning of the fourth line (see figure 3.1). The sign-in routine will involve them in more than writing their names. They will do assigned number work and individual writing stimulated by the chick paraphernalia and informational texts and by a newly posted poem.

"Visit the number chart," Mrs. Poremba directs. "You might want to visit the table and do some looking, and you might want to visit the easel."

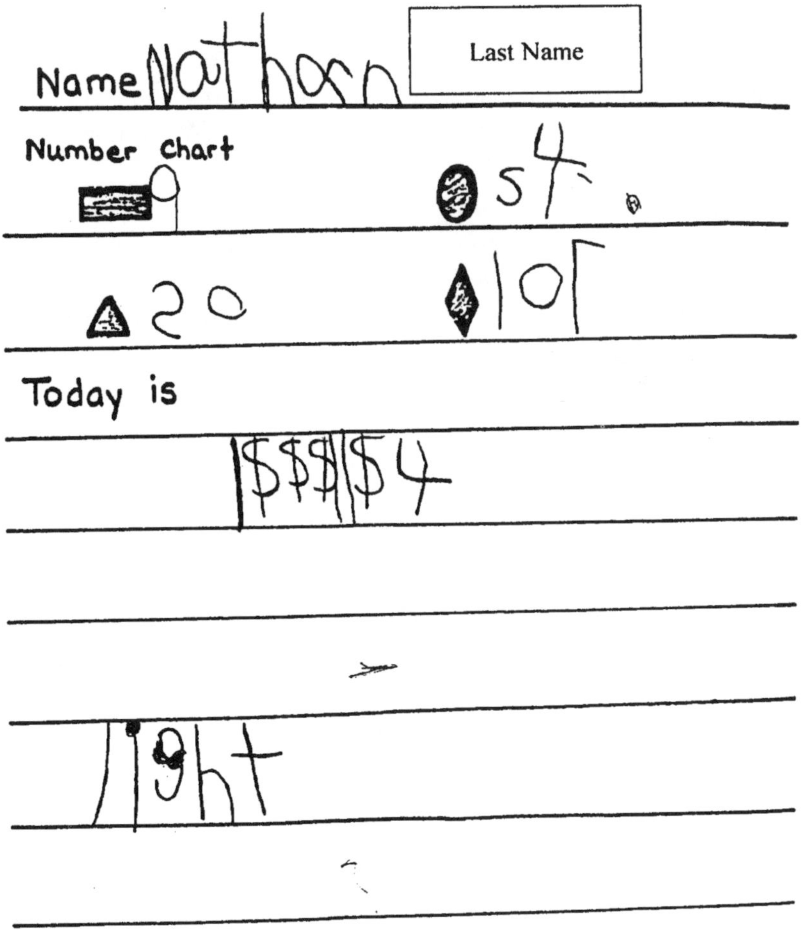

Figure 3.1. Nathan's May 9 Sign-in Sheet

The number chart is a poster on which the numerals *1–110* are displayed in rows of ten. Today, four numbers are masked, *9* by a rectangle, *20* by a triangle, *54* by an oval, and *107* by a diamond. Today is the 9th day of May, Day *20* in the hatching cycle, the *154*th day of school. Below the words *Number Chart* on the kindergartners' sign-in sheets and next to the small drawings of those same shapes, the kindergartners are to write their guesses of what numbers are masked by the corresponding shapes on the number chart. This is their "number chart work," which all are expected to do. Other writing on sign-in sheets is optional.

At the easel is a playful poem that begins, *Peck, peck, peck* and then tells about a chick cracking its egg and emerging, neck first and leg last. Mrs. Poremba has copied the poem in alternating colors, black and green, for alternating lines, beginning with the title.

At the chick equipment display, Ian says, "Tomorrow the chicks hatch!"

"What's this?" asks Jason about the brooder box. "What does this say?" he asks about the label.

"'Brooder box,'" reads a classmate.

"This is what they look like right now," says a kindergartner, referring to the *A baby chick grows!* poster.

Jeff announces, "Ian, I'm gonna write all this down. Ian, let's write all this down. Are you gonna write that down, Nathan?"

"No," answers Nathan.

A minute later, Mrs. Poremba comes by. "Oh, Jeffrey, I see you're gonna be writing down new words!" And a bit later, "Well, Jeff, you're gonna give people good ideas by watching what you're doing today! What a good idea!" Figure 3.1 shows Nathan's sign-in-sheet writing today, and Figures 3.2 and 3.3 show Jeff's and Ian's.

Ben is a new student; he has been in Mrs. Poremba's class only two weeks. He comes by and reports to Mrs. Poremba, "The number chart was easy." He has recorded all correct numbers on his sign-in sheet.

Mrs. Poremba responds, "The number chart was easy for you today? Really?"

At a nearby table, Lauren and Mayra are conferring quietly about Mayra's number chart work. Lauren joined Mrs. Poremba's class on February 28 and Mayra on September 27. At first, Mayra spoke very little English. Her native language is Spanish, but she is comfortable speaking English now. She has a small personal number chart so that when she makes her predictions, Mrs. Roloff can give her immediate feedback.

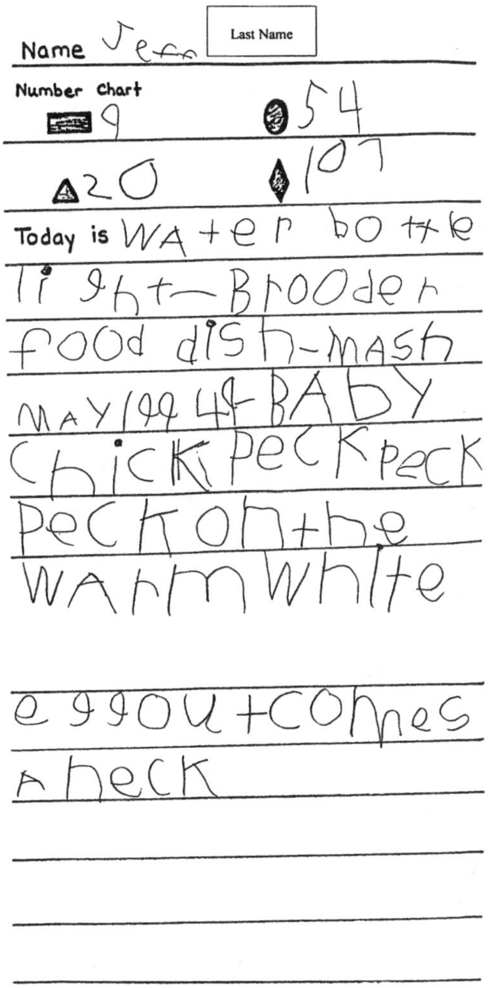

Figure 3.2. Jeff's May 9 Sign-in Sheet

But right now, it is Lauren who helps Mayra. Lauren leans over the chart, points to a number, and gives Mayra a serious but encouraging look.

Mrs. Roloff joins Mayra and Lauren. She points and leads Mayra in counting, "101, 102, 103, 104, 105, 106, 107." Then Mrs. Roloff directs Mayra's writing, "—one, zero, and then a seven. That's right. Good job, Mayra. Let's see if you're right." She unmasks the *107* on Mayra's personal number chart. Mayra cheers and hugs Mrs. Roloff. Lauren watches from beside Mayra. "Good job!" says Mrs. Roloff, returning Mayra's hug. "You went to a hundred and seven, Mayra! Let's talk about the numbers you

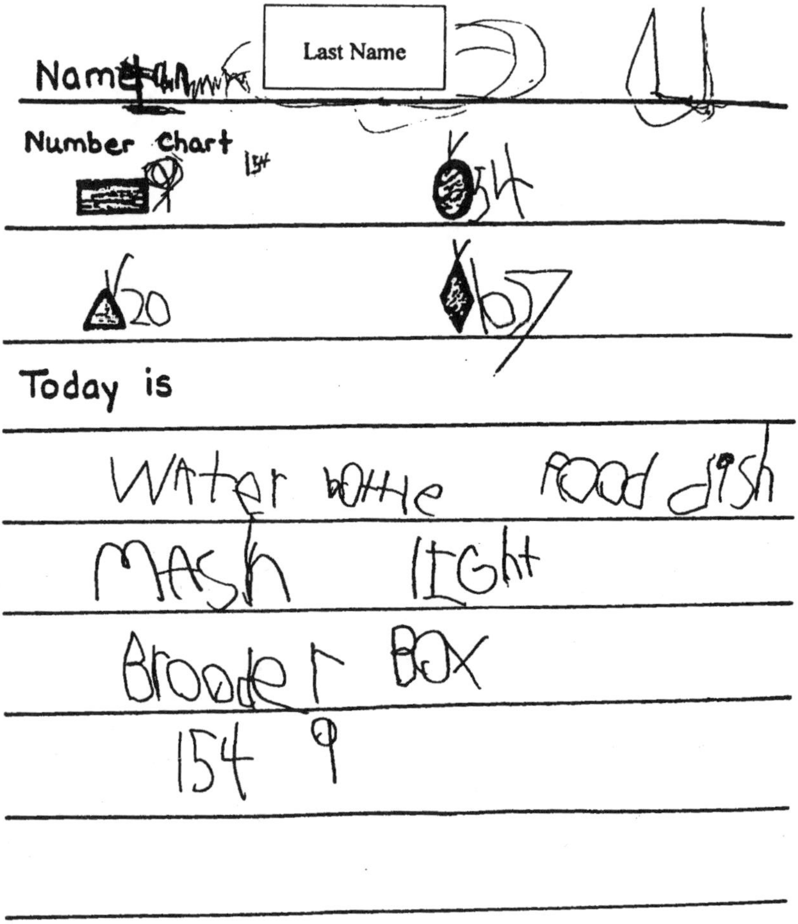

Figure 3.3. Ian's May 9 Sign-in Sheet

have down, so you remember, okay? What number did you say was by your rectangle?" Mayra's sign-in has mayra and her last name on the name line, with a backwards y and in shaky letters that sometimes dip way below the line, and correct number chart numbers. Later, she will also write mvsic / 1 (a scribble) 123 / S (slashes will indicate line breaks in children's writing).

Meanwhile, at the chick equipment display table, Freddy reports, "I'm done, Jas." He has written his first, middle, and last names, all the correct number chart numbers, and light mash / Food dish / WAteR bottle. Later, he will also write BAby chick / 154 789 / yes sunny Nocloudy No Rainy yes windy No snowy (with a backwards a) and on the back of his sign-in sheet, WADRM / WINdy / suop wA. He will get ideas for these words from the chick equipment display and from the group, beginning-of-the-day activities that will take place soon.

"How many more words do you have to write, Jas?" asks Ian.

"None!" answers Jason. He has finished copying labels on the displayed chick equipment (see figure 3.4).

"None?"

"I'm just—"

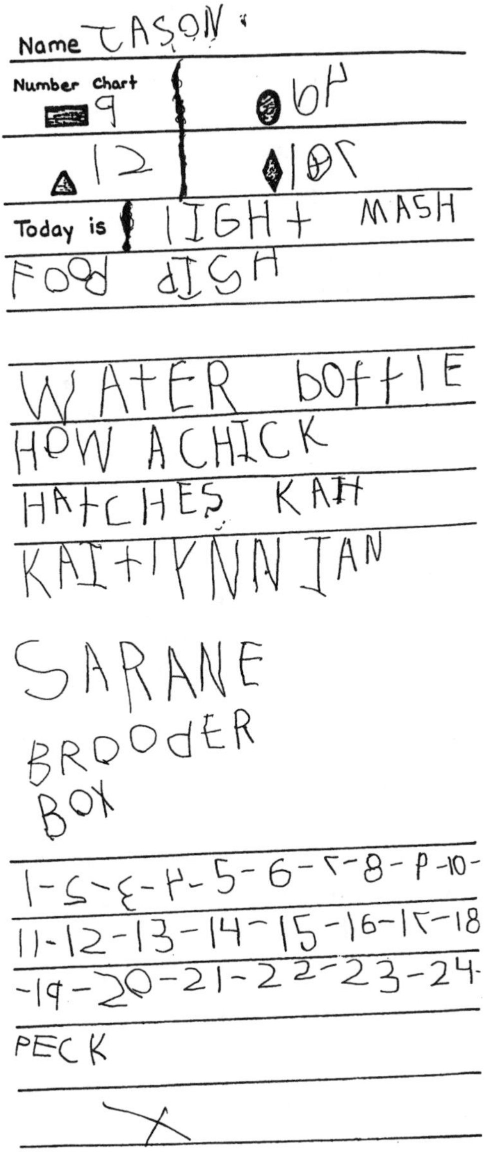

Figure 3.4. Jason's May 9 Sign-in Sheet

"I'm tired."

"Well, I'm writin' these now," explains Jason, who has moved on to copying words from the *How a Chick Hatches* poster. "What does this say, Mrs. Poremba?"

"This tells—" and Mrs. Poremba points and reads, "'How a Chick Hatches.' If you look at the different pictures—here I'll move this over—and you follow them around, it'll show you exactly what to look at to show how a chick hatches. This book right here also shows you what to look for."

Erin is talking to Mrs. Roloff about how to spell *Kelly*. Deborah has been pretending her name is Kelly, and Erin wants to make a record of this. "Well, it starts with kuh," says Mrs. Roloff.

"*K*," says Erin.

"Did you say *Kelly*?" asks Jeff. "My sister's name is Kelly."

"Now the small sound is an *E*," continues Mrs. Roloff. " Okay?"

"My sister's name is Kelly," Jeff repeats.

"*Kellllll-*."

"*L*?" asks Erin.

"That's right, an *L*," Mrs. Roloff confirms. "And then, I usually figure two *L*s. It's a double letter. And then *Kelleeeee*. What do you think is at the end?"

"*Y*?"

"Uh huh. There's a *Y* at the end."

Mrs. Poremba summons the kindergartners to group beginning-of-the-day activities with a song, "Come Sit Down—." The kindergartners call these activities "wall work" because they take place at the wall-like bulletin board that spans nearly the width of the room (see figures 2.1 and 2.2, chapter 2). Wall work routines include number chart work, helper naming, straw cups and number line work, calendar, weather report, and Words for Today writing.

The kindergartners join Mrs. Poremba's singing: "Come sit down. Put your bottom on the ground. Open up your eyes. Open up your ears. Come sit down. Come sit down."

THE NUMBER CHART ROUTINE

"The first thing we are going to do is our number chart work," says Mrs. Poremba. She calls on Ian, who chooses to report on the diamond, which Mrs. Poremba's kindergartners call a rhombus. "Ian, what do you know about the number behind the rhombus?"

"One hundred and seven."

"How do you know it's a one hundred and seven?"

Ian points to and identifies, "One hundred and six."

"'Cause you looked at the one hundred and six, and then what?"

"Then I knew it was one hundred and seven."

Mrs. Poremba asks Ian to show how he wrote 107 (see figure 3.3) and to unmask the *107* on the number chart. "There it is," she says. "Did you notice the way the one hundred and seven is written?" She directs the kindergartners' attention to their writing on their sign-in sheets: "Check to see if you wrote it with a one first and then a zero and then a seven. If you did, could you circle your one hundred and seven, so we know that you wrote it the way it was on the chart?"

Mrs. Poremba encourages more than one way to determine answers. Kaitlynn, for example, explains how she arrived at 107: "One hundred and ten, one hundred and nine, one hundred and eight, one hundred and seven."

"Oh, so you counted backwards to figure out the one hundred and seven?"

"Yeah."

"That's a good way to do it." Mrs. Poremba calls on Jeff for a demonstration with the oval and *54*, Tara G. with the triangle and the *20*, and Mayra with the rectangle and the *9*.

When Mayra arrives at the chart, she says simply, "Rectangle."

"Mayra's thinking about the rectangle," says Mrs. Poremba. "Mayra, what do you know about the number hiding behind the rectangle?" When Mayra is silent, Mrs. Poremba helps her to "count by *ones*" until they arrive at the *9* spot.

"That's good counting. That's right."

"I did the columns," says Kaitlynn.

"After nine comes eight," says Mayra.

Mrs. Poremba prompts a correction, "After eight comes—"

"Nine," answers a kindergartner.

"Thank you, Mayra, for explaining your thinking," says Mrs. Poremba.

Kaitlynn repeats, "I did the columns."

"You did the column way. That's an interesting way," responds Mrs. Poremba.

"I just looked at the nineteen, and then—" Kaitlynn demonstrates going up a column from *19* to *9*.

"That's a very good way to do it, Kaitlynn. There's more than one way to do your thinking on this number chart. There's lots of different ways."

"I counted all the numbers to one hundred," reports Mayra.

HELPERS

"That's a good thing to do, too, Mayra. Thank you, Mayra, for showing us the 9. Let's go over and pick our new helpers for today." Several kindergartners read Elizabeth's and Alyssa's names from the helper name cards as they say thank you to them for being yesterday's helpers. Then Mrs. Poremba says, "Elizabeth and Alyssa, you were great helpers!"

"Thank you, Alyssa," Mayra adds.

Mrs. Poremba draws the name cards for today's helpers, but she does not show them to the kindergartners. She begins one of the class's favorite routines, a kind of guessing game. This game gives the kindergartners important practice identifying letters, visualizing print in their minds before seeing it on a card, and talking about letters and their positions in words, for example, first and last. Literacy experts have for a long time known that such print awareness is a necessary prerequisite to learning how to read and write (Clay 1975; Templeton 1980). Mrs. Poremba asks, "What information would you like today?"

Eric C. asks for the first helper's initials, and the class correctly guesses that the helper is Kaitlynn.

"Today's a special day," says Kaitlynn, "because, because, um—" Kaitlynn can barely express her excitement. "—Friday I came here, back and, and today I'm the helper, and—"

"We're excited for you, Kaitlynn, and it's wonderful having you back," says Mrs. Poremba. Meagan asks for initials for helping to guess the second helper, but Mrs. Poremba suggests trying a different way for the second name.

"How many letters?" asks Meagan.

"How many letters? Okay. Six."

Several kindergartners speculate: "Could be—" "Meagan!" "It could be you." "It could be Nathan." "It could be Meagan."

"Lots of people with six. I think we probably need more information. Freddy, what would you like to know?" Mrs. Poremba has a look of alertness, attention, genuine asking, and openness to the kindergartners' responses to this guessing game. She really wants to know what they think.

"What's the first letter in their first name?"

"An *S*."

"Sarah," suggests Jason, forgetting about the 6-letter restriction.

"It could be Sarah," says Mrs. Poremba.

"Steven!" say several kindergartners.

"Well, Steven, what do you think?" asks Mrs. Poremba.

"I don't know."

"How many letters in *Steven*?"

"Six," answers Steven.

"Six letters in *Steven*. What's the first letter?"

"*S*," answers Steven.

"Steven!" says another kindergartner.

"Are you sure it's you, Steven?"

"Yes."

"Steven!" repeats the other kindergartner.

"Or do you need more information?"

Steven decides that, just to be very sure, he would like to know the last letter of the helper's last name, and Mrs. Poremba tells that it is *K*.

Several kindergartners disagree about who it can be: "Steven!" "No!" "Yeah!"

"He said the very last letter of his last name. It would be the last letter that this person would write in their last name." Mrs. Poremba helps the kindergartners to compare Sarah's and Steven's last names. Sarah's ends with *E*, Steven's with *K*. Then she asks, "Do you know for sure who it is now?"

"Steven!" call two kindergartners.

"Steven, are you certain? Okay." Mrs. Poremba shows Steven's name on the card.

"'Steven!'" several kindergartners read.

"It sure is Steven." Mrs. Poremba pins the name cards of the helpers on the Helper Tree on the wall work bulletin board. And she calls attention to the record-keeping function of writing: "If you want to remember that Kaitlynn and Steven are helpers today, what could you do?"

"Look at the board," answers a kindergartner.

THE STRAW CUPS AND NUMBER LINE ROUTINE

Next in wall work are the straw cup and number line routine for keeping track of the number of school days and the calendar activity.

As Kaitlynn flips the numerals on the straw cups to show *154* for 154 school days, Deborah exclaims, "Hey! Today has a fif-, today has a fifty-four in it!"

"Oh, yeah!" responds a kindergartner in appreciation of this connection.

"Ah-ha!" says Mrs. Poremba. "Deborah just figured something out! Deborah, tell us about your thinking!"

"Today on the number chart we had fifty-four days."

"We had the number *54* on the number chart—" clarifies Mrs. Poremba.

"Yes," says Deborah. "And today is fifty-fo-, one hundred fifty-four."

"Isn't that amazing?"

"Yeah."

"I know why you picked that," says Tara G.

"Now do you know?"

"A *5* and a *4*—" says a kindergartner.

"We'll have to see if you can figure out any other things about those numbers I picked today."

THE CALENDAR ROUTINE

Helper Steven correctly predicts the dates (*7*, *8*, and *9*) that fill in the empty Saturday, Sunday, and Monday (today) spaces on the calendar. He also uses the pattern of shapes for this month to predict the shapes of the cards on which the dates are written. This month's calendar pattern was only tentatively established on Friday, May 6, when for the first time, the shape for May 1, a daisy, was repeated. The pattern is daisy, tulip, butterfly, butterfly, butterfly; so now, the calendar shows a *1* on a daisy; a *2* on a tulip; *3*, *4*, and *5* on butterflies; and *6* on a daisy again. "Do you know what shape that *7*'s going to be written on?" asks Mrs. Poremba.

"A purple tulip," Steven answers.

"A purple tulip? You think so? Why do you think so?"

Steven points to the tulip for May 2.

"Because after the daisy, comes a purple tulip?" asks Mrs. Poremba. Mrs. Poremba removes the cut out shape with a *7* on it from her calendar envelope. It is a purple tulip. "Steven, look at that!" she says. With May 9 in place, she asks, "And we've been, our eggs have been in the incubator how many days?"

"Twenty."

"Boy, there's lots of number things to think about when we do the calendar."

"Tomorrow's Hatch Day!" says Deborah.

"We'll probably start to see some hatchings tomorrow," confirms Mrs. Poremba. "That's right. Very nice, Steven. Thank you."

"Mrs. Poremba, I noticed something," says Freddy.

"I did, too," says Kaitlynn.

"What did you notice, Freddy?"

But Kaitlynn says it first: "On the number chart is, has a *9*, too." She has written a backwards *9* on her sign-in sheet after *Today is*.

"There's a *9* on the number chart?" asks Mrs. Poremba. "Ah ha. One of our numbers on the number chart was a *9*."

Deborah notes that twice, now, an important wall work number matches a number work number. "Two!" she shouts.

"And look-at," continues Mrs. Poremba, "we put a *9* up today."

"Two!" Deborah shouts again. "Two times! Two things! Straws and calendar!"

"So far, straws and calendar. That's absolutely right."

THE WEATHER REPORT ROUTINE

The class reads the date from the calendar together. Kaitlynn places the *Music* card on the chart that tells the special class for each day, and Steven leads the Pledge of Allegiance. Then it is Kaitlynn's turn to be the helper for the weather report. She clasps her hands before her as she stands at the wall work bulletin board beside a vertical display of five weather words with pictures: *sunny*, *cloudy*, *windy*, *rainy*, and *snowy*. Behind each is a sliding card that can be moved to the right so that the word *Yes* is exposed or to the left so that *No* is exposed. Above this "weather graph" is a title card: *Today's Weather*. Kaitlynn waits for her classmates to settle down after stretching and moving to that end of the bulletin board. Her serious face is framed by blond bangs and other strands of hair that have failed to participate in a long ponytail. Over white pants, she wears a light-blue-and-white-striped dress with matching blue buttons down the front. It functions as a top rather than a dress; its long sleeves are three-quarter length now and its short flared skirt is more like a ruffle than a skirt. Her eyes dart to her left to Mrs. Poremba and back at the class. Mrs. Poremba is sitting beyond the right edge of the group, in the blue wooden arm chair by the easel. "One, two, three. Kindergarten check time!" Kaitlynn says.

"Oh, I think Kaitlynn's looking for attentive body language," says Mrs. Poremba. "Erin, can we see your attentive body language? What I want you to do is this: Kaitlynn is going to be showing you her ideas about today's weather. I want you to look at what she does and think about what Kaitlynn is showing you about her ideas. So you'll have to watch Kaitlynn and you'll have to watch the weather graph. You might even want to do some guessing to see if you can guess what Katilynn is going to say about the weather today. Let's give them a moment to do some guessing, Kaitlynn, okay?" Mrs. Poremba directs the class, "Can you guess by just whispering to someone close to you?"

Whispered *yes*es and *no*s drift among the group of kindergartners.

Kaitlynn waits patiently, uncharacteristically silent and still, her hands still clasped before her. "I heard some people making some guesses," observes Mrs. Poremba. Kaitlynn begins to sway back and forth, and twice she glances out the window.

"Okay, Kaitlynn—"

As if released from a tether, Kaitlynn turns and heads for the classroom door, in the corner beyond the lockers that are behind the wall work bulletin board.

"—I think we're ready for you to show us your idea," continues Mrs. Poremba. Kaitlynn has propped open the door and is outdoors now on her weather reconnaissance mission. Erin holds up her clipboard. "Oh, Erin showed me her guesses by writing down the *yes*es and *no*s she thought she would see on the graph today. Erin, when Katilynn is finished, you can check to see if Kaitlynn's ideas match yours. That was a very good way of showing us your thinking, Erin." On the back of her sign-in sheet, Erin has written in a column, yes / NO / yes / NO / NO, with backwards ys. On another sheet of paper, Erin also writes the same column of her *yes* and *no* guesses and next to that a matching column for Kaitlynn's reports (see figure 3.5).

Kaitlynn is back. She slides the *Yes* and *No* strip for *sunny* so that only the *Yes* shows to the left of the weather word, then resumes her clasped-hands stance.

"I was right," says Jeff in an uncharacteristically soft voice.

"Did you, was your guess right?" asks Mrs. Poremba. "You made a prediction, Jeff. That's called a good guess."

Kaitlynn now proceeds with all the remaining cards, displaying *No*, *Yes*, *No*, *No* for *cloudy*, *windy*, *rainy*, and *snowy* respectively.

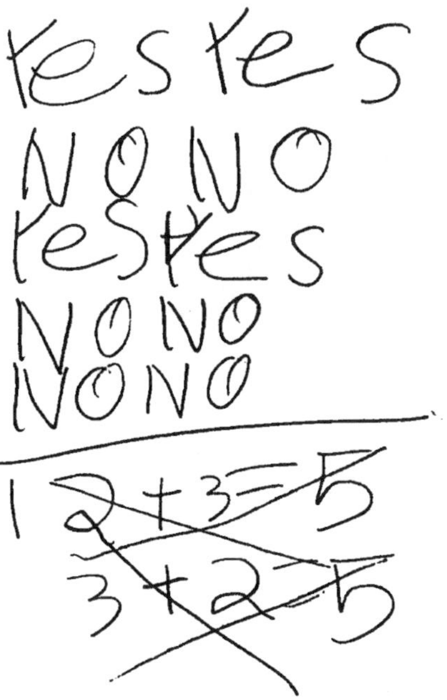

Figure 3.5. Erin's May 9 Weather Report Predictions

"Ah ha!" says Mrs. Poremba as the children begin to talk to one another about Kaitlynn's report and their predictions. "Was that what you predicted?" asks Mrs. Poremba.

Jeff shows that he knows what *prediction* means. "When you were weighing me, she said 70 first, before I weighed myself, and I weighed 70."

Mrs. Poremba responds, "She made a very good prediction, didn't she?" Now, she directs the whole class, "Look at what Kaitlynn said today."

"Hey, look at mine," says Erin, displaying her written predictions.

"Did your ideas match Kaitlynn's idea, Erin?"

"Yeah."

"Did it? All right!"

A chorus of kindergartners claims the same distinction: "So did mine!" "So did mine!"

"Would somebody like to tell us what Kaitlynn's ideas are, using words? Alyssa, would you like to do that?"

Alyssa reads, "'Yes sunny; no, no cloudy; yes windy; no, no rainy; no snowy.'"

"Thank you, Alyssa! Would somebody like to tell us about Kaitlynn's ideas using numbers? Tara."

"Two *yes*es plus three *no*s make five altogether," answers Tara G.

"Elise, can you think of a different way to say it using numbers? Thank you, Tara."

Elise responds, "Three *no*s plus two *yes*es equal five altogether."

"Ah ha! Interesting ideas," Mrs. Poremba comments. Meanwhile, Erin writes $2 + 3 = 5$ and $3 + 2 = 5$ below her *yes/no* predictions (see again figure 3.5). Mrs. Poremba asks, "Kait, would you like to do our Numbers Today, our Words for Today, I mean?"

Kaitlynn answers immediately, "Yes."

THE WORDS FOR TODAY ROUTINE

As she stands and gets a black marker from atop the wall work bulletin board and hands it to Kaitlynn, Mrs. Poremba suggests to the class, "I want you to be thinking about special words that tell about today. You might even want to be thinking about what's happening with our chicks and how close we're getting to Hatch Day. Maybe those might give you some ideas for things we could put on our word list for today."

Kaitlynn writes the date at the top of the Words for Today chart, an eight-and-one-half-by-eleven-inch sheet of paper (see figure 3.6) that is pinned to the wall work bulletin board below a card displaying the month and year as a model.

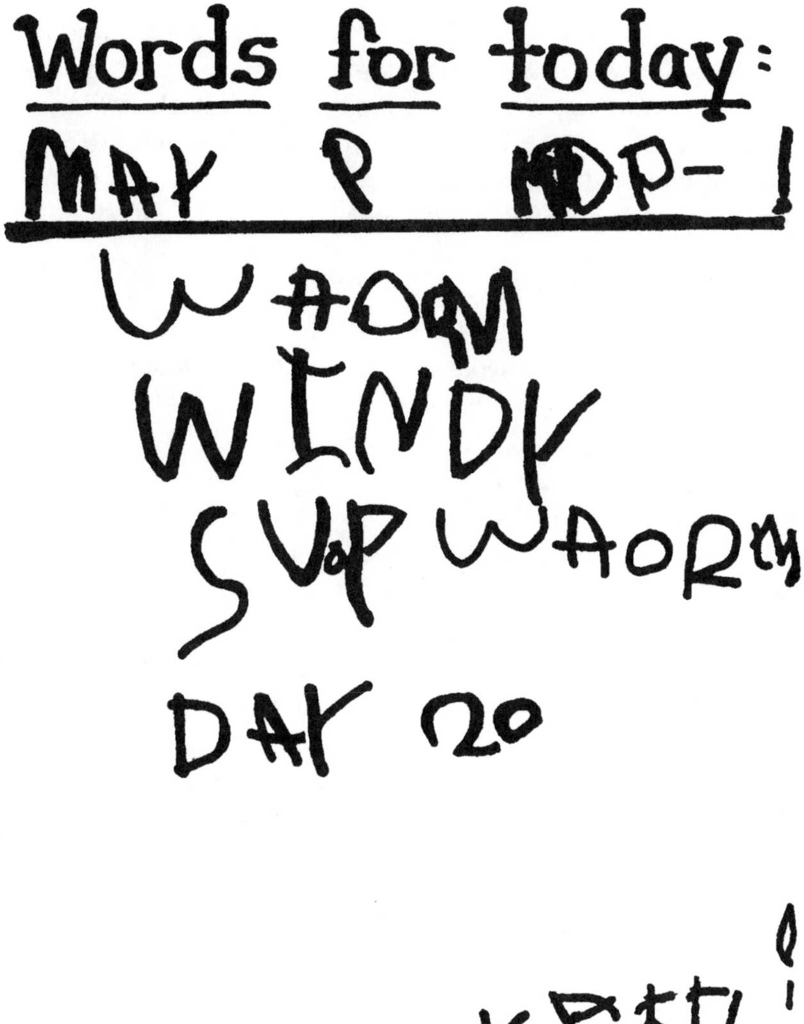

Figure 3.6. Kaitlynn's May 9 Words for Today

Meagan suggests the first word for Kaitlynn to write: "*Warm*."

"*Warm*," echoes Mrs. Poremba.

"I'm hot," says a kindergartner.

"We've had that word a lot recently," continues Mrs. Poremba.

Kaitlynn turns immediately to the Words for Today sheet and writes **WAOM**. Her classmates are quiet and attentive.

"Kaitlynn, I'm interested in your ideas for spelling the word *warm*. What were you thinking of?"

Kaitlynn points to her writing as she explains, again with no hesitation, "That's the *O*, I heard 'Wohhhhhhh.'" Kaitlynn draws out the *oh* sound, and even when she stops making the sound, she keeps her finger on the *O* that she wrote and she holds her mouth in an *O* shape. And Kaitlynn has listened well, for there is an *oh* sound in *warm*; though we spell it with an *A*, this vowel sound matches the vowel sound in *form*, not the vowel sound in *farm*.

"Okay," says Mrs. Poremba.

"And then, and I knew that—"

"You forgot the *rrr*," Nicole interrupts. (Nicole has been in Mrs. Poremba's class since November 1.)

"—the *M* was at the end," Kaitlynn continues.

As Kaitlynn stands ready for a second suggestion from a classmate for a word for today, Nicole repeats, "You forgot the *rrr*: *warrrm*."

Kaitlynn turns back to the Words for Today sheet and writes an *R* before her *M*.

"You forgot the *R*," adds Nicole.

"Oh, I see you put the *R* in before the *M*," observes Mrs. Poremba. "Did what Nicole say help you to think about that *rrr* sound in *warm*?"

"Yeah."

"Nicole, that was very good thinking. Does somebody else have a good word for our list today?" Several hands go up, and Kaitlynn calls on Tara G.

Kaitlynn completes her Words for Today writing from Tara G's suggestion of *windy*, Nathan's *super warm*, and Mrs. Poremba's *Day 20*—"because today is the twentieth day our eggs have been in the incubator" (see again figure 3.6.). She copies *windy* from the weather chart, sounds out *super* (saying "Ooooo" as she writes the *U*, and, after completing the *P*, "Ooooo" again, whereupon she decides to squeeze a very small *O* between the *U* and the *P*), copies **WAORM** from her writing of *warm* for the first word for today, and writes **DAy** without hesitation. As she is about to write *20*, Kaitlynn says, "Oooops!" and measures the space between **SUoP** and **WAORM** with a finger, moves that finger to hold a space after **DAy**, and writes **20**.

"Thank you, Kaitlynn," says Mrs. Poremba. "Kaitlynn, can you read the words on our list that we have, for us, please? Could you read everything that you wrote down today?"

Kaitlynn points with her marker as she reads the date and then, "'Warm, windy, super warm,' and 'Day 20'"

"Ah ha! An important thing—"

"Mrs. Poremba!" interrupts Freddy. "I noticed something."

"What did you notice, Freddy?" Mrs. Poremba asks.

Freddy goes to the Words for Today sheet and points, "The first two of 'em, they both started with *W*."

"Said absolutely correct. *Warm* and *windy* both started with the sound of *W*."

Mrs. Poremba gives the kindergartners an opportunity to read what they have written on their sign-in sheets: "Thank you, Kaitlynn. Can you take a moment to look at a friend's sign-in sheet and ask them to read something to you that they wrote down? Ask your friend to read something to you."

All the kindergartners do this. Ian scoots up to Ben, points at his own sign-in sheet and reads, "'Water bottle, food dish'" (see figure 3.3). Erin is on Ian's other side. She reads from her sign-in, "'Kelly, Maggy, Ian, Meagan, Sarah, Kaitlynn, Alyssa, Zack, Tara.'" And, indeed, those are the first several words she has written on her sign-in sheet after *Today is*.

"I wanna write—" Jeff tells Mrs. Poremba, pointing to the easel. He is still copying from the poem there.

"You writing the whole poem, Jeff?" asks Mrs. Poremba.

"Doesn't that look like a crooked *T*?" Jeff asks Mrs. Poremba, pointing to a *K* in his copy work. The two slanted lines of his *K* do look like a *T* leaning against the letter's vertical line (see figure 3.2).

"Is that what you think? I've never thought of a *K* looking like a crooked *T*, but now that you say it, I guess I can see what you mean.

Sure. It looks like the *T* is kind of leaning over." Jeff leans to his left in imitation of the crooked *T* in *K*.

I collect the sign-in sheets, and as Tara G. hands me hers (see figure 3.7), I say, "Thanks, Tara. Great writing! Boy, you wrote a lot."

"I filled my whole sign-in sheet."

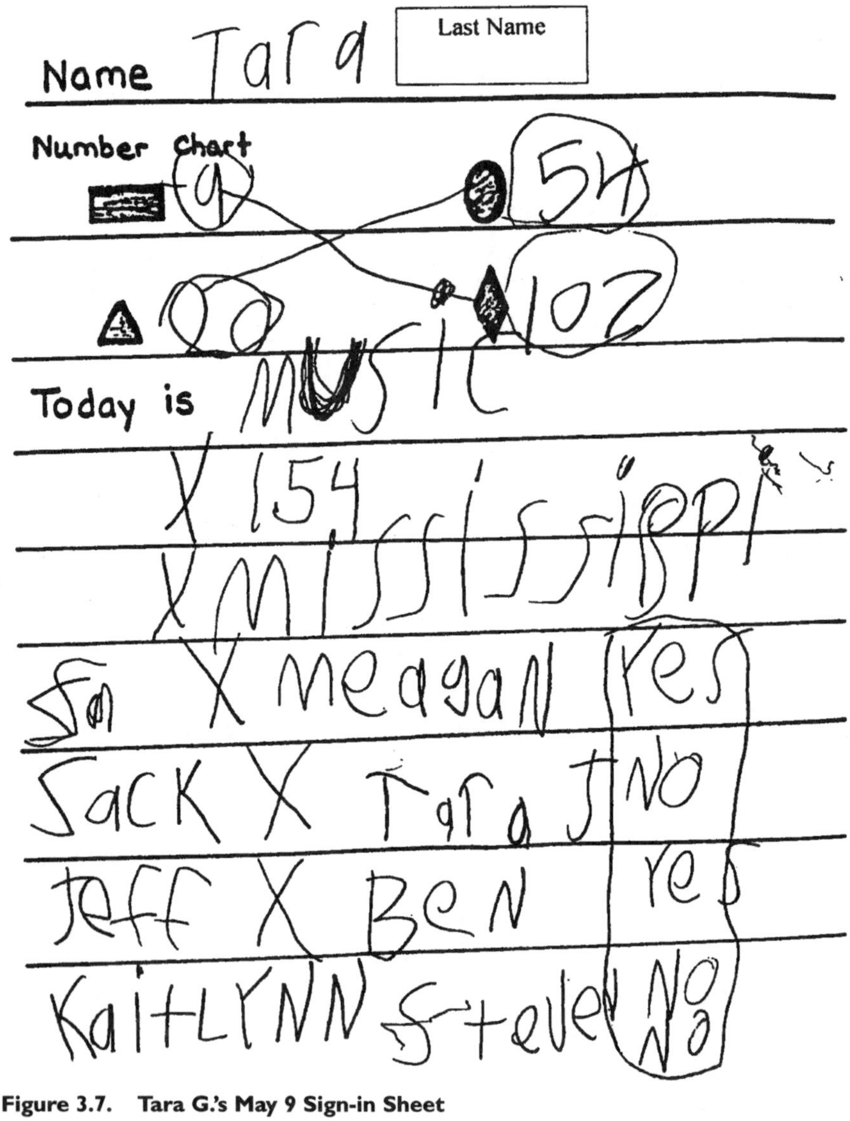

Figure 3.7. Tara G.'s May 9 Sign-in Sheet

THE HEADLINE NEWS ROUTINE

Often on Mondays, the class sits in a circle and takes turns telling briefly—in just a headline—something about themselves, often something about their just-finished weekend. And so, after wall work today, Mrs. Poremba directs, "And how about if we meet back in the Block Center for our Headline News today?"

"Show and tell" is a widespread kindergarten activity, but in Mrs. Poremba's class it has evolved to include both relevant talk about the current unit and personal talk, often accepted, when the need to communicate is pressing, with winking disregard for the "just a headline" rule. Today's is typical Headline News, with a wide variety of offerings. Among them are Jeff's "On Wednesday, I saw a fox," Ben's "I went to the neighborhood park yesterday," Erin's "Yesterday, um, me and my friends, we, um, had a water balloon fight," Deborah's "Two days, I saw Mrs. Poremba—two times, Friday night and Saturday afternoon," Elizabeth's "I write chalk on the driveway," and Mayra's, "Uh, my, my moth—, my mother's earrings to me."

"They're beautiful earrings," Mrs. Poremba responds, "Are they brand new?"

"Yeah. They're green earrings."

"They *are* green. I really like them! Thank you."

Mrs. Poremba calls on the next kindergartner, but Mayra objects, "No, I have one more!"

"One more? Okay. Thanks for reminding me."

"Um, my mom—"

"Show everybody," Mrs. Poremba whispers. "Tell us. What happened?"

"Um, my mom painted my fingers."

"They're beautiful! Beautiful fingernail painting!"

"Let's see!" say several girls.

"Thank you, Mayra."

On this day before the chicks are expected to hatch, Elise has a hatching story. "Last week, um, there, um, was kildeers in our garden, and we got to see 'em hatch."

"What is a kildeer?" asks Mrs. Poremba.

"A bird."

"What does it look like?"

"I don't know."

"Do you remember what color a kildeer is?"

"No."

"Did you just see the babies hatching, or was the mother, um, nearby, too?"

"Yes."

"The mother was nearby, too? That's a lucky thing to see, then. Thank you."

When it's Nathan's turn, he says, "I need more thinking time."

"Okay, Nathan. Jason's turn."

"Me?" asks Jason.

"Mmm hmm."

"Already?"

"Mmm hmm. Already, Jason."

"Um, I went to Nathan's house yesterday."

"Thank you, Jason."

Jeff asks, "What did you do, play in the creek? You played in the creek?"

Nathan indicates no. "But we did go on my log bridge," he adds.

"Oh, yeah, we did. We did," says Jason.

Another boy asks, "Did you guys—" and his voice trails off.

"It's not like a footbridge," says Nathan.

"A tree fell over it, over it, and we crawled across it."

"I know—" says a kindergartner.

"—a storm," says Freddy.

"Thank you, Jason," says Mrs. Poremba.

Jason's story primes Nathan. He waits for the next speaker to finish and then announces, "Now, I'm ready."

"Okay, Nathan, go ahead."

"Um, when we were crawling over the bridge, um, I saw the, um, I think I saw the dinosaur's teeth, um—"

"Tooth," corrects a kindergartner in a quiet voice.

"—Ja—it was over the bridge," Nathan continues. "Jason can't see it, couldn't even see it."

"I wasn't in the middle," Jason says.

"What did you think you saw?" asks Mrs. Poremba.

"A dinosaur tooth," says Tara G.

"Ah!" responds Mrs. Poremba.

"It could have been a leaf," suggests a kindergartner.

"I wonder," says Mrs. Poremba.

"It wasn't a leaf," says Nathan. "It was under the bridge. It wasn't on the side of the bridge." Nathan isn't finished: "*And* I have another thing to tell. Um, there's, there's, um, baby birds in our, um, in our bird, um, um, house."

"Lots of baby birds are hatching this time of the year. You're right."

Kaitlynn's turn is predictably long. She has a lot to tell about her just-finished vacation, and she has a gift for gab. She begins with a warning: "I have a lot to tell. See, I went to Georgia, and I swimmed with my friends, and it was really fun because I went off a slide and I went off a diving board, and I got this new ring that's really pretty. And we played in the ocean, and the friends that I have is Chris and Adam."

"*My* friend's name is Adam," notes a kindergartner.

"Oh, oh," says Nicole, "you shouldn't play in the ocean. Salt water sharks." A few days ago, Nicole had told the class about a surfer's being attacked by a shark because the shark had mistaken the surfer for a seal, the shark's favorite food.

Kaitlynn continues: "*And* then we had lots of fun until we had to go home, *and* I have some, I have a *lot* to show." Then hurriedly and urgently, as if she knows she has already far exceeded the headline limitation: "I only have two things: I have tan."

"It's beautiful, Kaitlynn, just beautiful," responds Mrs. Poremba.

"Now these," says Kaitlynn about her shells.

"Thank you, Kaitlynn."

Jason has a proposal: "Shouldn't she, um, put it out on—take 'em out of the bag and like set one next to the other one—"

"Would you be interested in looking at Kaitlynn's shells today, Jason?"

"Yes."

"Kaitlynn, if I give you some magnifying glasses, would you, would it be okay if friends came over to look at your shells?"

"Yes."

"Thank you."

Freddy's turn, like Kaitlynn's, involves something special he has brought to school. "Um, one day my mom was cutting the grass, and she went, she was near our evergreen trees, and we found a robin egg there."

"And you brought it with you, didn't you?" To the class, Mrs. Poremba adds, "If you would like to visit Freddy's robin egg center, you can come right up over here. He has it all set up. Be careful, because there's a light that can get warm, so make sure you don't touch the light. It could burn you. And—"

"Can we, um, touch the robin egg?" asks Nicole.

"—today," continues Mrs. Poremba, "Freddy wanted to do something special with it. What did you want to do, Freddy?"

"Candle the egg." Candling is shining a powerful light through an egg, a process Mrs. Poremba and the kindergartners have already performed twice with their chicken eggs, on days seven and fourteen of the incubation process.

"Yeah. He made a sign. Do you want to tell us about the sign you made?" Freddy's sign is NO next to a drawing of an arm and hand and yes next to a drawing of two eyes.

Freddy begins to read, "'No touch—'"

"What did you want to tell us about this?" asks Mrs. Poremba.

Freddy repeats, "'No touch. Only—'"

"'Yes,'" reads a kindergartner.

"'—yes look,'" continues Freddy.

Mrs. Poremba makes sure the kindergartners understand Freddy's written directive, but then he seems to change his mind, at least somewhat: "Um, this morning, I was letting 'em touch only if I was there and I was holding it very gently. Could they do that, at free-choice time?"

"Well, you need to decide," says Mrs. Poremba. "Well, your sign says something different."

"I know. It's only if I'm away."

"Okay."

"If nobody, if I'm not around there, then the sign, um, tells 'em not to touch."

"You need to know—" begins Mrs. Poremba.

"If I'm arou—"

"Okay, go ahead."

"If I'm around, they could touch, but I'll have to tell them."

FREE-CHOICE TIME

After everyone has a turn for Headline News, Mrs. Poremba announces free-choice time. She reminds the class of the chick equipment display. "Make sure you visit the red table and the orange table and look very carefully at what you see there because after choice time is over, we're going to be talking about those things today. I want you to see them. Let me show you what the clock looks like right now." It's a few minutes after ten o'clock. Mrs. Poremba moves the hands on a demonstration clock. "And when choice time is over, when I ring the bell, it's going to look like this. Right in between the *4* and the *5*. Okay?"

"We get a lot of choice time," notes a kindergartner.

Jason disagrees: "No."

"If you need to go to the library, please do that. Mrs. Roloff will have a snack table set up. If you need to return, um, a classroom book—think right now: How many of you need to go to the big library today? Okay. How many of you need to return a classroom reader? How about you, Eric? Okay. Do those jobs first. Are you ready to go?"

"Yeah," say several kindergartners.

Some kindergartners choose to join Freddy by his incubator, where he is ready for the candling of the robin egg. Mrs. Poremba arrives. "Are you ready?" she asks. She unplugs Freddy's warming light and plugs in her candling light.

"I see it!" exclaims a kindergartner.

"Well, we've got an air sac," observes Mrs. Poremba.

"Yeah, we've got an air sac," agrees Tara G.

"No tubes!" notes Lauren, who remembers the tangle of tubes that were visible during the class's candling of their chick eggs several days ago.

"Any food tubes?" asks Mrs. Poremba.

"No."

"I see a little gray part on the bottom," says Tara G.

"Yeah," agrees a kindergartner.

"There's an air sac."

"Well, we definitely have an air sac," says Mrs. Poremba. "All eggs have air sacs."

"Oh, I know!" says a kindergartner. "The chick is in there."

In fact, there is no robin growing in the egg, but Mrs. Poremba wants Freddy to arrive at that conclusion himself. He is not inclined to do that.

"It's just pretty small probably," suggests Freddy.

"It's what?" asks Mrs. Poremba.

"It's pretty small probably. That's why we can't see it."

"There is not a chick," asserts Nicole.

"You don't think that there's a robin growing in there?" asks Mrs. Poremba.

"It's so small," says Freddy.

After more looking and more disagreement about what the light reveals, Mrs. Poremba suggests, "We'll have to watch it. Maybe we can candle again tomorrow to see if it's changed at all." And she emphasizes what she can truthfully say, "That air sac just shows up so beautifully. Isn't that interesting, that even robin eggs have air sacs at the top?"

Freddy begins writing a record of his classmate's positions about the viability of his robin egg. He draws ovals, like those on the class's egg-candling chart. That chart has one oval for each of the eighteen eggs in the incubator, and *yes* or *no* for the candling results at Day 7 and Day 14. Freddy's chart has one oval for each person he polls about his one robin egg. So far he has three ovals, each followed by a **yes**. "Kaitlynn said, 'Yes, there is a chick,' so I'm writing it," he explains.

Eric C. and Meagan are examining Kaitlynn's shell collection, using magnifying glasses that Mrs. Poremba has set out. They are deliberate, focused, and quiet.

"You want this one?" Eric asks in a low voice. And after another minute of quiet study, "Look at this one."

Eric leaves and Tara J., Tara G., and Alyssa join Meagan. "Let's dump 'em all out," suggests Tara G.

"No," answers one of the girls.

"Let's ask Kaitlynn," says another. "She's over there by—"

"Kaitlynn!"

"Kaitlynn!"

"Come here. We have a question for you." Kaitlynn joins the group.

"Can we dump these out? Tara wanted to know."

"Yes," admits Tara G.

"Can *I* dump 'em out?" asks Kaitlynn.

"Yes."

"Whoah!"

"There's so much little ones!" says Tara G.

"I know, there's a lot of little ones."

"How awesome," says Tara G. "This looks like a crystal ball."

"Excuse me, Kaitlynn."

"Wow, Georgia must be a pretty neat place!" says Tara G.

"Yeah, I wish I was gonna go there," says Tara J.

Other free-choice activities today include playing with modeling dough at one of the big tables and pizza parlor pretend play at the Housekeeping Center. Both of these are student-initiated activities, and they sometimes overlap as when Deborah, at the modeling dough table, makes a pizza after consulting with the pizza parlor group. Pizza parlor play includes play with writing. At one point, Ben is poised with pencil, clipboard, and a small sheet of yellow paper, ready to take my order.

"—thin crust, pepperoni, with black olives," I say. "And are you offering any drinks this week?"

"Yeah," answers Ian.

"How about a large root beer?" I ask.

Ben produces four lines of scribble writing, one each in response to my *thin crust*, *pepperoni*, *black olives*, and *root beer*.

At the flannel board, another group tells the story of *The Very Hungry Caterpillar*, using the book by Eric Carle (1992) and felt story props that Mrs. Poremba used when she told the story last Thursday. Most kindergartners move from one activity to another and manage time for a stop at the snack table. For a long time, Freddy remains focused on his robin egg project. He approaches the shell display with his survey. "Alyssa, do you think a chick's growing in there?" When he gets no response, he repeats, "Alyssa, do you think a robin's growing in there?"

"Yes," answers Alyssa.

Tara G. returns the talk to the shells by describing as she works: "I just got one more, and it iiiiiiis—this one. You have some neat ones, Alyssa."

Finally, Freddy leaves his survey to take up storytelling at the flannel board. He is there with Kaitlynn when she calls, "Mrs. Poremba, it's time to ring the bell."

Mrs. Poremba answers, "No, we have—look at the clock."

"Oh."

"A little bit more time. If you want to finish telling *The Very Hungry Caterpillar*, I think you can do that. Boys and girls, the snack table will be closing soon."

Ian is at the pizza parlor cash register. "Do you know what twenty-five plus ten is?" he asks his mates.

"Thirty-five," one of them answers. "Thirty-five."

Mrs. Poremba reminds the pizza parlor boys, "Guys, just remember when I ring the clean-up bell, you have a lot of cleaning up to do."

Tara G. asks at the pizza parlor, "How much do I have to pay?"

"There you go. Want anything to drink? Root beer's free tonight," says Ian. "Root beer's free tonight. Here's your root beer. It's free tonight."

"Hey, how much do I pay you?" asks Nathan.

"Nine hundred and sixty-five dollars," answers Ian.

"Guys, clean up!" urges one of the boys. And soon Mrs. Poremba rings the bell and directs, "I'll meet you on the carpet. We're going to talk about our things right up here on the table." After a minute she reminds, "Ian, let's take a trip to see how the Housekeeping Center looks. There's still some things on the floor that shouldn't be."

READ ALOUD AND DISCUSSION TIME

After free-choice time, Mrs. Poremba reminds the class that their chicks are expected to begin hatching tomorrow. She reads to them from *Inside an Egg* (Johnson 1982), one of the books on display with the chick equipment, about their chicks' being so big now that they fill their eggs and about each chick's having a bump on its beak called an egg tooth for breaking out of the shell. She reads about how the chicks on Day 20 use their beaks to break the air sacs inside the eggs, so that they begin now to breathe air rather than to get oxygen "through the red tubes" that the kindergartners had seen in their last candling of their eggs. "Today, on Day 20, our chicks are starting to breathe real air from their air sac on top of the egg," Mrs. Poremba explains. Then she leads the kindergartners as they feel their own lungs expand and contract during breathing. "We're going to feel our lungs breathing real air. We're going to feel our lungs filling up, and we're going to feel our lungs getting smaller and letting air out. Lungs are inside your body, and that's what holds the air that you breathe. Well, chicks have lungs, too." After some time breathing in and out and feeling the changes in the size of their chests, the kindergartners look at a photograph in *Inside an Egg* of a chick inside its shell at Day 20. "I wanted to tell you that now our baby chicks have everything they need," says Mrs. Poremba. She reads more and the children discuss more from the book.

Then they talk about the displayed chick equipment, beginning with the brooder box. "Boys and girls, this is not any ordinary box. This—Why don't I take the name off, so you can see it?—is our—" Mrs. Poremba displays the *Brooder Box* sign and pauses, giving the kindergartners a chance to read it.

"'Finger paint box,'" reads one kindergartner

"What a good guess! What good reading!" responds Mrs. Poremba.

"'Big box,'" reads Erin.

"'Brrrrrrr,'" read Tara G. and Kaitlynn at the same time.

"'Brooder box,'" reads Lauren.

"This is our—" Mrs. Poremba points and reads, "'brooder, box.' That's a home for chicks."

Mrs. Poremba explains about the water bottle: "We'll turn it over like this, and the water will dribble out into the orange tray, and the chicks can drink from it in there. That's why this says 'water bottle.' They need water to drink. And this is a special kind of water bottle that's designed especially for baby chicks. It helps to keep them safe when they're drinking their water. Baby chicks, if we put a bowl out, it could happen that a baby chick could fall in the bowl, and chicks have actually drowned—not since we've been using a water bottle like this."

This talk leads to Jeff's voicing a worry. "What if they have a heart attack?" he asks.

"What do you mean, Jeff?" asks Mrs. Poremba.

Jeff's answer is too soft for me to hear.

"Well, Jeff, I suppose it would be possible for us to have a chick that was not healthy. And if that happens, we'll have to talk about how to deal with it, what we can do to help the chick. That's a very good question."

"We'll get a chick doctor," suggests Jeff.

"Mmm hmm. A chick doctor—"

Jeff has scored a winner. Much talk erupts among the kindergartners about this intriguing idea.

DAY'S END

After music class with the school's music teacher and a visit from Nicole's mother, who brings a grown chicken, a pet on Nicole's family's farm, it is time to go home. When the kindergartners are lined up at the door, Mrs. Poremba leads them in singing a good-bye song that is posted over the door. This is sung to the melody of *Frere Jacques*. The words declare that kindergarten "is so fun" and announce the next day that the kindergartners will see one another. For this, the text has removable cards for the names of the days of the week. Earlier in the chick hatching countdown, the class changed the last line of the song from *Everyone, everyone* to *Cheep, cheep, cheep. Cheep, cheep, cheep.*

"Are we all ready?" asks Mrs. Poremba. But Jeff has bumped someone. Mrs. Poremba tells him, "Moving fast and running and rushing, you could bump someone, and that hurts. That's why we need you to move more slowly, so you don't bump into people and hurt them."

"I couldn't see. Everybody was blocking my way," says Jeff.

"Okay, so when that happens, rather than pushing your way through, just wait, and when you see a space, then you can move through. Okay?" Now, to the whole class, "Let's say good-bye to Monday." Mrs. Poremba removes the *Monday* card from the song poster.

"'Bye, Monday!" the kindergartners shout.

"And let's say hello to Tuesday." Mrs. Poremba places the *Tuesday* card in the song poster.

"Hi, Tuesday," say a few kindergartners.

"Are you ready? Tomorrow, we might want to say—" Mrs. Poremba was about to suggest a new ending about Hatch Day.

A kindergartner interrupts: "Mrs. Poremba?"

This interruption and the lateness of the time cause Mrs. Poremba not to finish her suggestion. She only says, "Shhh. Let's sing our song. Okay?"

Everyone reads and sings together, loudly and with spirit, and using the posted ending: "'Cheep, cheep, cheep. Cheep, cheep, cheep.'"

Kaitlynn, however, returns to the idea of a new final line for the song. "We could say, 'Chi-icks hatch! Chi-icks hatch!'" She sings her suggested new words.

"For tomorrow, that would be a good way to end our day," agrees Mrs. Poremba.

SOURCES OF THESE CHANGES?

It is easy to notice how Mrs. Poremba's kindergartners have changed in 154 days. They are truly at home in a room that encourages many kinds of learning. They move easily from one routine to another. They engage in productive free-choice play. They read and write in a variety of ways, in a variety of contexts, and for a variety of purposes. They show respect for one another in all sorts of interactions, whether around a planned display of chick equipment, in a group activity such as wall work, or in an individual project such as Freddy's survey. Their learning builds from previous experiences, whether in the current several-week-long chick-hatching unit or in the yearlong evolution of routines such as Straw Cups or Words for Today. With unobtrusive supervision and gentle guidance, Mrs. Poremba shows them that sometimes rules can be flexible, when there is no harm and when they are onto something, such as when Kaitlynn goes beyond the "just a headline" restriction for Headline News or when Nicole interrupts Kaitlynn's Words for Today writing to note the need for an *R* in *warm*.

What are the origins of these accomplishments? How do Mrs. Poremba and her students establish productive routines? What makes a science unit work as a context not only for science learning but also for learning about reading and writing, speaking and listening, cooperating and collaborating? To find answers to these questions, we will follow in the next several chapters the evolution of several important routines and the history of two units of study.

FROM MRS. POREMBA

The spring chick-hatching season in kindergarten is one of my favorites. It is the catalyst for rich conversations and so much learning. Children are drawn to making connections across the curriculum as they read, write, listen, speak, count, measure, compare, analyze, and predict about the wonderful events that are unfolding. The literacy routines established earlier in the year now take on a new relevance as they reflect our new classroom focus.

Literacy routines provide daily opportunities for children to practice, refine, use, demonstrate, and develop their skills and knowledge. I believe the most valuable literacy routines are flexible and accommodate a wide range of students. For example, emergent readers and writers can successfully participate in signing in alongside more accomplished readers and writers because all of them approach the task at their own levels. The Words for Today routine is different each day depending on the student leader and the group-generated teacher-facilitated conversations that arise.

While literacy routines are predictable and familiar, they are not cookie-cutter tasks where all children are doing the same things in the same ways. They provide a meaningful structure but a structure that is far from rigid. On the contrary, they can be highly personalized, unique, and refreshing because individual, unique, refreshing children are empowered to make these routines their own.

4

PLEASE SIGN IN.

As long ago as the first half of the previous century, research about children's signatures revealed developmental progressions that reflect increasing motor control, greater awareness of letter features, and growing knowledge that letters are discrete units (Hildreth 1936). Clay (1991, 98) notes, "A child's name has singular importance as he embarks on learning about literacy, both for the child's management of his own learning about print and for the observant teacher trying to understand his pattern of progress." Harste, Burke, and Woodward (1981) and McGee and Richgels (2000) have described sign-in procedures in which even preschool children write their names daily on a sign-in sheet. Fisher (1998) describes several sign-in procedures for kindergarten. When children sign in every day, they learn that writing can serve real-life purposes (the attendance-taking function), they gain practice in letter formation, and their teacher gathers valuable documentation of the students' developing writing skills. This chapter shows how daily signing in evolved during the first two months in Mrs. Poremba's kindergarten to serve many more functions than just the attendance-taking function and gave her kindergartners a social context for developing and practicing many kinds of writing beyond signature writing. As the kindergartners initiated these additional kinds of writing, Mrs. Poremba responded with just the right encouragement and support.

EXTRA WRITING ON SIGN-IN SHEETS

Beginning with the second day of school, Mrs. Poremba's kindergartners start their day by signing their names on one of several sign-in sheets that she places each day at the big tables at one end of the room (see figure 4.1). She checks the sheet at each table to see that everyone there has signed in and then dismisses those children so that they are free to take up other activities around the room before whole-class, wall work time is called. This sign-in procedure gives kindergartners direction; with it, they have an everyday first routine. It also provides them practice writing their names and an opportunity to visit with tablemates before they are dismissed.

Already in the first two weeks of school, signing in shows two characteristics that will have powerful ramifications for the kindergartners'

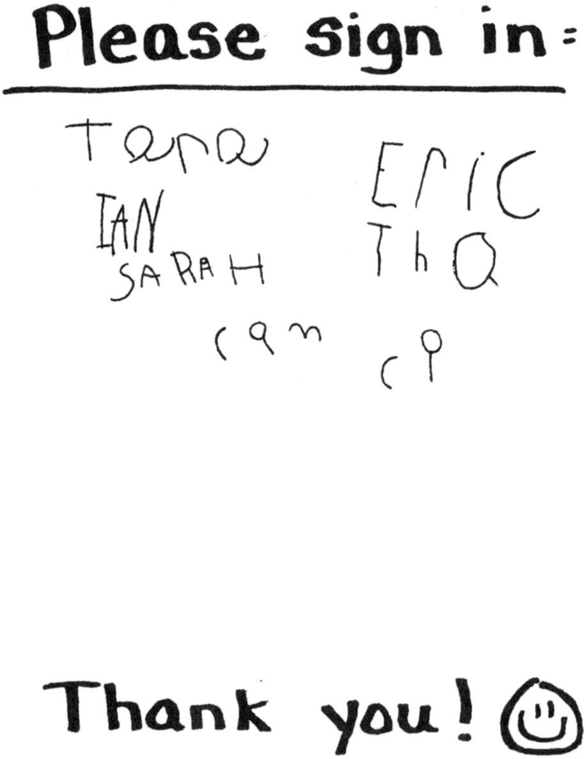

Figure 4.1. August 31 Sign-in Sheet

writing development. They begin writing on their sign-in sheets a small number of words other than their names, and they make signing in a social event. On September 3, Steven writes **Kitt** (modified to **Kit** on September 8); on September 8, Ian writes **OFF NOON**; and on September 10, Jeff writes **no**. The amount of such writing will increase dramatically over the next few weeks.

The orange table's signing in on September 13 is an example of the enthusiasm and the interaction that accompanies the kindergartners' extra sign-in writing. Steven is the first to write. He writes **StEVEN**, **KKit**, and **Stop** (with backwards **S**s). And he copies the first four letters of *Please*: **Plea**.

While Steven writes, Nathan rehearses for his turn. "*N-O, no. N-O, no.*"

When Mrs. Poremba arrives to dismiss the orange table, Steven is still writing; he has just finished the *a* in *Please*. "Are you done signing in? Who wrote that *Stop* word? Steven? You used to write *Kit*. Now, you're writing *Kit* and you're writing *Plea* and you're writing *Stop*. You know a lot about writing, don't you Steven? Can you pass your sign-in sheet to another friend?"

Nathan gets the sign-in sheet next. "Come awwwn!" complains Eric C., and Nathan quickly writes his first name and then the word he had rehearsed, *NO*.

"What are you doing? *N-O. N-O, no*?" comments Eric.

"*N-O, no. N-O, no*," answers Nathan.

"*N-O, no*," echoes Eric.

"And this goes with this," explains Nathan.

Now Eric interjects, "Do you know how old my brother is?"

"How, *N-O, no*?" responds Nathan, joking and returning the conversation to its established subject. Eric is not amused. Nathan tries to appease Eric: "I was gonna say eight."

Eric begins again, "Do you know how old my brother is?"

This time Nathan answers, "Eight."

"No," replies Eric.

"Nine, ten, eleven, twelve, thirteen, eighteen, nineteen," continues Nathan.

"My sister's twelve," says Steven. "She gots a gerbil."

Nathan responds, "Gerbils. Oh, they always . . ." and the conversation swings to gerbils.

Eric finally gets his turn to sign in. He writes his first name and then begins a copying job that will take several minutes, past the start of wall work time for the rest of the class, and will eventually include his writing Please / signin :, and Thank You ! s (with backwards es). Eric was the first to do this sort of copying from the preprinted words on the sign-in sheet. At his first signing in on the second day of school, he wrote Tha / cam ca under his name, the first letters of *Thank* and of his last name (see figure 4.1). And in the days between then and now, several kindergartners copied all or parts of *Please sign in:* and *Thank you!*

Today, Jeff shows how familiar these words have become. He walks by Eric and observes, "You're making *Please sign in*."

CONNECTIONS

Throughout the school year, Mrs. Poremba helps students to make connections between one literacy event and another. This helps beginning readers and writers to understand the importance of meaning in written language. Reading and writing events are not isolated and random. They are intentional and communicative. Early in the year, signing in offered many opportunities to emphasize connectedness and meaning. As the kindergartners enter the room on Tuesday, September 14, they visit with one another and their teacher. Today, this includes commentary about the weather: "Icky rain out there!" "Good thing I brought a umbrella to the um—Teacher, good thing I brought a umbrella to my bus stop."

As Mrs. Poremba greets the children, she collects the large envelopes in which notes are sent to and from school. "I'll take white envelopes!" she announces. "Thank you!" And she calls children's attention to a four-line poem about rain that she has copied onto large chart paper and posted at the easel: "You might want to stop and look at the poem before you go to your table. . . . Make sure you stop off and look at the poem. . . . Stop on off and look at that poem. I wonder what that poem could be about."

Later in the day, the children read the poem with Mrs. Poremba. Two days later, on September 16, the poem is posted on the wall near Ian's table.

In what will soon be a trend in Mrs. Poremba's classroom, Ian copies on his sign-in sheet from writing available around the room. He is copying the word *rain* from the poem (see figure 4.2). "I'm copying," he tells Mrs. Poremba. She asks him and Freddy, who is nearby, what they think this word says.

"Raining," guesses Freddy.

"Those rainy days of summer," suggests Ian.

Later, at wall work time, Mrs. Poremba displays kindergartners' sign-in sheets for their classmates' responses. "Oh, look at this one!" she says about the yellow table's sign-in sheet (see figure 4.2).

Figure 4.2. Ian's September 16 Sign-in Sheet

"I wrote my name two times," Ian points out.

"Yes, I noticed."

Kaitlynn erupts, "Oh! I can see *off*!"

"Can you see *off*, Kaitlynn? Where?" Kaitlynn points to where Erin has written OFF. "Oh my goodness! Erin, Kaitlynn pointed to your word. Thank you, Kaitlynn. There's *Off—O-F-F—Off*."

"And *No*, *No*," Kaitlynn adds.

And Eric D., "And there's an *N-O*."

"*N-O*, our good old"—she pauses ever so slightly, and several children join her in finishing—"*No* word."

Ian jumps up and points to where he has written and circled RAIN. "What about *this*?" he asks.

Mrs. Poremba does not answer Ian's question. Instead, she promotes discussion. She says, "Holy cow! I wonder what this says. Ian, where did you find that word: *R-A-I-N*?"

Ian answers, "Over on the poem." On the posted text, the word *rain* appears four times, twice as *Rain* and twice as *rain*, never as *RAIN*. Ian has transposed to all capitals in his writing RAIN. (Yesterday, Ian had written YEIIOW after his name, copying from the color label at his, the yellow, table. He—incorrectly for the *Ls*—transposed the lowercase letters on the label to capitals using a laminated alphabet card at his table as a guide.)

Mrs. Poremba, who had talked with Ian while he was writing RAIN, has returned the poem to the easel in anticipation of this opportunity to reinforce Ian's and to invite his classmates' attention to print. "I moved the poem right up here," she says. "Can you show us where you found it? Go touch it on the poem where you found it." Ian does this. "Right there," says Mrs. Poremba.

"Right where?" asks a classmate.

"Right there," says Ian, pointing again.

Mrs. Poremba adds, "I wonder what that says!"

"I'm sure I don't know," answers Tara G.

"You don't know?"

Several children pick up the refrain, "I don't know."

"I wonder how we can figure out what it says," challenges Mrs. Poremba.

Several children immediately respond, "Read it!"

"Oh, of course! Would you like me to read that poem for you?"

"Yeah." "Yeah."

Since the very first day of kindergarten when Mrs. Poremba taught the class to sign "Good Morning," she occasionally teaches the American Sign Language manual sign for a special word or phrase. This keeps the kindergartners involved by giving them something to do with their hands; it reinforces the meaning making that is at the core of language, whether spoken or written or manually signed (manual signs stand for words, and written strings of letters also can stand for words); and it is fun. "Okay. As a matter of fact, I'll teach you how to sign that very important word." Mrs. Poremba makes her fingers go up and down while drawing her hand down before her.

Mrs. Poremba uses this new sign to focus children's attention as she reads. "Every time we say the word *rain*, can you sign it for us?"

"Yeah." "Yeah."

"You have to listen carefully, and you have to be ready for the word *rain*. Here we go."

The children watch intently as Mrs. Poremba points and reads the poem from the chart paper. They sign the word *rain* every time she reads it.

"Now we know what that word says," she concludes. "Great stuff goin' on here!"

UNPLANNED CONNECTIONS

Mrs. Poremba's efforts to make connections between literacy events do not always go as planned; however, they usually result in learning, both hers and her students'.

During signing in on Tuesday, September 14, Nathan writes NathanNO and a small picture, the outline of a wavy form. "I wrote *shark*," he announces, pointing to the shape. "That's a shark." And then he reads, "'*N-O*, no, shark.'"

Later, Mrs. Poremba stops at Nathan's table. She looks at the sign-in sheet and reads, "'Nathan No.'"

Nathan tells her, "No sharks!"

"No sharks?"

"And I made a shark there."

"I like your writing, Nathan."

Ian, standing nearby, informs Mrs. Poremba, "I wrote *no*, too."

"You wrote *no* also. You really know how to write *no*."

Later that day, at wall work time, Mrs. Poremba displays Nathan's and his tablemates' sign-in sheet. "Whoah!" the children react.

"My goodness! We have so many writers here."

"Look at what someone put in," a classmate says in reference to Nathan's drawing.

Mrs. Poremba waits while the class studies this.

"No," says one kindergartner.

"'No sharks,'" reads Ian.

"Oh! Nathan is the one who wrote this! Nathan, can you tell us about your writing? We really like it. It says," continues Mrs. Poremba.

"'No sharks,'" repeats Ian.

"'Nathan—,'" reads Mrs. Poremba.

"'No-shark,'" finishes Nathan.

"'No-shark,'" repeats Mrs. Poremba. "Wow. That's important."

Three weeks later, on September 28, Ian writes IAN NO on his sign-in sheet and below that NO BEAR (see figure 4.3). He copies BEAR from a Bear Facts chart, another text that has been posted near his table. The class had composed this chart on September 17. After a discussion of the differences between real bears and bears in make-believe storybooks, they looked at informational books about bears and dictated "bear facts" to Mrs. Poremba, Mrs. Roloff, or me. We wrote what they dictated on index cards and assembled the cards on this chart for the class to read and discuss together. As with YEIIOW and RAIN earlier, Ian prefers uppercase letters; he almost always writes in uppercase. He uses a laminated alphabet card at his table to find and copy the uppercase letters that correspond to the lowercase letters on the Bear Facts chart.

Ian's transposing from lower- to uppercase shows that his writing is not random copying. He makes it his own. His attention to print is driven by personal motives, by his own striving for meaning. Although he is not yet a conventional reader or writer, he knows what he is doing with his sign-in writing.

Figure 4.3. Ian's September 28 Sign-in Sheet

When Mrs. Poremba comes to the yellow table, she reads Ian's writing, "'Ian No-Bear.'" She uses the same inflection as she has in the past for Nathan's *no-shark*.

"No. They don't go together," objects Ian.

"Oh. 'Ian. No. Bear,'" Mrs. Poremba reads, stopping after each word.

Ian is satisfied: "That's how it is."

Mrs. Poremba's intention to highlight a connection between Nathan's and Ian's writing is derailed, but she learns that Ian has made a different, equally important connection between his own writing and a whole-class text. And their conversation shows that he is aware of the two very different sources of his writing NO and his writing BEAR and that he intends for a reader to preserve that difference.

WHOLE-CLASS CELEBRATIONS

Mrs. Poremba's celebration of Nathan's *no-shark* writing is just one occasion of her inviting her students to observe and learn from one another's work. Some days she directs their attention with a particular objective in mind. Other days, what they notice, and therefore what become topics of discussion and learning for all, is surprising and fortuitous, often topics that would be missed if the content of every teacher–student exchange were teacher-driven and preplanned.

On September 14, the same day as Nathan's *no-shark* writing, Meagan stops by the red table where Kaitlynn is signing in. "What are you trying to make it?" she asks.

"*N*," answers Kaitlynn.

"*M* or *N*?"

"*N*."

"That goes like that. That's an *N*," Meagan says, making a proper *N* below Kaitlynn's signature.

"Hurry up!" Jeff tells Kaitlynn. He hasn't yet had a turn to sign in on the sheet they share.

At wall work time, Jeff brings his table's sign-in sheet to Mrs. Poremba. Besides writing his name below Kaitlynn's, he has turned the N that Meagan wrote there into NO.

"Thank you, Jeff. My goodness, lots of people are putting that *no* word on today, aren't they?"

Eric D. tells that it is he who wrote Pleasesigin and Thank You! s at the bottom of his and Jeff's and Katilynn's sign-in sheet: "Teacher, I wroted all that."

"Did you do all that today, Eric? My goodness that was a lot of writing."

Two school days earlier, on Friday, September 10, Mrs. Poremba had added four horizontal lines to the sign-in sheet, not to mandate writing on the lines, but to give each student a clearly defined space for the extra writing that so many of them want to do. Now, she feels they are ready to talk about that. "How about if we look at sign-in sheets for just a moment?" she asks. "When you first came to kindergarten, on the very first day I believe"—actually it was the second day—"we had a sign-in sheet out at your table, and it looked something like this—" She shows an old sign-in sheet, with no horizontal lines.

"But it's different," observes a kindergartner.

"But it's different," repeats Mrs. Poremba. "What's different about it?"

"The lines," answer several children.

"Yeah. We added some lines to the sign-in sheet."

"What's the lines for?" asks Freddy.

Mrs. Poremba wants the kindergartners to arrive at their own answer. "That's a very good question. Does anybody have an idea?"

"I know," says Jason.

"Jason, what do you think the lines are for?"

"To separate them," answers Jason.

"To separate the names. You're using that word *separate* that we learned the very first day. How about you, Kaitlynn?"

"So you can put your names on them."

"And not higher than the line," adds Jason.

"Oh, it helps you keep your letters not higher than the line?" And so writing on the lines is Jason's, not Mrs. Poremba's idea, and she does not impose it on the others. "Erin, how about you?"

"You put one name on it."

"One name?" Mrs. Poremba repeats. "So one name goes on a line. Very interesting. Any other ideas about the sign-in sheet? Has it been helping you to know where to put your name?"

"Yeah," answer several children.

Mrs. Poremba is ready to go on to other lessons to be learned from today's sign-in writing. "Oh. You know, I noticed—here's a sign-in sheet right here, and we do have quite a bit of things on this sign-in sheet. Eric wrote his name, and Kaitlynn wrote her name, and Jeff not only wrote his name, but he wrote another thing."

"'No,'" read several children.

"There's that *N-O*. That *No* word. And Eric wrote a lot down here. He was telling me all about that."

But Eric D. is less interested in his own work that is on display than in his buddy Eric C.'s work. "Look at Eric," he says. "He's still writing." Eric C. is alone at the tables, still adding to his sign-in writing.

"Yeah. Eric is—"

"Where's the dots?" asks a kindergartner who has observed that Eric D.'s copy of *Please sign in*: is without the colon. "He forgot—"

Mrs. Poremba reads, "'Please sign in. Thank you!' He even remembered the smiley face."

"What about the dots?!"

"Hmmm. He decided not to do those."

"Because I didn't have that much room," explains Eric.

Mrs. Poremba holds up the yellow table's sign-in sheet.

"Full!" declares one kindergartner.

"That's a full one," agrees Mrs. Poremba.

"And I see that *N-O* again," says Kaitlynn.

"There it is! What does that spell, Kaitlynn?"

"*No*!" answers a chorus of voices.

"*No* and *yes*," says Erin, with reference to Ian's writing, OFF NO.

Mrs. Poremba points and asks, "*No* and—?"

"I wrote that!" declares Ian.

"Is *yes* on here?"

"No. That's *off*," explains Ian.

"Oh, that says *off*."

Ian directs the class's attention to his writing JANINE: "And then look on the bottom."

"What does that say, Ian?"

"'Janine.'"

"Janine. That's Ian's sister."

"And then I have another sister, but I can't remember [how to spell] her name."

"I bet you'll learn how to do that." And indeed, on September 22, Ian's sign-in writing includes LARSSA for his sister Larissa.

Today, Mrs. Poremba continues reading: "So we have 'Erin' and 'Sarah' and 'Jason' and 'Ian. Off, no, Janine.' Extra things on that one."

Eric D. remarks, "When I was a three year old, I had a teacher named Janine."

"Did you really? I wonder if she spelled her name the same way Ian's sister does. Now, look at this one." And Mrs. Poremba displays the sign-in sheet on which Eric C. has just finished writing. He has filled all the spaces left by his tablemates Steven and Nathan with his writing **Pleas-esign: / NoThank Yo / u! s** (with backwards **e**s).

Jason observes, "Teacher, you know—there's the dots."

"Where?"

Jason points to the colon following Eric's **Pleasesign**.

"Did you do those two on the end also? Did you make those dots right there?" Mrs. Poremba asks Nathan.

"No," answers Nathan.

"No."

"I did," says Eric C.

"But Eric did. That says, 'Please sign in' and there's the little dots right there."

"They're not little!" protests a kindergartner, who is right—they are rather large.

"'No—thank you'?" Mrs. Poremba continues. "Did you write that, too, Eric?" His classmates laugh, and Mrs. Poremba repeats, "'No thank you.' I like that, Eric. And there's the face right there. And Steven is writing a lot up here." Mrs. Poremba points to the top line of this sign-in sheet, where Steven has written **StEVEN 4 KKit / Plea** (with a backwards **S**). "I asked Steven about it. You know what Steven told me? Is it okay if I tell them what you told me?"

Steven agrees.

Mrs. Poremba lets the kindergartners know that copying without being able to read is all right. "Okay. When I was looking at Steven's, I noticed that he wrote *Steven*, and he wrote a *4*, and he wrote the word *kit*. And I asked him about these letters." She points to Steven's **Plea**. "You know what he said? 'I was just writing letters.' Isn't that a good idea? He knows a lot about writing. Good for you, Steven. Well, it's real interesting how each sign-in sheet was special today."

NAME WRITING

Although many kindergartners quickly moved beyond name writing, for others signing in remained an opportunity to practice the sometimes difficult task of writing their names, and it allowed Mrs. Poremba to notice when they needed extra support. On Thursday, September 16, the thirteenth day of school, Kaitlynn declares, "I love writing my name." She has written it twice.

On Monday, September 20, Sarah's name is all in capitals. She has had trouble writing the *S* at the beginning of her name (see figure 4.4). Last Friday, when Mrs. Poremba had complimented Sarah's *S* writing, her tablemate, Erin, had explained, "I teached her." Today, her *S* is smaller and floating higher than the rest of the letters; it is Erin's work, over Sarah's earlier erased attempt that had looked like a backwards *C*. In fact, Erin writes Sarah's *S* the next two days, too.

On September 22, Mrs. Poremba greets Sarah, "How are you today, Sarah? You know, I've been thinking about something last night. I've

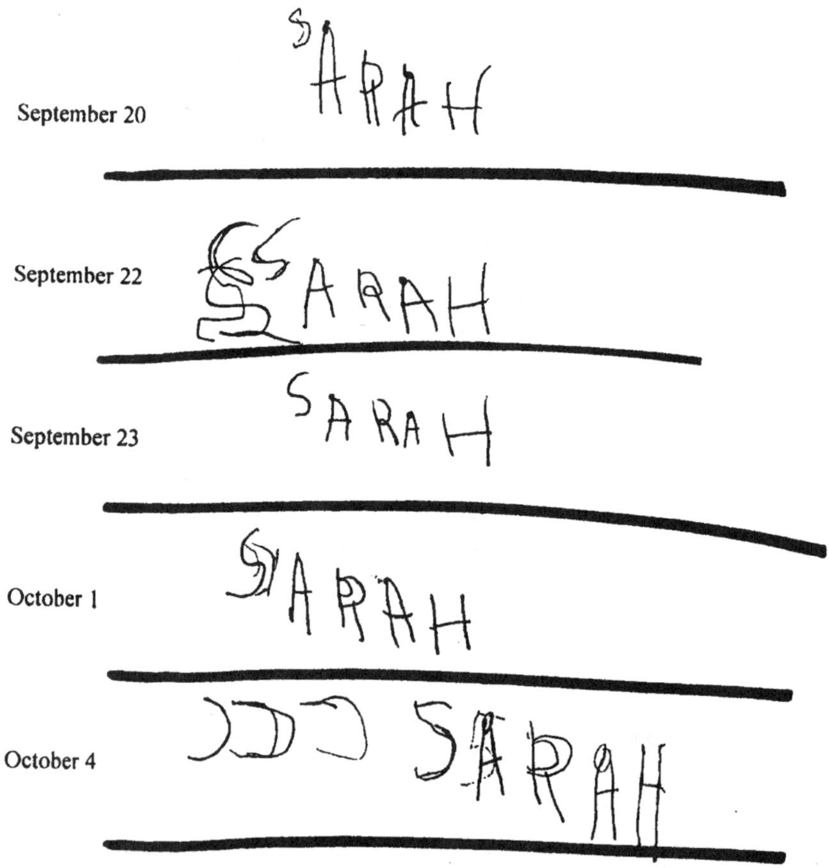

Figure 4.4. Sarah's Signatures

been thinking about how hard it is to write *S*s, and I'll show you something later that will help you."

When it is Sarah's turn to sign in, Erin again writes Sarah's *S*. Mrs. Poremba comes by and comments on her *S*.

"I did it," explains Erin.

"Did you have some help? I'm trying to think of a way that will help Sarah with her *S*s. I've got a few ideas. I was thinking about that last night. Jason?"

"Trace this with the *S*," suggests Jason.

"Trace with an *S*. That might be a good idea. I like that idea."

The next day, Thursday, September 23, the eighteenth day of school, Sarah says to me as she signs in, "I didn't have any trouble with my *S*!"

And when Mrs. Poremba asks Sarah how she learned to do *S*, Sarah answers, "She teached me," indicating Erin.

On October 1, Sarah is first with the sign-in sheet at her table. She makes a false start on the letter *S*, erases and writes it again. She says, "*S*, I'll try it—I'll make it again. Let me try it one more time." She makes an *S* that looks more like a question mark without the dot than an *S*.

Erin says, "No! No."

"Yeah, that's an *S*. See?" Sarah points to the *s* in *Please* as proof. "Yup." Now, Sarah goes to the next letter in her name. "*H*!"

Erin says, "Not an *H*."

"*A*!" says Sarah.

"*A*."

Sarah continues, "*R*! *H*."

Erin coaches, "*A*!"

"*A*. Then when do you make the *H*?" Sarah finishes writing her name.

Now Erin erases and rewrites Sarah's *S*.

Sarah protests, "Hey! That's my *S*!"

Erin says, "That's a *G*. Go like this, like that!"

On the next school day, Monday, October 4, the twenty-fifth day of school, everyone at Sarah's table has his or her own sign-in sheet, and Sarah's tablemates are filling those sheets with much writing in addition to their names.

Mrs. Roloff asks, "Are you all going to do a lot of writing?"

Sarah answers, "Uh-uh. I'm just going to write my name."

And she does just that, but puts a lot of effort into it, including erasing three backwards *C*s—false starts at *S*—and then making a recognizable *S*, though it is composed of a backwards *C* with a cap on it, like you'd put on a 5.

On November 1, Sarah applies what she knows in a new context. During wall work, Mrs. Poremba shows the class a card on which is written the name of one of today's two helpers. "And here's our next helper."

Some children read, "'Sarah!'"

Others say, "'Steven!'"

Sarah says, "It's me. Because there's an *A*."

"What do you mean, Sarah?" asks Mrs. Poremba.

"Because after the *S* comes an *A*."

"In Sarah's name," Mrs. Poremba points to the name on the card, "it starts with an *S*. And right after the *S* is an—"

Several kindergartners say, "*A*."

"—*A*, right there. And Steven's name—Steven, what comes after your *S*?"

Steven answers, "A *T*."

"A *T*. We'll put Sarah's name right up there." Mrs. Poremba posts Sarah's name on the Helper spot on the wall work bulletin board.

RELATED HAPPENINGS DURING SIGNING IN

By mid-September, signing in had already become a big part of the beginning of the day in Mrs. Poremba's kindergarten, and as we will see, it would evolve into an even more powerful literacy routine during the coming weeks. It never, however, occurs in isolation. Interactions, conversations, other learning activities, many of them impromptu, happen at the same time.

Friday, September 17, the fourteenth day of kindergarten, begins with a crisis. The children report to Mrs. Poremba that Elise has left her book bag outdoors. "She ran outside to go get it." "She had someone else's book bag."

"Oh, I'll bet she'll be back," Mrs. Poremba responds. Then she asks a visiting grown-up, "Would you like to run down and see how she's doing?"

Kaitlynn, Erin, Jason, and Ian are first to their tables. Elise arrives with her book bag and a sad face. "So your book bag is safe, and so are you," says Mrs. Poremba to Elise in a consoling voice and patting her on the shoulder. Then she reminds the whole class in a businesslike voice, "I'll take envelopes."

Kaitlynn, Erin, and Ian return to their lockers to retrieve their home–school envelopes from their book bags. As the children hand her their envelopes, Mrs. Poremba thanks them. "Thank you, Alyssa." Alyssa is already on her way to the name board, where the kindergartners move their name cards from a poster to an envelope attached below it to indicate that they are present, but she turns back as Mrs. Poremba continues, "Alyssa, it was nice seeing you after school, yesterday." Alyssa beams.

Eric D. approaches on tiptoes, arm extended. "Here, my bear's in here," he says. An at-home project, as part of the class's bear unit, is to color a cut out figure of a bear and dictate (for a grown-up to write out) a story about the bear. Mrs. Poremba takes Eric's envelope.

Eric tugs and straightens first one T-shirt sleeve, then the other, and nods as Mrs. Poremba asks, "Did you make it already? You did your story already?!" Then he crosses his arms with satisfaction, as Mrs. Poremba exclaims, "Oh boy, oh boy!"

Then Eric steps forward to point to his bear as Mrs. Poremba removes it from the envelope. "I dressed my bear. He has clothes on."

"Oh, you have a bear in clothes! What a wonderful bear you did, Eric!"

Then Eric moves toward the name board, again adjusting his sleeves and suspenders.

Meanwhile, all the children find their way to their tables and begin signing in. Kaitlynn runs to her table, announcing, "I got this first." She quickly writes her first name twice. She calls across the room, "I'm writing my name two times, Ian." And on the third line of the sign-in sheet, Kaitlynn writes NO (with a backwards N).

At one point, as they await their turns to sign in, Jeff and Eric twirl their pencils. Their dropping the pencils and reaching across one another to retrieve them escalates to a friendly pencil sword fight. But when Eric stops and holds his pencil still, Jeff picks up the tempo, wrapping repeatedly at Eric's pencil until he knocks it right out of Eric's hand. "Stop it!" Eric protests. He picks his pencil up from the floor and approaches Mrs. Poremba. "Teacher, Jeff's hitting me with his pencil."

Mrs. Poremba wants to be sure that Eric and Jeff learn an important lesson about getting along with one another in kindergarten. She answers, "Oh! Do you need some help in handling that, Eric? I heard you use your words a minute ago. Did that seem to help?"

Eric immediately takes his seat again at the table.

Mrs. Poremba crouches to Jeff's level and puts an arm across the back of his chair. "Did you understand Eric's message? Was it pretty loud and clear? What does he not want you to do?"

"Stop hitting his pencil."

"And you understood that? Are you going to be able to stop?"

Jeff nods.

"I'm glad," says Mrs. Poremba, and she pats Jeff's shoulder and moves on to the adjoining table.

Kaitlynn finishes her turn by writing ON (with a backwards N) at the bottom of the sign-in sheet, and Eric is next. Jeff has been sitting by, waiting for his promised turn long enough: "Are you going to write your name, Eric, or not?!"

But the whole group is about to follow another diversion.

Tara G. announces, "It's the fourteenth day of school!"

"Yeah," Kaitlynn replies, turning around to look at the big wall work bulletin board, across the top of which is a number line with numbers through *13* for yesterday, the thirteenth day of school.

Eric D. disputes this, "It's the seventeenth." He points toward the bulletin board on which is displayed the calendar bearing numbers through yesterday's date, the sixteenth. He begins pointing with his pencil and counting, "Sixteen, seventeen." But he can't stop, "Eighteen, nineteen, twenty." Now, he stops, acknowledging by wrapping his own head with his pencil that he has obscured his point by counting too far. Then he returns to writing his name.

"No. Past thirteen," says Jeff.

Eric responds, "Really, really, it's supposed to be thirteen."

"No," says Tara G.

"I'll show you where thirteen is," says Jeff, and he and Kaitlynn jump up and go to the bulletin board. Both of them point out the *13* on the calendar, Monday's date.

Tara joins them, but she points to the *13* on the number line, the one that supports her contention, which started all this, that today is the fourteenth day of school.

Eric is on his way, too. He only makes a perfunctory jab at the top row of dates on the calendar, as if only to claim participation in this new game before immediately heading back to the table lest he lose possession of the sign-in sheet. Tara and Jeff follow him.

Kaitlynn stays to point to and count with the numbers on the calendar. She stays in sequence through *7*, but then skips down to *12*. When she returns to her table, her group is listening to Mrs. Poremba.

"The afternoon kindergartners really liked looking at your sign-in sheets. You know, Jeff, when they saw your name, they said, 'Boy, does Jeff write his last name well!'"

Eric wants in on this praise, "Did they look at my last name?"

"They did, and I told them about your idea of writing it on the chalkboard and practicing. And they thought that was a really good idea."

Kaitlynn says, "Mrs. Poremba, I know how to spell *on*: *O-N*."

"That *is* the way you spell *on*."

FREDDY "WRITES THE ROOM."

On September 22, Freddy is the last kindergartner writing on his sign-in sheet (see figure 4.5). He is walking around the room looking for print to copy. Eventually, he fills all the space around his name on his line of the sign-in sheet and the spaces below that line and at the top of the page.

He talks to me about his writing. "I'm doing Kleenex." He gets up and down from his table near Mrs. Poremba's desk to check his copying of the print on the tissue box on Mrs. Poremba's desk. This box, however, is a different brand. "See, I wrote Kleenex," he tells me, again naming the most popular brand but pointing to his writing of the other brand name. "Can you read what else I wrote?" he asks.

I notice color words that Freddy has copied from the designators at the tables. I read "'Red,'" but then I add "No that's 'Freddy' when I notice that this RED is really part of his signature, FfREDDY, almost lost in the surrounding writing. I point to and read Freddy's green, yellow, Yes, No, and Book. I read the numerals 1 to 11 and an extra 2 (meant to be *12*), sprinkled in available spaces around the bottom of the sign-in sheet. Freddy has copied these from the face of the classroom clock. I'm not sure how to read ord.

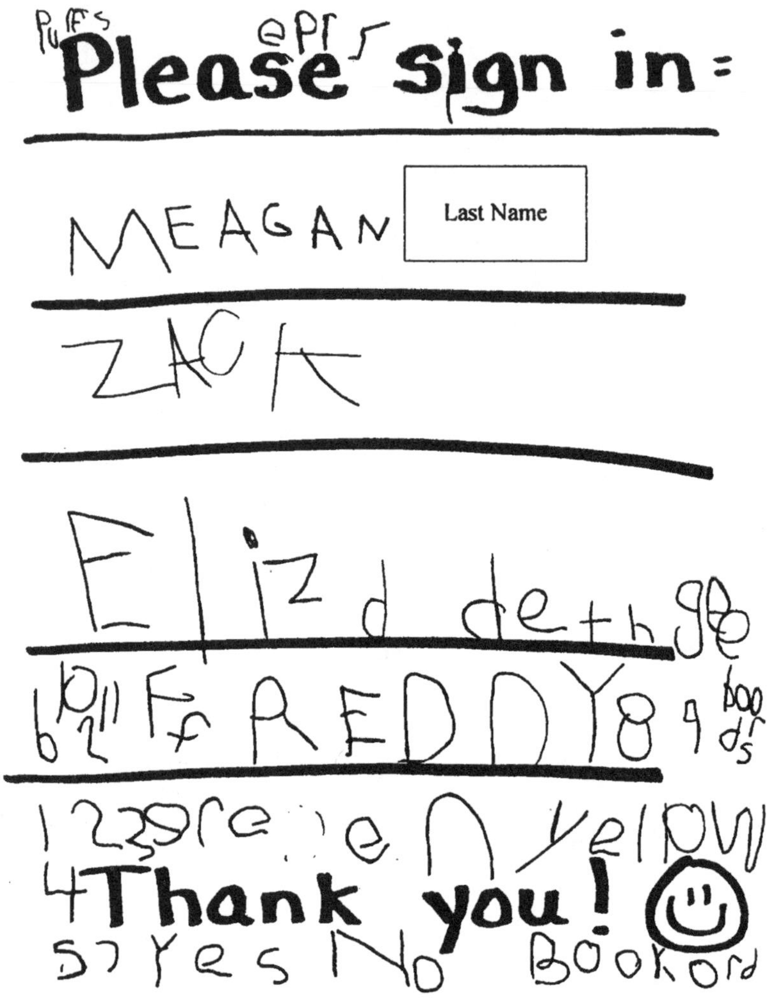

Figure 4.5. Freddy's September 22 Sign-in Sheet

I ask Freddy to read it, but he can't. "*You* can read it. Can't you read it?" he says. He is sure that I should be able to read whatever he has written. He has copied from reliable sources, and I am a reader. I begin to look for possible sources of **ord**. I suggest that maybe he was copying *geoboards*, a label on a bin on the math tool cart near Freddy's table.

"No, that's not where I was looking," he says.

Suddenly I spy a manila folder on Mrs. Poremba's desk bearing the label *Book Orders*. That's it; Freddy's **ord** follows his **Book** and lacks *ers* because he ran out of space in the bottom right hand corner of his sign-in sheet.

Now, I also notice where Freddy did write **geo / boor / ds**, in three tight rows of letters squeezed in the right margin of his sign-in sheet. This leaves only one more word for me to read, but I can't. It is **epZ** (with a backwards **Z**) at the top of the sheet. We are unable to find the source for this copying, but again Freddy insists I should be able to read it.

"That doesn't make a word," I say, and I note an erasure between the **p** and the **Z**. Freddy writes an **r** there. "Now it says 'appears,'" I say lamely, though we never find a source.

During choice time, Freddy shows his sign-in sheet to Mrs. Poremba. "Now tell me what it says," she urges.

"'Kleenex,'" reads Freddy. He points to his writing and again misreads it, using the name of the most popular tissue brand.

When Freddy can't read **Yes**, Mrs. Poremba points to **No**, which he can read, and now, this helps him to remember **Yes** as well. "I wrote *geoboard*," he says, and Mrs. Poremba finds it.

When he has trouble reading **yellow** and **green**, Mrs. Poremba reminds him of his source, the labels at the yellow and green tables. He seems not to want to use that aid and says, "Orange-yellow table," for **yellow**. But then with a sideways glance at the green table's label, he reads, "'Green.'" Freddy reads several of the numerals he wrote.

"What a good *4*!" comments Mrs. Poremba.

Freddy agrees. He tells Ian, "Look at what a good *4*." About that mystery word **eprZ**, Freddy tells Mrs. Poremba, "Dr. Richgels and I couldn't find it."

"Freddy, you did such good writing!" Mrs. Poremba says.

"Let's show the principal," suggests Freddy. Mrs. Poremba takes Freddy to the office, and when they return, she tells me that Freddy could read every word for Mrs. Larsen. This burst of writing by Freddy would be a preview of things to come for the whole class.

PERSONAL SIGN-IN SHEETS

It's Tuesday, September 28, the twenty-first day of school, and several elements of the kindergartners' sign-in procedure are about to come together in a way that will produce a new routine in Mrs. Poremba's classroom: personal signing in. Today's events will lead, by three weeks from today, to the kindergartners' using individual sign-in sheets, held on clipboards, for self-assigned writing practice, for copying classroom print, and for recording important information from the opening-of-the-day wall work.

For weeks already, many kindergartners have been writing more than their names on their sign-in sheets, and several have grown restless about sharing a sign-in sheet with two or three tablemates. Two weeks ago, on September 14, Ian waited for Jason to arrive and sign in. Ian wanted to be last so that he could use the bottom space on the sheet for extra writing. "I like to be last so I can write other stuff," he explained.

Today, at the yellow table, Erin and Sarah sign their names, and then Jason and Ian collaborate on filling the entire sheet with writing. Ian's contributions include the *no bear* writing described earlier in this chapter.

Jason has also written BEAR after his name (see figure 4.3), but he reports to Mrs. Poremba that he wrote it without having to copy. "I just know how it goes."

Later, Ian has written SOO in the space after Sarah's name. He is not satisfied with the first letter of this word. He erases it and writes Z. "*That's* a Z!" he says. He asks Jason what his word says. "Don't tell him," he tells me.

"'Zoo,'" reads Jason.

Then Ian writes CENTER. He copies from the Housekeeping Center sign, again transposing from lower- to uppercase letters, but retaining a lowercase-style tail on his capital *T*. Again he asks Jason to read, but this time neither one knows the word. When I ask Ian, he walks across the room, points to the second word in the Housekeeping Center sign, and says, "It's *that*!"

Ian joins his classmates for wall work, and Jason continues writing. Jason writes his name once more and then writes rows of letters from his name, especially *A*s and his signature backwards *J*s. These and several zigzag lines are almost a decorative, space-filling motif. His other writing includes repetitions of CAT, MAT, BAT, HAT, NO, and FFO.

Freddy also stays at his table writing on his sign-in sheet while his classmates begin wall work (see figure 4.6). He, too, will fill a sheet with his writing. It is not as filled as Jason's, but it is all his work. Today, Freddy takes his sign-in writing in a new direction, where, soon, all his classmates will follow. He is the first kindergartner to have his own sign-in sheet.

Freddy takes his sign-in sheet to the wall work area. He holds it in front of his classmates one at a time. "I did all of this," he says.

"Freddy did a lot of writing," says a kindergartner.

"You did a lot of writing?" asks Mrs. Poremba. "I'm anxious to see it, Fred."

Freddy thrusts his sheet in front of Mrs. Poremba.

"Wooo! Did you do all of this?!"

"Yes."

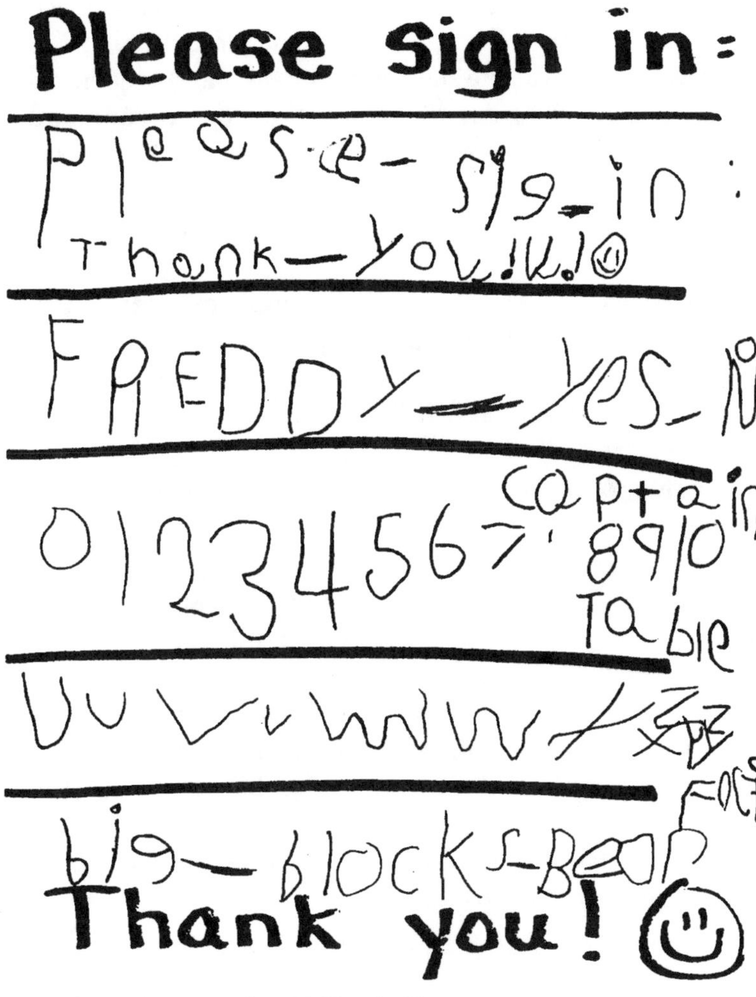

Figure 4.6. Freddy's September 28 Sign-in Sheet

YOU'RE WELCOME TO GET ONE.

The next day, Wednesday, September 29, the twenty-second day of school, Freddy again asks Mrs. Poremba for his own sign-in sheet. She shows him where the sheets are stored and invites him to take whatever he needs. Again, he does much self-assigned copying, though his efforts are cut short by a class field trip to a fire station. On this Wednesday, both Freddy and Ian use commercial print on available objects as models for their sign-in writing. This will become a popular strategy as their classmates expand the scope of their sign-in writing over the next several weeks.

Freddy's sign-in writing includes **Cheese / Cottage FRIENDy**, copied from an empty cottage cheese carton in the Housekeeping Center. Ian copies **O'GLUE** from a glue stick in the supply canister on his table.

The next day, Thursday, September 30, the twenty-third day of school, Ian and Jason follow Freddy's lead. They notice that he has created an opportunity to write more by using his own sign-in sheet. Ian does not hesitate, while Jason needs a little prodding, to obtain their own sheets.

At the yellow table, Jason, Ian, Erin, and Sarah are signing in. Erin and Sarah are first. And then Jason writes his name and **DOGCAT** under his name.

"You guys!" protests Ian, who still hasn't had a turn with the sign-in sheet.

"I'm going to do something else," says Erin about her intention to write more.

"I'm gonna go and ask the teacher for a new sign-in sheet for me and Jason!" says Ian. Then to Jason, in a quieter, almost conspiratorial voice, he adds, "Okay? Jason, would you like that, if I go ask—"

"Yeah, yeah, yeah!" Jason responds.

When Ian returns, Jason clarifies, "How about they use—those two, they get to use that one, and we get to use this one?"

But now, Ian has an idea to assure that he will not have to wait or share any longer: "How about we both get our own?"

"Ask the teacher if we could do that," suggests Jason.

"No, we, we *can*," asserts Ian, confidently.

"Go ask the teacher," persists Jason.

"Look, *they* get their own," Ian counters, perhaps referring to Freddy.

"Ask the teacher—"

Ian quotes Mrs. Poremba: "'You're welcome to get one.' Remember?" Though his words speak of confidence, Ian whispers conspiratorially, "So she won't care!"

"Why do you have two sign-in sheets?" asks a passing kindergartner about the two sheets for the four kindergartners at the yellow table.

Ian replies in a loud, almost defiant (but perhaps a bit guilty) voice, "Because we like to write a lot!"

Ian persists, "Jason, she said we're welcome to get a sign-in sheet. So that means, like, I could—"

"Ask the teacher," Jason whispers.

"—get one!" continues Ian. He gets up from his chair and is back in a few seconds with his own sign-in sheet. He immediately writes his name.

Ian begins writing on the second line of his sign-in sheet (see figure 4.7). He writes B and then rests his right elbow on the table and his chin

Figure 4.7. Ian's September 30 Sign-in Sheet

in his right hand, looking to his right at the *What bears look like* subtitle on the Bear Facts chart. His eyebrows make raised arches as he studies the chart. Then he sets down his pencil, and like an office worker consulting a reference book with the calm of routine, he reaches for and unfolds the laminated alphabet card in the supply caddy beside him at the end of the yellow table. Consulting the card, he transposes lowercase letters to uppercase as he continues writing BEARS. Yesterday, Ian had copied WHAT from this same source, the subtitle *What bears look like*. Today, he is starting with the next word, *Bears*.

THESE ARE TWO SEPARATE WORDS.

As wall work time approaches, Mrs. Poremba assures all the kindergartners that there is more than one all right way to do sign-in writing. She announces, "Those of you who are ready on the carpet, we can start our wall work. Those of you who are still writing, you can finish up and come over when you are ready." The latter group is Ian, Jason, Freddy, Zack, Kaitlynn, Eric C., and Tara J., and even among them, there are many personal goals to attain. Freddy, for example, is again filling up his sign-in sheet with self-assigned copying from models all around the room, something the whole class will, within three weeks, institutionalize as the Writing the Room routine.

Freddy is up on his knees on his chair, leaning across his table, as he copies from a wooden plaque attached to the front of Mrs. Poremba's desk: A CLASSY / TEACHER (see figure 4.8). The writing on the plaque is in block uppercase letters, each almost squared-off, and there is a decoration of flowers. Freddy makes his letters in the same squared-off style and includes some floral decoration in crayon. When he finishes that, he changes writing styles to copy a very different model, the more fluid font in the sign that identifies the Writing Center.

Meanwhile, Ian draws a vertical line after BEARS. "These are two separate words," he says, and then he begins to copy LOOK from *What bears look like* on the Bear Facts chart. After that, his writing is accompanied by careful examination of his pencil. He studies the side of his pencil, then he writes a letter, over and over again. "I wrote a really silly thing," he tells me. "You know what I wrote?"

Figure 4.8. Freddy's September 30 Sign-in Sheet

"What?" I ask. When Ian shows me his sign-in sheet, I read, "'*Jurassic Park*!' Where did you get those words?"

Giggling, Ian shows me his pencil.

Meanwhile, Jason stands up, leans across the green table to look at Freddy's name tag, and leans back to his place. He does this several times. Then he turns to me, points to his writing, and says, "Dr. Richgels, I writed *Freddy*." He points to his friend.

"Good for you! Good job!" I reply.

Jason sits down again and immediately looks down at the front of his sweatshirt. He pulls the shirt out from his body. After a bit, he turns to me. "Dr. Richgels, what does this say?" On his shirt, in an arc above the curved back of a large cartoon of a zonked-out dinosaur figure is printed *ZONK-A-SAURUS*.

"Well, let me see. 'Zonkasaurus,'" I read.

"Which way do you start?" asks Jason. "This way?" He points from his left to his right, which is backwards for someone reading the shirt.

I answer, "It starts over here with a Z."

Jason looks down at his shirt front, then writes, looks down, then writes.

I'M GLAD YOU'RE LISTENING EVEN THOUGH YOU'RE STILL DOING YOUR WRITING.

As wall work finally begins, only Ian, Jason, Freddy, and Eric C. are still writing on their sign-in sheets, but they keep an ear tuned to what is happening with the rest of the class. Jeff is the helper for calendar time. He puts the *29* in place for yesterday since the class had not done calendar work because of a field trip. "Now, Jeffrey, the twenty-ninth day of September was when we went on our field trip."

"That was Wednesday," notes Tara G.

"That was Wednesday," confirms Mrs. Poremba. "But we've been to school one more day." Mrs. Poremba points to the empty space after the *29* on the calendar. "Let's go back to our *20*, and let's count on after *20* to see what we're going to end up with right back here. Put your eyes on the *20*. Are you ready? Twenty."

Mrs. Poremba points to the dates as the kindergartners count together, "Twenty-one, twenty-two, twenty-three, twenty-four, twenty-five, twenty-six, twenty-seven, twenty-eight, twenty-nine—" She points to the empty space for today's date.

"—thirty!" the kindergartners say together.

"Thirty is today. Do you know what *30* looks like?"

In the discussion that follows, one kindergartner suggests, "A *zero* and a 3, a *zero* and a 3," and the class debates what is the correct order of the digits. Ian and Jason are still writing at their table, all the way across the room from the wall work area. "A 3 and an *oh*!" Ian shouts.

Mrs. Poremba asks Ian, "Is it an *oh*, or is it a *zero*?"

"You scared me!" says Jeff.

"Zero!" answers Ian.

"A *zero*? Ian, I'm glad you're listening even though you're still doing your writing." Mrs. Poremba shows the *30* date card. "Is this what you made in your mind?"

"Yeah!" shout several kindergartners.

LOTS OF WAYS TO WRITE

As the children have a stretch after wall work and then settle down at Mrs. Poremba's blue chair, she says to Eric C., "Eric, I don't think I've ever seen you write so much." She holds his sheet so that everyone can see (see figure 4.9). "Look at all that Eric wrote today." Mrs. Poremba is about to recognize and validate several sign-in writing strategies that kindergartners used today. These strategies will thereby be available to more kindergartners as this routine evolves into daily individual practice and record making.

"Oh!" "Wow!" say kindergartners.

"Eric, where did you get all of your ideas for your words?"

"I was thinking."

"You were thinking about them? And, and, did you write down what you were thinking about? Eric?"

Eric remains at his place in the back row on the carpet. He nods.

"You wrote down what you were thinking?" Except for his name and Pleasesienin: / ThankYou!, the sources of Eric's writing are less clear than many other kindergartners' obvious copying. Mrs. Poremba asks, "Did you see these words anyplace?"

Eric shakes his head.

"They were just up here in—"

"I seed them in my brain."

"You saw them in your brain! That's a neat plan. Freddy, tell me about your idea." But the class is not ready to listen. "Let's have a kindergarten check time," Mrs. Poremba says. "One, two, three, kindergarten check

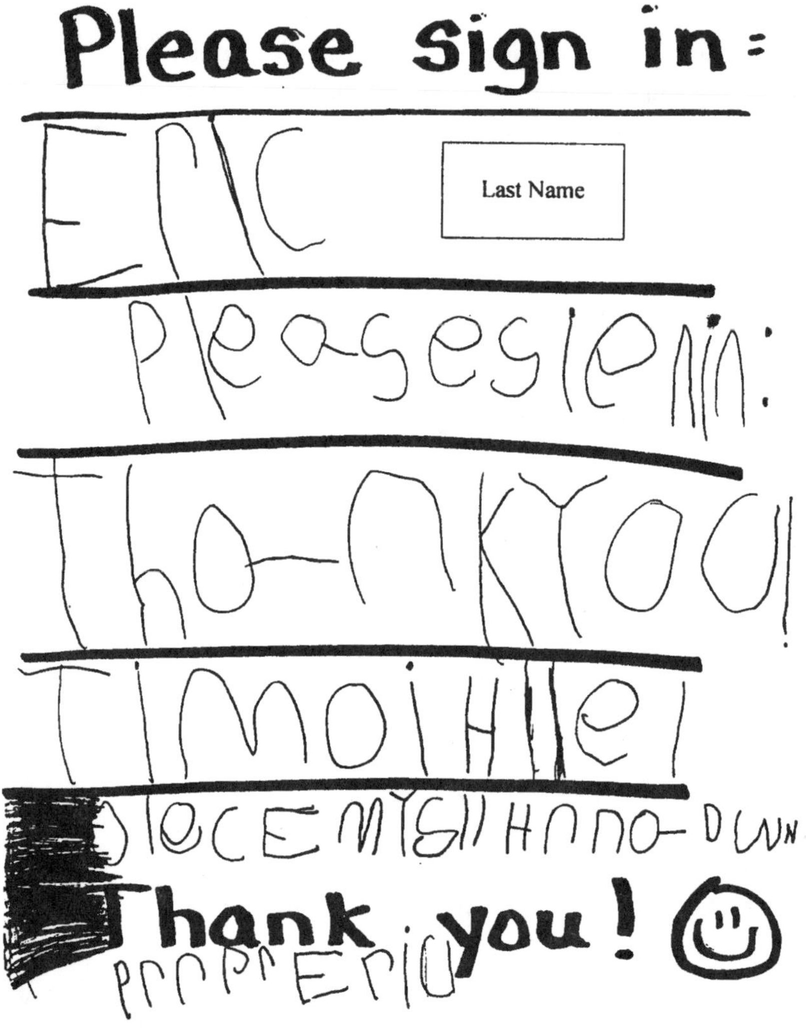

Figure 4.9. Eric C.'s September 30 Sign-in Sheet

time." Now, the class is ready. "Freddy, tell me about your ideas, and where you got your ideas for your words. What did you do? Eric got his in his brain. What did you do?"

Freddy was sitting in the back of the group, but by the time Mrs. Poremba finishes this list of questions, he is standing beside her as she displays his sign-in sheet. He has his hands in his pockets and looks out at the class proudly. "I looked at stuff," he says.

"You looked at stuff! What do you mean, you looked at stuff?"

"I saw 'em."

"Where did you see them?"

"Over there," answers Freddy pointing toward the Writing Center.

"Go show us where you found your ideas."

Freddy goes to the Writing Center bulletin board.

"Use your eyes. Follow Freddy with your eyes," Mrs. Poremba tells the class, but soon all but Tara J. leave the carpet to join Freddy, who is pointing to the words *Writing Center* on the bulletin board. Those words are in large black letters in a web cast by a large Spider Man figure.

As the crowd returns to the carpet, a kindergartner says about Freddy's other sign-in writing, "And he write this, this here."

"This, too," says another.

Eric D. points to the A CLASSY TEACHER sign on the front of Mrs. Poremba's desk. "And he wrote these."

Mrs. Poremba recaps: "Freddy, you got your ideas by looking at words around the room. Eric got his ideas by thinking about what was in his mind. It's a different way to do it."

"And I looked around the room, too," says Ian from his place on the carpet.

"Ian—I wanted to show you Ian's sign-in sheet—Ian, tell me where you got your ideas."

Mrs. Poremba holds up Ian's sign-in sheet (see figure 4.7), and the class responds, "Whoah!" "Oh!" Some kindergartners laugh in delight and dismay. Ian goes to Mrs. Poremba's side.

"Let's listen to Ian and see where he got his ideas."

"I got, I got—" Ian points to his name first, "This is just my name." Then, he points to NON. "I got, I got—This is—I just wrote this word."

"'No,'" reads Tara G.

Ian begins to correct her: "No, that—"

But Mrs. Poremba interrupts, "Okay. Was that an idea that you had in your mind?" Mrs. Poremba points to NON on the sign-in sheet and then to her head. "Or did you see it somewhere?"

"Mind."

"You had it in your mind."

"I was about to write *noon*—" *Noon* has been one of Ian's favorite words since the fourth day of school. "—but I messed up, so I decided—"

"I see some, three stars, right there," says Tara G. about Ian's triangle and two stars.

"I don't see any," says Eric D.

"Who made those stars?" asks another kindergartner.

Ian points to the interlocking-teeth design. "I got this idea from Jason." And, indeed, Jason has filled in empty spaces on his sign-in sheet today with a similar design.

"Okay. So you can get ideas by looking at what other people are doing, too," says Mrs. Poremba, nodding.

Ian points to BEARS. "'Bear facts,'" reads a kindergartner.

"And I got that, and I got this from the Bear Facts," Ian says, pointing across the room.

"From the Bear Facts paper that we did?" confirms Mrs. Poremba.

Ian nods and then points to LOOK, but Mrs. Poremba and Tara J. are ahead of him. Mrs. Poremba points to JURASSLC, and Tara says, "And I know where you got that other word."

"Where did you find this word?" asks Mrs. Poremba.

Tara answers for Ian, "Um, from the Jurassic Park pencil."

Ian looks at Tara with a smile and says, "Right!"

Now Ian points to his JURASSLC and then turns to address Tara: "Yeah, but this doesn't say whole Jurassic Park." Ian knows that *Jurassic Park* is two words. He points to PARK on the next line. "*This* says Park."

"Very interesting," responds Mrs. Poremba. "So you wrote the *Jurassic* part here—"

"'Look!'" reads Ian, interrupting and pointing up to his LOOK. "That's what that says." Then he points to his writing of his sisters' names below the last line of the sign-in sheet. "And these are just words that I had in my mind." And finally, pointing to THANK yOU!, "Or I could just copy 'em from the sign-in sheet."

"Oh, so, so you can find words by looking around the room to copy."

"Right," says Ian, nodding.

"You can find words that are just in your mind."

Ian nods.

"And you found words that are written on the sign-in sheet to use."

Ian nods again.

"You have three ways that you found your words. Thank you. You know, I wanted to show you Jason's sheet, also."

Mrs. Poremba holds up Jason's sheet, and the class responds as they did to Ian's: "Whoah!" "Oh!"

"Jason, do you have a moment, do you have a moment to tell us about where you get your ideas for your writing?"

"I copied stuff."

"Come on up, Jason, and show us that."

Jason stands next to Mrs. Poremba, a hand at his face, not looking nearly as confident or in-charge as Ian had during his turn. But, with no hesitation, he offers already a second explanation for his writing: "I know how to spell stuff."

"You know how to spell it? So, do you get your ideas from looking at something or do you have them in your mind already?"

"I have them in my mind already."

"You have them in your mind already. Were all of these ideas from your mind—"

Jason nods.

"—or did you, did you look anywhere to get your ideas today?"

Jason shakes his head.

"These are all ideas from your mind?" Mrs. Poremba turns Jason's sign-in sheet so that she can read it. "Boy!"

"Except *bear*," Jason says, in a quiet voice, his hand still at his face, now tugging on his chin.

"Except for what?"

"*Bear*."

"Except for *bear*?" Mrs. Poremba turns the sign-in sheet toward the class again. "Where's *bear*? Do you remember where you put that?"

Jason has been standing slightly behind Mrs. Poremba, so he leans around the sign-in sheet she holds before the class and peers at his own writing.

"I can't find the *bear*. I did the *bear*."

"You did *bear*. Do you remember where it is on your sign-in sheet?"

"Here it is," Jason says in a quiet voice, pointing.

"Here, you found it!" Mrs. Poremba points, "Here's the *B* and the *E* and the *A* and the *R*. Where did you find that word *bear*?"

Two days ago, Jason told Mrs. Poremba about his writing BEAR, "I just know how it goes." But today he remembers his source. "On the Bear Facts," he says, and in one motion, he wipes his nose with his arm and points across the room at the Bear Facts chart.

"On the Bear Facts," echoes Mrs. Poremba. "Okay. So you did look around to find one of your words. The other ones came from your mind."

SO, YOU CAN ALSO LOOK AT YOUR CLOTHES IF THEY HAVE WRITING ON THEM?

Jason makes a move to return to the carpet, but I ask, "Jason, do you remember when you asked me what it says on your shirt, where it says *Zonkasaurus* on your shirt? Did you use that on your sign-in sheet?"

"Yes."

"Did you?" says Mrs. Poremba. "So you can also look at your clothes if they have writing on them?"

"And you can look at your pants," suggests a kindergartner.

Mrs. Poremba begins, "Pants might have—"

"I know," says a kindergartner. "I have writing on—"

"You do have writing on your clothes today," confirms Mrs. Poremba.

"I have writing on my leg!" says a kindergartner.

"Even on your leg! So we can look for writing on our clothing, too."

"I have writing on my shoes!" says Eric D.

"Even on shoes there can be writing?!" responds Mrs. Poremba.

"I have writing inside my shoes!" says Tara G.

"Tara found writing inside her shoe!"

"I did, too," says a kindergartner.

"We both have the same," says another.

Soon, many kindergartners are declaring writing discoveries on their persons.

"Mrs. Poremba, I can, I can read this," says Tara G., pointing to writing on the bottom of her shoe. Her reading is lost amidst much kindergarten talk, as classmates begin comparing discoveries of writing on their clothes and shoes.

"Wow, even on the bottom of shoes we can find words sometimes." Ian has been sitting cross-legged behind Tara G. He tumbles sideways in an effort to search the bottom of his right shoe for writing. In the front row, Jeff checks the bottom of his right shoe and holds that foot up for Mrs. Poremba's inspection. She speaks to the whole class, following up on their interest. "I want to give you a moment to look around at your friends'—I want to give you a moment to look at your friends' clothing, look at your friends' shoes, and see what you can find when you look. Look over your friends!" As the kindergartners do just that, Mrs. Poremba grasps Jeff's foot and reads from the bottom of his shoe, "It says, 'Power Lights.'"

Shouts of "I found—" "I found—" "I found—", always with the next word obscured, surface during the noisy, eager search-for-print that ensues.

EVERYONE WRITES THE ROOM.

Almost three weeks later, on Wednesday, October 20, the thirty-sixth day of school, the whole class, not just Freddy and Jason and Ian, have taken up personal sign-in writing. Mrs. Poremba facilitates this move by providing just the support, in materials and encouragement, that the kindergartners need to make best use of all the print displayed in the room. As the children arrive, they go to their tables to sign in, but many are attracted to the Writing Center where a new bulletin board displays cutouts of Halloween figures, each labeled: *pumpkin*, *ghost*, *witch*, *owl*, *Frankenstein monster*, *bat*, *skeleton*, *black cat*. Soon there is a crowd of kindergartners at the Writing Center, wanting to copy the Halloween words onto their sign-in sheets. "There's not enough chairs over here for us," reports a kindergartner.

"Ohhh," sympathizes Mrs. Poremba. "Well, you could stand, you could sit right there, you could pull a chair up."

Kindergartners talk about access to the Writing Center: "I'm sitting there." "I'm standing here." "Make two rows." "Yeah, make two rows." "Oh, can I have that one?" "No, you can go get a chair." "This is the boys' table." "No!" "Is this okay?" "Yeah."

Zack asks, "Who hit my sign-in sheet?"

Jeff makes a claim: "Jason, I'm sitting there!"

"Boy, we need a bigger table back there, for all that writing," says Mrs. Poremba.

"Jason, can I have my place back?" asks Jeff.

"I don't know where to sit," answers Jason.

A second row of chairs is forming. "Jeff, you want to use this? You can sit in the second row and use this clipboard," I suggest.

"I don't need that," answers Jeff.

"Well, this is so you have something hard to put under your paper."

"We need to make some more clipboards, I think," says Mrs. Poremba. Soon she is distributing clipboards that she had obtained recently for a future math project. They are lap boards with clothespins for holding the paper in place.

"Mrs. Poremba, when we finish this, can we—" says a kindergartner.

"Yup," answers Mrs. Poremba, "you can go around and write—"

"Hey, where did that pencil go?" asks a kindergartner over the rest of Mrs. Poremba's answer.

Mrs. Roloff helps: "Guys, I have some clipboards here, if you'd like to put your paper on a clipboard."

"I do!" "I do!" "I want one!" answer several kindergartners.

Much talk follows: "Where did you guys get those clipboards?" "I got a clipboard!" "Me, too!" "Want to write *Bat Man*?" Ian writes and reads, "*B-A-T. M-A-N.* 'Bat Man,'" copying from his Bat Man tissue pack. Even children at tables want clipboards.

Soon kindergartners are carrying their clipboards and pencils all around the room, copying other writing on bulletin boards, signs, and labels. From this day on, signing in will be this extended activity that the kindergartners will come to call "Writing the Room."

Jeff, Zack, Jason, Ian, Erin, Steven, Eric D., and Freddy are at the Writing Center in two rows. Sarah, Elizabeth, Tara G., Nathan, Mayra, Eric C., and Elise are at their own table places. Tara J. and Elise are at the Bear Facts chart.

"Zack, do you have any ideas on some words you might want to work on?" asks Mrs. Poremba. "Oh, you're going to do your special, favorite word, aren't ya?" For several days, Zack and Eric D. have been writing the word *oval*, copying from labeled geometric shapes displayed on one wall of the classroom. Zack writes **oval** again today.

"I'm writin' some *new* words," says Jeff.

"What are you writing?" Jason asks Zack. "What's your favorite word? What are you writing?" Jason is to Zack's right and Jeff to his left at the writing center table. Zack turns to his left and leans back around Jeff in order to see the shapes displayed on the wall across the room. He finishes copying **oval** from there.

"Can you read that?" Zack asks.

"'Oval,'" one of the boys reads.

"That's it. It's *oval*, I knew it," says Eric D. from his place behind Zack in the second row of pulled-up chairs.

"He got it," says Zack.

"You forgot to close it up," Jason says, pointing to Zack's o. Zack corrects that oversight. Zack turns all the way around to face Eric as Eric writes oval.

Eric says, "I'm gonna write *oval. O-, O-V*, ohvee!" He laughs.

"Here's how I'm makin' it," says Jason. He writes ovol on his sign-in sheet.

To an inaudible question from Zack, Eric D. answers, "No, I'm makin' it small." And it's true: his oval is much smaller than Zack's. By the end of sign-in time, Eric will write his first and last names and, copying from the new bulletin board and from other places around the room, bat skeleton I ghost / oval rat I Reading I left I right / 36.

When he shows his writing to Mrs. Poremba, she asks, "Oh, *owl*? *Oval*? You wrote that word *oval*? You and Zachary love to write *oval*. That's what I see on your sign-in sheet a lot." Mrs. Poremba notices other words that Eric D. has copied: "Oh, I see *bat*, and I see *skeleton*, and I see *ghost*. And I also see *oval*."

During wall work, Eric D. will still be writing on his sign-in sheet from his table place. But he will participate in the class's activities, including writing 36 on his sign-in sheet during straw cup time to memorialize today's being the thirty-sixth day of school. From this date on, kindergartners will use their personal sign-in sheets on clipboards in this way, to record important ideas from wall work activities and other beginning-of-the day happenings.

"I'm writing some *new* words," Jeff repeats. "I'm writing new words." When he is finished writing today, his sign-in sheet will be packed with small, neatly written words, copied from the new Halloween bulletin board and from the Color Cats bulletin board.

Freddy copies witch, owlt, bot, and Frankenstein / monster from the Halloween bulletin board. Meagan and Deborah have moved chairs to the open gold-carpet space before the Color Cats bulletin board. (Deborah joined Mrs. Poremba's morning kindergarten a month ago, on September 21.) They sit with their feet propped on the radiator that runs below the bulletin board and write on the clipboards in their laps. Meagan writes black- / red-blue / PumPkin-6 green (with a backwards g) / MeaganW-purple / yellow-brown-green / orange / color-cats / white-big-blocks-bat witch. She has copied big blocks from a label in the blocks play area adjacent to the Color Cats bulletin board. On the back of her sign-in sheet, she draws a jack-o-lantern, three rabbits, and two eggs, and she twice writes pumpkin.

The fact that Deborah is wearing purple knit gloves does not seem to interfere with her writing. Mrs. Poremba comes by and observes, "Deborah's looking at her color words. Deborah, how is it writing with gloves on? Is it more difficult?"

"No," answers Deborah.

"What you might want to try—just to see what it feels like—is take your one glove off. See what it feels like when you hold your pencil without your glove, and see which way you like best, see which way works the best for you. Do you want to take it off?"

Deborah declines. She writes in big, faint letters DEBORAH / brown / colorccA / tsred.

Tara J. and Elise have been copying from an old source of Ian's, the Bear Facts chart. Tara writes some bears are / drown and They / have white claws. In addition, her sign-in sheet will have Green Tara J / blue TyRaNNOSAURUS / purple ON NO / drown (with backwards Ns). Tara, approaches Mrs. Poremba. "Mrs. Poremba, look-at."

Mrs. Poremba reads Tara's sign-in sheet, "'Some bears are brown and they have white claws.' You were looking at bear facts! Show me where you found that, Tara."

Today, Elise writes cut pumpkin / BARFACtSglue / TriAngle / red / reFrigerAtorgreen (cut and glue are copied from posted art project directions; TriAngle from the same shapes display where Zack found *oval*; and reFrigerAtor from the Housekeeping Center). Tara G. writes greeNorange / rcd purple / MOM DAD / blueeasel block / JUStIN LOVE (with a backwards J). Tara's color words are in crayon to match the named color, including black crayon for block, which was intended as *black* not *block*.

YOU'RE WORKING ON *PUMPKIN*? AND WHERE ARE YOU IN THE WORD?

Sarah is alone at the yellow table. She still has less enthusiasm for extra writing than many of her classmates. Today, she has written SARAH / MOM / NO and her last name, and she is now working on copying the word *pumpkin*. At each table is a miniature pumpkin on which Mrs. Poremba has taped a small label, pumpkin. Mrs. Poremba quietly takes a seat across the table from Sarah. She asks, "What are you working on right now, Sarah? You're working on *pumpkin*? And where are you in the word?"

Sarah points to the m in the label

"Do you know what letter that is?"

Sarah shakes her head.

"It's an *M*." Mrs. Poremba points to the letter. "Like *Mmmmonday* starts with *M*, doesn't it? And *muddy*." Sarah has seen those words on the calendar and among the More Weather Words that kindergartners have suggested that Mrs. Poremba write as part of their opening-of-the-day routine (see chapter 5). Mrs. Poremba asks, "How will you write the *M*?"

Sarah rests her head on her right hand, her elbow on the table, her pencil still in that hand. She doesn't write or answer.

Mrs. Poremba traces the m on the label with her finger and says, "You make a line down and then a hump and another hump." Sarah completes her writing of PuMPKin, with a capital *M* with no humps and unlike the lowercase m in the label that Mrs. Poremba has traced and described. Sarah makes her u and n in PuMPKin as curves with tiny added-on lines, in the upper-left part of n and the lower-right part of u.

WE REALLY WANT TO SEE YOUR WRITING

Now Mrs. Poremba gives the kindergartners procedures that will help to make today's Writing the Room a permanent institution in their classroom. She says, "Boys and girls, I need you to look at me for a moment. I have a very important announcement. I, I need to see your sign-in sheet. So before you put it in your book bag, before you put it in an envelope, you need to make sure that you give it to me. It's very important that I and Dr.

Richgels look at your writing every single day. We really want to see it. We'll make sure that you get it back, but we need to see it. So when you're finished, please bring your writing to us. If you make sure that your name is on it, we'll always know who to give your writing back to. Okay? And I have a special place to put clipboards when you're finished, our special box that we'll put our clipboards in. Make sure that you leave your clip on it."

Mrs. Poremba begins, and the class joins her, singing the "Come Sit Down" song, to the tune of *Frere Jacques*. During the wall work time that follows, Mrs. Poremba discusses many students' writing. Zack has written less than many of his classmates did, but she celebrates what he has written: "Zack wrote one of his most favorite words again, good old *oval*. He loves that word. You know what, Zack? I bet you're going to get so good at writing *oval* that you won't even need to look at the *oval* sign. I betcha pretty soon you won't have to look at it."

"I don't, I still—right now, I don't," says Zack, who had leaned way around Jeff to see the shapes display when he copied *oval* today.

"'Clock,'" reads Elizabeth from her sign-in sheet. She has copied **PleszCek** (with upside-down **e**s) under a message, written by an adult helper, *Please check and return daily*. And she has written **clock / pumpkin / Elzabeth / E** (with a backwards **n**).

"You wrote *clock*. Good writing, Elizabeth, and good reading."

"How do you like mine, Mrs. Poremba?" asks Tara G. about her sign-in writing.

"You know what, Tara? How do *you* like yours?"

"I like mine."

FROM MRS. POREMBA

I first considered using signing in with my kindergartners after I read Bobbi Fisher's book *Joyful Learning* (1991). Fisher cites Harste, Woodward, and Burke's *Language Stories and Literacy Lessons* (1984, 22), with its plea, "Let them 'sign in,' please!" As you can see, people who know much more about literacy development than I do have given the practice of signing in their stamp of approval. I have modified their ideas to make them my own, and each year signing in looks a little different in my classroom because I am learning, too!

My classroom signing in evolves with my students' developing literacy abilities. At the beginning (see figure 4.1), the sign-in sheet is simple, and I watch to see how comfortable students are with writing their names. I make decisions about what support individuals need based on my observations. For example, some children need help with their first names, as Sarah did, while others are interested in and ready for last-name writing. I teach children how to use resources, such as name labels found in our classroom for models and pencil grippers for fine motor support. Soon all children are making progress and having personal success.

The addition of lines to the sign-in sheet (see figure 4.2) is to help children begin to organize print on paper. These lines provide some spatial structure and gently support children without overdirecting them as traditional three-lined handwriting paper might do. I also encourage children to pay attention to the print on the sheets and the names of their classmates. I ask them to think about and talk about what they notice. I want them to think critically about print. Sign-in writing and talk with their classmates about that writing are great catalysts for such thinking. Conversations around signing in, such as those you've seen in this chapter and in chapter 1, provide the foundation for children's later, more sophisticated discussions about literacy.

Writing the Room is not the only possible, student-directed evolution of sign-in writing. For many years, children's initiatives have centered on a daily sign-in question. Some years, later in the first semester, I introduce simple yes/no questions (using rebuses where helpful), for example, *Can a dinosaur jump?* (see figure 1.1, chapter 1). Reading and answering the sign-in question are social literacy experiences. Children cooperate, collaborate, and often negotiate as they strive to make sense of the question. This past year, I began typing the sign-in question, using a computer connected to a large overhead monitor, in addition to writing it on the sign-in sheet. Children started their discussions about the question of the day the moment they walked in the door and looked at the monitor, even before they had their coats off! They also started thinking of possible sign-in questions and were delighted when their suggestions appeared on the monitor the next day. One child's suggestion was *Do you like salami?* I never would have thought of that question!

When wh-questions (for example, *What is your favorite color?* and *When is your birthday?*) replace yes-no questions, possible answers become more varied. Signing in becomes even more a social literacy experience, with lots of interaction among the students. They help each other locate resources in the room (such as our word wall, charts, and books). Students have even gone beyond suggesting sign-in questions to composing their own sign-in sheets, with such questions (from this past year) as *Do you have a van?*, *Do you like chocolate or vanilla?*, and *Do you like dogs or cats?* Children use their literacy skills and understandings to write their questions, interview their classmates, and record their answers. They "report out" their findings at the end of the day (for example, fifteen children like dogs and ten like cats), and they brainstorm new questions for the next day. Over the course of the year, kindergartners gradually become the eager owners of signing in!

5

WORDS FOR TODAY

It is Tuesday, September 14, the eleventh day of school, near the end of wall work. Mrs. Poremba says, "I want you to be able to see this part of our working board right now." She directs the children to the weather report board. This is a laminated chart with picture and word entries that read *sunny*, *cloudy*, *windy*, *rainy*, and *snowy*, each of which has its own movable *Yes* and *No* strip (see figure 2.2, chapter 2). When the strip is centered, the *Yes* appears at the left of the weather word and the *No* appears at the right of the weather word. Each strip can be moved to the left so that only the *Yes* shows to the left of its weather word; or it can be moved to the right so that only the *No* shows to the right of its weather word. "I want you to use your eyes to get ideas about what this could be about up here."

WHAT CAN YOU SHOW US?

Mrs. Poremba is using the What Can You Show Us? routine (Richgels, Poremba, and McGee 1996). Its essential element is the children's reading whatever parts they can in whatever ways they can from a new posted text, even before the teacher reads it.

"Sunny and rainy," suggests Kaitlynn.

But Mrs. Poremba reminds her to raise her hand. When Kaitlynn complies, Mrs. Poremba says, "Kaitlynn has her hand up. Kaitlynn, what's your idea?"

"Uh, today is a rainy day, and I found a rainy day right—here." Kaitlynn points to the rainy picture part of the *rainy* entry on the chart.

"How do you know that says *rainy*?" asks Mrs. Poremba in a curious, soft voice.

"Because, because I can tell because of gray clouds."

"So the picture helps you to read the word *rainy*," confirms Mrs. Poremba. "Thank you, Kaitlynn. Does anybody else have an idea they want to tell us? Steven, come on up." As Steven hesitates before the weather chart, Mrs. Poremba prompts, "What do you notice?"

"It's rainy," says Steven, pointing to the same picture that Kaitlynn had.

"You noticed the same word. Do you notice any other things up there, Steven?"

Steven points to the picture part of the *cloudy* entry and says, "Cloudy."

"Oh, he can read *cloudy*." Mrs. Poremba points to the word part of the entry. "What else can you read, Steven?"

Steven proceeds in the same way to read the next entries by looking at the pictures, and Mrs. Poremba confirms and again points to the words. "'Windy.'"

"He can read *windy*."

Now the children are joining Steven, "'Snowy.'"

"He can read *snowy*."

"'Sunny.'"

"And you can read *sunny* up there."

Now children are calling out what they can read, "I can read *sunny*."

Ian says, "I can read all of them, too!"

"Can you read those too, Ian? Don't the pictures help with reading?"

"I can read all of them!" says Eric D.

"They really help. And you can read them all, too, Eric. Yes, Zack?"

"I can read every one of them!"

"Well, Zachary, why don't you read them for us?"

"'Snowy, rainy, windy, cloudy, sunny!'" reads Zack without hesitation, tracing his fingers left to right across the word of each entry in turn.

Mrs. Poremba whistles in admiration and says, "That's quite a reader we have here, guys."

"I can read it, too," adds one more kindergartner.

A WEATHER REPORT

Now Mrs. Poremba directs the kindergartners' attention to the movable *Yes* and *No* strips, with both the *Yes*es and the *No*s showing. "I'm interested in something else, though. I see some words on the right side here."

"'No,'" read many kindergartners together.

"There's a word you can all read, and many of you are writing that word." (Mrs. Poremba is referring to their sign-in sheet writing.) "It's a word—"

Many children call out, "'No.'" Others, reading the words to the left, add, "'Yes.'"

Jason says, "Teacher, teacher, I noticed—"

Mrs. Poremba reminds the children to take turns. Then she says, "Lots of you know that *no* word."

Sarah says, "Yes."

"Sarah, did you have something to show us? Come on up, Sarah."

Sarah points to one of the *Yes*es.

Meanwhile, another kindergartner is still looking at the five *No*s and reading, "'No, no, no, no, no.'"

"Sarah, you pointed to this word down here. What do you want us to know about that word?"

"'Yes.'"

"It says 'Yes.' Can you read the other words there, too? On this side? Can you read those words? Can you touch them and read them? What does that say?"

"'Yes. Yes. Yes. Yes,'" reads Sarah, as Mrs. Poremba points to the other *Yes*es.

"Oh! Did you see Sarah? Did you listen to her, Zack? Thank you for reading today, Sarah."

Jason persists: "I noticed something. There's all *Yes*es on this side and all *No*s on this side."

Sarah and Jason have looked closely at and made an important discovery about these functional words. They do not need to do isolated visual discrimination exercises on reading readiness worksheets.

"He noticed that there were all *Yes*es over here, and all the *No*s were over here," confirms Mrs. Poremba. "Thank you very much." Now, Mrs. Poremba points to the title at the top of the weather chart. "The words up here say, 'Today's Weather.' And this is where we'll do our weather report. This is something new for Mrs. Poremba. I haven't done weather this way before, but I thought a lot this summer, when I was home getting ready for kindergarten, about how to make this better for you. And I want to try it to see what you think. You see, the *Yes* and the *No* will help us to tell about"—and she points again to the title—"'Today's Weather.' So when I look at the word *sunny*, is today sunny?"

"No."

"No. So I'm going to push the *Yes* sign in and there is the *No*. It is not sunny. Is it cloudy?" And Mrs. Poremba proceeds to elicit and display a full weather report: *No* for sunny, *Yes* for cloudy, *No* for windy, *Yes* for rainy, and *No* for snowy. "Look at that!"

"'No, yes, no, yes, no!'" reads one kindergartner.

"It makes an *E*!" declares another, referring to the three *No*s extending from the right side of the weather chart like the three arms of an *E*.

"You made an *E* and an *F*!" declares Jeff, noticing also the two *Yes*es extending from the left side of the chart like the arms of a backwards *F*.

"Oh, I sure did! How many *No*s do we have today?"

"Three!" answer several kindergartners together.

"How many *Yes*es do we have?"

"Two."

MORE WEATHER WORDS

Next, Mrs. Poremba leads a discussion of the two *Yes*es and the three *No*s using the math words *less* and *more*. Then she continues, "I have something else I want to show you on our weather report here. Here it says, 'More Weather Words.'" Mrs. Poremba points to a sheet of paper pinned to the bulletin board next to the weather chart (see figure 2.2, chapter 2). "Now there might be other weather words that we don't have here on our list that you can think of that tell us about today's weather. Does anybody have any more weather words?"

Steven has the first suggestion: "It's muddy."

"*Muddy*! Oh my gosh, that's a great weather word. I'm going to write that word right here on our 'More Weather Words.' *Muddy*. What does it start with?"

"*M*," answers one kindergartner.

"It starts with an *M*—"

"Teacher, you know what?" asks Jason.

"Hang on—I'm working. I'm working. I have to think about what I'm doing," says Mrs. Poremba as she finishes writing **muddy**. "There's the word *muddy*. It really is muddy."

With this, Mrs. Poremba is initiating what others have called Shared Writing, a technique by which the teacher and students together create a text, but the teacher does the actual writing (Tompkins 2000). We will see that as the More Weather Words routine evolves, it will take on the characteristics of guided writing, in which the teacher supervises, but the students do the actual writing (Tompkins 2000).

"Tara, do you have a weather word for us?"

"Rainy!" "Puddles!" call out other kindergartners while Tara J. says, "Wet."

"*Wet*! *Wet*! That's a great weather word!" responds Mrs. Poremba.

"I was going to say that!" declares Jeff.

"Me, too!" "Puddles! Puddles!" shout others as Mrs. Poremba writes **wet**.

"People are shouting at me. That makes it hard for me to know who to call on. If you have an idea, raise your hand," counsels Mrs. Poremba in a very quiet voice. "So far we have 'muddy.' We have 'wet,'" she reads as she points to the words. "Erin, do you have another weather word for us?"

"Puddles," replies Erin.

"*Puddles*!" echoes Mrs. Poremba.

As she writes, Ian asserts, "I came up with that word."

"Me, too." "Me, too," say two others.

"No, you guys followed after me, but I came up with it," says Ian.

"Hey, we have four *B*s," observes Eric D. about the four **d**s in **muddy** and **puddles**.

"'Puddles!'" reads Mrs. Poremba. Then she asks Eric, "What did you notice?"

"We have four *B*s."

"The four *D*s right here? Here's two *D*s right there and right here?"

"Yeah."

"Any other weather words you want to tell me about?" She calls on Eric C.

"Rainy," he suggests.

"*Rainy*? I think we already have that one on our list here. That was a good word, but we have it on our weather chart. These are words that we don't already use." She calls on Eric D.

"Puddle," he answers.

"I think we've got it right here—'puddle.'"

Jason says, "Dark."

"Jason?"

"It's dark out."

"Why is it dark out, Jason?" Mrs. Poremba asks as she writes dark.

"Because when it rains it gets dark. Teacher?"

"'Dark,'" reads Mrs. Poremba. "Let's see if we can get these words now. Do you remember the very first word that Steven gave us?"

"'Mud.'" "'Muddy,'" read two kindergartners.

"'Muddy,'" reads Mrs. Poremba. "Do you remember?" she asks, pointing to the second word.

"'Wet!'" reads one kindergartner.

"'Wet.' Good. How about this one?"

"'Puddles,'" read several kindergartners.

"How about this one? That's Jason's word."

"'Dark!'" "'Dark!'"

"Good job on your weather words today! Everyday, I'll give you a chance to give me more weather word ideas. And we came up with four good ones today!"

"Teacher, I've got another one," announces Eric D.

"Do you have one? I'll tell you—tomorrow we'll do some more, but I think we need to do a little stretching. Can you stand up and do a stretch?"

Jeff asks, "Mrs. Poremba, can I read all of those?"

"Go right on up and do that! I'd love to hear you do that, Jeff."

Eric persists, "Teacher, I know—"

Jeff reads the weather chart, "'Sunny, cloudy, windy, rainy, snowy.'"

Mrs. Poremba whistles her approval and says, "That's great reading."

As the group breaks up, Eric D. continues, "I've got one for—damp."

"*Damp*! That is so good. Eric, I'm going to write that down. That is such a good word. Did you hear Eric? Eric came up with another word, *damp*. But what does *damp* mean?"

"*Damp* means wet," answers a kindergartner.

"Kind of wet," confirms Mrs. Poremba. "I need you to sit down in a circle."

"—dirty," says one kindergartner, trying unsuccessfully to get in one more word.

PAYING ATTENTION TO MEANINGS

On Friday, September 17, the fourteenth day of school, the first More Weather Word is Zack's suggestion, *muddy*.

Later, when Tara J. also suggests *muddy*, Mrs. Poremba says, "You agree with Zack."

Eric D. suggests *wet*.

Mrs. Poremba says, "*Www-et*. We've been using that word a lot lately, too. *Www-et*. Watch me carefully as I write that word. This is a word we've been using a lot. *Wwww—ehhh-t*."

Erin suggests *puddles*, and Mrs. Poremba reminds the kindergartners, "When I'm writing the words, be sure you watch."

Jeff suggests *kind of dry*.

"*Kind of dry*," echoes Mrs. Poremba. "Isn't that interesting that we had wet up here, and Jeff said we should put up *kind of dry*? Is some of those wet puddles and the wet grass starting to dry up?"

"Yeah," answer several kindergartners.

"*Kind of dry*. Let's put that up here. 'Kind, of, dry'" reads Mrs. Poremba as she writes, and she is joined by a few kindergartners.

"Look at that." She points and reads, "'Kind, of, dry.' Okay. We'll take one more. Steven, go right ahead."

"Damp," says Steven.

"*Damp*. What does *damp* mean?"

"Not real wet," answers Steven.

"That's a very good way of telling us what damp means. I like that idea." Mrs. Poremba says the first sound and then the whole word: "*D-damp*."

"*D*," say several kindergartners.

Mrs. Poremba writes **damp**. "Well, I think we have room for at least one more."

Ian suggests *yucky* "because it's yucky out and there's lots of mud." After Mrs. Poremba writes the word and she and the students note its two *Y*s, Eric D. says, "Hey, it looks like a cradle. It looks like a cradle."

Mrs. Poremba echoes, "It looks like a cradle."

Eric explains, "The two *Y*s are holding it up."

HOW WORDS LOOK AND LETTER–SOUND RELATIONSHIPS

The next school day, Monday, September 20, the fifteenth day of school, the kindergartners suggest many of the same More Weather Words. That's all right with Mrs. Poremba. She knows that beginners enjoy and benefit from familiarity with a small set of words. Today, she will use More Weather Words to invite the kindergartners to pay attention to how words look, including the comparative length of words, and to emphasize letter–sound relationships.

Zack suggests *muddy*.

"Zack, I wonder what letter *mmmuddy* starts with," says Mrs. Poremba. "I bet Eric knows that." Earlier Eric D. had noted, "There's an *M* on *music* [on the Today We Have chart] and an *M* on the calendar [*Monday*]."

Eric says, "*M*."

"There's that *M* again," confirms Mrs. Poremba. "I'm going to write the small *M*, though. *Muddy* is *M-U-D*—"

She is interrupted by kindergartners' shouting out new suggestions for words. "I'm not even finished writing *muddy* yet. I just have the *mud* part." She finishes writing and says, "Now it says *muddy*."

Meagan suggests *puddles*.

Mrs. Poremba says the beginning sound: "*P-p-p-*."

"*P*!" say several kindergartners.

Mrs. Poremba confirms, "It starts with a *P*. Watch me write that *P*. Listen to *puddles*. I think you're going to like the way it's spelled. It's *P-U*. Watch this: *D-D-L-E-S*."

Eric D. observes, "Hey, we got four *D*s. Four *D*s in both of them!" Eric had made a similar observation on September 14, but he had called that day's four *D*s four *B*s. Today, he gives them their correct letter name.

Mrs. Poremba asks, "There's what?"

"Four, four, four *D*s in both of them."

"Oh, you noticed the two *D*s in *muddy* and the two *D*s in *puddles*? And two plus two makes four, you're right."

Steven suggests *wet*.

"*Wet*. We have that word up here a lot on our graph, don't we? *Wwwet*. Starts with a *W*. It's a small word. Watch me write that. *W-E-T*. Look at how small, only three letters in *wet*. It's a small word."

Eric C. suggests *damp*. When asked what it means, Eric says, "*Damp* means that it's puddly."

Mrs. Poremba emphasizes the first sound: "*D-d-damp*."

"*D*," says a kindergartner.

"Watch me spell the word *damp*," directs Mrs. Poremba.

"Five *D*s!" says Jeff.

Mrs. Poremba identifies the letters as she writes damp.

Erin suggests *cold*.

"I'll spell *cold* right here," again ensuring that the kindergartners look at the words. "It's *C-O-L-D*. *Cold*."

Elizabeth suggests *damp*.

"You agree with Eric," says Mrs. Poremba.

Jeff says: "A little windy." But Mrs. Poremba asks if it is windy now, and Jeff admits that it isn't (today's weather report helper had chosen *No* for *windy*), and so she doesn't write *a little windy*.

Freddy suggests *wet*.

"You agree with Steven," says Mrs. Poremba.

Tara G. suggests *dirty*.

"*D-dirty*"—Mrs. Poremba says the beginning sound twice—"starts with a *D*."

Erin notes, "That's a new word."

"It is a new word. And there's an *R* and a *T*. And watch the last letter, Jason. I want you to look at the last letter I'm going to write and see if another word has that *Y* on the end of it."

"The top one." "The top one," say two kindergartners.

"Do you remember what that first word was?"

"'Muddy,'" reads a kindergartner.

"'Muddy.' It has a *Y* at the end also. Look at that, *dirty* and *muddy*. Both with *Y*s at the end."

Eric C. suggests *cloudy*.

"*Cloudy*" echoes Mrs. Poremba. "You agree with the weather graph, don't you? See where we already have that word up here?"

"Yeah."

So Mrs. Poremba does not write *cloudy*, but she advises, "If you ever need to know where to look for *cloudy*, Eric, you can always check our graph."

Zack suggests *soaking wet*.

"We've got the *wet* part right here," responds Mrs. Poremba, pointing to the third word on today's More Weather Words list.

"But we don't have *soaking*," notes Zack.

"We don't have the *soaking* part," Mrs. Poremba agrees. "How about if I put the *soaking* part near the *wet* word? Will that help you? Okay. *Soaking*."

Jason says, "I realized something." With two fingers he points to the two ds in muddy.

"Oh, you noticed these two *D*s. How about if I circle them?"

Then Jason points to the ds at the beginning of damp and dirty.

Eric D. says, "And there's two other *D*s."

"Where's the two other *D*s?" Mrs. Poremba asks.

Eric shows the two ds in puddles.

Another kindergartner notices the d in cold.

Mrs. Poremba circles them all. "Look at all those *D*s we have today," she says.

Eric counts them, and Mrs. Poremba confirms, "Seven *D*s. Wow. That's a lot of *D*s for one day!"

Mrs. Poremba's class won't need a Letter of the Week bulletin board featuring the letter *D*.

FINAL *Y*: THIS IS REAL HARD STUFF.

Three days later, on September 23, it's no longer muddy and soaking wet outside, but the kindergartners continue to like those words. Although

Mrs. Poremba expresses skepticism (she tells that on her way home the previous day, she noticed that it wasn't muddy any more), she lets the kindergartners dictate these favorite words and makes use of them. So More Weather Words diverges from its expressed goal of elaboration of the weather report.

When Steven suggests *muddy*, Mrs. Poremba directs, "Help me spell the word as I write the letters."

"*M-U—*" say several kindergartners.

"What comes after the *M-U*?" asks Mrs. Poremba.

"*D*," say several kindergartners.

"How many *D*s?"

"Two," say several kindergartners.

"Two. Okay."

A kindergartner repeats the letter name: "*D-D*."

"And there's our *D*," says Mrs. Poremba as she writes the second *D*. "Now what's at the end of *muddy*?"

Erin says, "*Y*." Other kindergartners repeat, "*Y*."

Elise suggests *damp*.

Sarah suggests *windy* but changes her suggestion to *cold* when she is led to agree that it is not windy outside.

"That's in my name," says Zack about the *C* in *cold*.

Tara G. suggests *wet*.

Mrs. Poremba asks, "Is *wet* gonna be a long word or is *wet* gonna be a—"

Erin interrupts, "Short!" and others echo that.

"Only three letters," predicts another kindergartner.

Mrs. Poremba confirms this by writing **wet**.

"Teacher, teacher, teacher!" calls Jason.

Eric D. suggests *slippery*.

"I wonder if *slippery* is going to be a longer word or a short word?"

"Long," say several kindergartners.

The kindergartners identify the letters of *slippery* as Mrs. Poremba writes them, but some say "*Y*" even before she writes it. They show that they know that *slippery* ends like *muddy* and all the words on the weather chart, *sunny*, *cloudy*, *windy*, *rainy*, and *snowy*.

Jason makes this explicit: "You know what? Two *Y*s, at the bottom and the top." (The top word is *muddy*.)

Mrs. Poremba confirms, "Jason noticed that there's a *Y* at the bottom and a *Y* at the top—"

Jason adds, "And there's a *D* on every single word." But Mrs. Poremba asks Jason to check that out, and he amends his observation, "All of the words except for the bottom two." (They are *wet* and *slippery*.)

Zack suggests *soak*.

As they discuss this suggestion, Mrs. Poremba and the kindergartners begin saying *soaking* instead.

"Watch what's the last letter of *soaking*," says Mrs. Poremba, again directing the kindergartners' attention to how words look. "It might surprise you."

When they identify the **g** at the end of **soaking**, Tara G. says "That's a new letter."

Mrs. Poremba agrees: "We haven't talked a lot about that *G* have we?"

Zack suggests, "Let's go hunting for those."

Mrs. Poremba suggests they might do that later, maybe during choice time.

On Tuesday, September 28th, the twenty-first day of school, Elise suggests *wet* for More Weather Words. Mrs. Poremba talks about wet grass. The kindergartners know that *wet* is a short word, and they help Mrs. Poremba to spell it.

Next, Steven says, "Dry." Either he disagrees about the appropriateness of *wet* for More Weather Words or he demonstrates how far this exercise has moved toward word play with favorite words rather than elaboration of the weather report.

"*Dry*," echoes Mrs. Poremba. "Tell me about the *dry* part today, Steven."

"My driveway was dry," says Steven without hesitation.

"Oh, was the grass wet, but the driveway was dry?"

"We learned a new word," notices Erin.

"Watch this one," says Mrs. Poremba.

And the kindergartners identify the letters as she writes them: "*D-R-Y*."

On Friday, October 1st, the twenty-fourth day of school, the first three More Weather Words are *cold*, *muddy*, *dry*.

Next, Freddy suggests *frosty*. Yesterday one of the words was *frost*.

"Was it frosty this morning again?" asks Mrs. Poremba.

"No," say several kindergartners.

Mrs. Poremba says, "Listen to—I just want Freddy to explain his thinking."

Ian says, "It was frosty in my bathtub!"

"Tell us about *frosty*, Freddy."

"It was."

"Tell us about it."

"It was yesterday."

"Yesterday. Did we have *frost* in our weather words yesterday?"

"Yes," say several kindergartners.

Mrs. Poremba displays yesterday's More Weather Words. "Let's look at our weather words. This is yesterday's weather words. On Wednesday—on Thursday, we wrote these."

"'Cold,'" reads Ian. "We got it up there."

"We've got *cold*," agrees Mrs. Poremba.

"'Frosty!'" reads Zack.

"We wrote *frost* yesterday," says Mrs. Poremba in a calm, even voice, pointing to yesterday's word.

"Now we have *frosty*," notes a kindergartner. "Not *frost*."

"We didn't write *frosty*," confirms Mrs. Poremba. "It's a little different. Do you want me to write *frosty* up here?"

"Frosty the Snowman!" says a kindergartner.

"Wait until you see how you write *frosty*. I want you to look at *frost*, and I want you to watch this, Erin. Take your eyes and watch me write. Here's *frost*, but I'm gonna write *frost-y*."

Eric D. says, "*E*, it's gonna be a *E* at the end."

The kindergartners say the letters as Mrs. Poremba writes, "*F-R-O-S-T*."

"Oh, my gosh!" says Tara G.

"Here's the *frost* part," says Mrs. Poremba, pointing to what she has written so far. "Watch this. Watch it."

Eric repeats his prediction, "*E*."

"*Y*," say several kindergartners as Mrs. Poremba writes the last letter.

"Oh, my gosh!" repeats Tara.

"Now watch this." Mrs. Poremba points and reads, emphasizing the last sounds, "'Mudd-y, frost-y.' They both end with a—"

"But what about in the middle?" asks a kindergartner.

"—*Y*."

"'Muddy, dry, frosty,'" reads Ian.

A kindergartner notices that *dry* isn't on yesterday's list.

"*Dry* wasn't on this list," agrees Mrs. Poremba, "but Ian brings up a good point. There's a *Y* on the end of *dry*. What do you think, Ian?"

Ian can't put his finger on the difference in the final sounds of *dry* and the other two, *muddy* and *frosty*. And so Mrs. Poremba does not pursue this. She only says, "This is real hard stuff."

"Hey, there's three *Y*s," says Eric D., "Make a triangle."

"This is real hard stuff," repeats Mrs. Poremba. "There's *muddy*, *dry*, and *frosty*. All end with a *Y*. We'll talk more about that another time. Ian, I want you to keep thinking about that. We'll see if that happens again."

What the children are ready for is the purely visual task of noticing *Y*s in words. Mrs. Poremba asks the class, "Any other words here that end with a *Y*, from yesterday?"

"No." "No" say several kindergartners.

Kaitlynn notices the *Y*s at the ends of all the weather chart words, *sunny*, *cloudy*, *windy*, *rainy*, *snowy*.

"*Y* is at the end of a lot of words," says Mrs. Poremba.

Zack mentions the *Y* in *yes*.

"But is the *Y* at the beginning or at the end in *yes*, Zack?"

"Beginning," answers Zack.

"It's at the beginning," confirms Mrs. Poremba. "But it's also at the end in lots of words."

Kaitlynn notices the *Y* in *your* in Aunt Edith's and Uncle Wally's letter, posted nearby. Another kindergartner notices the *Y* in *Wally*. Elizabeth finds the *Y* in *Gym* on the Today We Have chart. And Mrs. Poremba leads talk about the beginning, the middle, and the end of words.

By November 4, Thursday, the forty-seventh day of school, Mrs. Poremba devotes much of her More Weather Words talk to sounds that letters stand for. She begins, "This is the time of the day that we write new words. We write words on our weather words sheet that help us to know about the weather. The words also, the writing that we're doing now, also helps us to learn a lot about spelling and writing."

Nicole makes the first suggestion: "Chilly."

"*Chilly*!" Mrs. Poremba asks, "What do you know about the word *chilly*?" She emphasizes a sound that the kindergartners might be able to match with a letter: "Does anybody know anything about the word *chillll-y*?" And when she writes the word, she calls attention to spelling conventions: "*Chilly* starts with this sound. Listen carefully. *Ch, ch, ch, ch, ch, ch, ch*. I'm gonna put down the letters that make that *ch* sound. A *C* and an *H* together make the *ch* sound in *chilly*!"

By this time of the year, the kindergartners have individual sign-in sheets with them on clipboards during wall work (see chapter 4). So Mrs. Poremba suggests, "If you want to write *chilly* down on your sign-in sheet, this is a good time to do it." And Elise, Allysa, and Zack do that.

Nathan suggests *crummy*.

Mrs. Poremba asks, "Is it kind of a crummy November day? I agree. Nathan, watch this. You might want to have your pencil ready for your word. Okay? You ready, Ian? Okay. *C-cr-ummy* starts with a *C-R*. That's the *cr* part. Now, I'm gonna do the *ummy* part. *Ummy* is *U*, and there's a double letter here."

"*M*," says a kindergarnter, "*mmmmm*."

"Hear it? *Crummmmm*"

Now several kindergartners suggest, "*E*."

Now Mrs. Poremba feels that the kindergartners are ready for the explanation that she had declined giving a month ago: "Sometimes the *Y* makes a sound like *E* on the end of a word."

Nathan does copy his suggested word, *crummy*, on his sign-in sheet. So do Alyssa, Freddy, and Ian.

Mayra suggests *muddy* for the next word.

Mrs. Poremba says, "You know what, I would have guessed my whole paycheck on that! *Muddy*. Boys and girls, we've written the word *muddy* a lot!" But Mrs. Poremba's patience about writing *muddy* almost every day for a month pays off. She asks, "What do you know about *muddy*, Mayra?"

And Mayra is able to say, without hesitation, "*M*."

"It starts with an *M*. Put your *M*s down. That's the very first letter." And she leads the kindergartners through the spelling of *muddy*. Freddy, Alyssa, and Elise copy it on their sign-in sheets.

READING AND WRITING

On Tuesday, November 16, the fifty-fourth day of school, I am the teacher for wall work, and rather than writing More Weather Words on the posted form on the bulletin board, I ask the kindergartners to write their own More Weather Words on their sign-in sheets: "We're gonna do something a little bit different for More Weather Words today. There are lots and lots of ways to write, and you folks are so good at writing. When I look at your sign-in sheets everyday, I see all the wonderful writing that you kindergartners can do. And one of the ways that you can write is by copying what somebody else wrote. Today, when you were writing the room, I saw you all over the room copying down things. Some of you were copying other people's name collars."

"I was!" "I was!" shout several kindergartners.

"Some of you were copying words from the Writing Center bulletin board."

"I was!" "I was!"

"Some of you were copying words from our Thanksgiving [words displayed on the] easel."

"I was copying the color words," says Tara G.

"Mmm hmm. That's one way to write. And sometimes when we do More Weather Words, Mrs. Poremba or Mrs. Roloff or I write a weather word up there and you copy it down. That's a good way to do it. Today, we're going to do a different kind of writing. This time it's going to be a kind of writing where you think about what to write, and you write down what you think. . . . I want each of you to think about your very own weather word and don't say it to anybody else; just say it to yourself. And listen to the sounds in the word, and when you come to a sound that you know how to write, write that sound down. . . . It doesn't have to be the way that I write it when I put it on the More Weather Words. . . . When you're finished writing your own weather word, draw a circle around it and bring me your sign-in sheet."

Later, during free-choice time, I show the kindergartners their sign-in sheets and ask them to read the circled words. Jeff correctly reads his sunny; Tara J. her wet; Erin her cool, cold, and wet; Jason his cooL and cloudy (with a backwards y); Alyssa her cool; Kaitlynn her cruMMy (with a backwards y); and Tara G. her wet. Eric D. reads his cood as "cold." Elise reads her MuddY correctly, her chlly as "chilly," her coLd as "cool," and her cooL as "cold." Deborah reads her fiziz COLD (with backwards zs) as "freezing cold." Ian reads his GOAMWN as "gusty" after I prime him with the first sound and his MTNMAX as "muddy." Meagan reads only the last sound of her cool and wet after I sound out the beginning and middle sounds of each. Sarah can't read her PARtiES; she says, "I don't know how," even when I point out her source in the Thanksgiving word list on the easel.

MOVING BEYOND WEATHER WORDS

By Monday, November 29, the sixty-first day of school, the kindergartner weather reporters often have displayed *Yes* for *snowy*, just from wishful thinking. Today, the class erupts in cheers when Tara J. is able truthfully to display that *Yes*. And when Nathan is called on for the first More Weather Word, he wants *snowy*. And Freddy suggests *ice*.

"That's a short word," says Erin after Mrs. Poremba writes ice.

But the rest of today's words are typical of the group's tendency to digress from weather words for this routine. Steven suggests *Christmas*.

"I wonder if *Christmas* is a short word or a longer word," says Mrs. Poremba.

"Longer," say several kindergartners.

Allysa suggests *holiday*.

"That's not a weather word," notes Jason.

"It's not a weather word, but is it a good word?" asks Mrs. Poremba.

"Neither is *Christmas*," says a kindergartner.

"*Christmas* isn't really a weather word either," agrees Mrs. Poremba. "You know, maybe what we need to do, instead of calling these More Weather Words, is just call them More Words."

"More *any* words," suggests Tara G.

"Let's try *holiday*. *Hhhhah-liday* starts with the same letter as *Hhhhah-loween*."

"*H*!" say several kindergartners together.

"It's an *H*. Watch this. *Holiday* is *H-O-L*—that's the *hol* part. Now, I'm gonna do the *ih, holi-day*."

"*D*," says Kaitlynn.

"*D-E*," says another kindergartner.

"*D*—" begins Mrs. Poremba.

"*A-Y*," finishes Tara G.

"*A-Y*," echoes Mrs. Poremba. "Got it, Tara."

"I was looking at the day of the week," explains Tara.

Next, Erin wants *Santa Claus*.

"Now, Erin, I want you to think about what you just told me. How many words is that?"

"Two," answers Erin.

"Two, one for *Santa* and one for—"

"*Claus*," say several kindergartners.

"Okay, I'll do the *Santa* part first. *Santa* is *S-A-N*—That's the *San* part; now, I'm gonna do the *tuh*. *Santa*—"

"*Claus*," says a kindergartner.

"You have to leave a finger space," says another.

"Finger space for *Claus*? Okay. *Claus* is *C-L-A-U*— Ooo, I can just barely fit that last letter on. *Clauzz*"

"*S*," says Erin.

"That's right, Erin."

WORDS FOR TODAY

On Tuesday, January 4, the seventy-fifth day of school, Mrs. Poremba says, "Some of you noticed that I changed our words up here. Instead of saying More Weather Words, I just said Words for Today." She models something else new, writing the date first at the top of the words list. Ironically, all the words that kindergartners suggest today are weather words: *snowing*, *winter*, and *cloudy*. The holidays are over, and the bitter winter weather is on everyone's mind.

Actually, Mrs. Poremba writes the word *winter* twice.

When Elise suggests *winter*, Erin says, "We never had that word!"

"Elise, what do you know about the word *winter*?" asks Mrs. Poremba.

"*W*!" say several kindergartners.

"It starts with a *W*," says Elise.

"It starts with a *W*. Anything else you know about that word, Elise?"

"Just like *wet*," notes a kindergartner.

"It starts like *wet*," agrees Mrs. Poremba. "When we wrote the word *wet*, we would always write the *W* first. Do you hear anything else in *winnnn-ter*?"

"*N*," say several kindergartners.

"*Nnn-nnn-nnn*," says a kindergartner.

"I wonder what letter might make that sound? What would you write for that sound?"

"*N*!" say more kindergartners.

"Sure, we would do the *N*."

A kindergartner makes the *T* sound: "*T-t-t-*."

Mrs. Poremba confirms this: "I hear the *t* also. *Win-t*. I'll put the *t* down. What is there on the end—"

"*Rrrr*," says a kindergartner.

"—of *winterrr*?" finishes Mrs. Poremba.

"*Rrrrr*!" "*R*!" say several kindergartners, some saying the sound, others naming the letter. Tara G. says both: "*Rrrr—R*!"

"Could be an *R*?" asks Mrs. Poremba. "Would that make sense? Let's see what we've got here." She has written wntr. She reads, "'Win-ter.' Did we get it? What we did is we wrote down the big sounds that we hear."

Tara asks, "But is that how you write it?"

"Let me show you what's missing," says Mrs. Poremba. "I'll write it down here, and I'll show you all the sounds, the big sounds *and* the little sounds."

"We missed the *E*," says a kindergartner.

"Watch this. You might be surprised about this," says Mrs. Poremba.

"I think there is an *L*," says another.

"When you write down the big sounds and the little sounds, you would spell it *winnn-terrr*." She writes winter.

"Oh yeah, that's what I think it is," says Tara G. "I thought it would be *I*."

"There is a *E*, though," observes a kindergartner.

"The *I* and the *E* are the little sounds," explains Mrs. Poremba. "And sometimes they're harder to hear when you're spelling."

"No," asserts Tara. "I can hear the *I—ih-ih-ih-ih*."

"I can hear it, too. I sure can," says Mrs. Poremba.

Later, when Mrs. Poremba asks about the spelling of the end of *cloudy*, Tara shows that she can also use the copy strategy. "I know it's a *Y*."

"How did you know?" asks Mrs. Poremba.

"I'm looking at the weather report," says Tara.

On Friday, January 14, the eighty-fourth day of school, Mrs. Poremba displays on the easel a page from the local newspaper. The headline is "Brrrrr!" and below that, "Arctic weather is no blast for workers." Monday, January 17 is the Martin Luther King Jr. holiday, and on the next two days, there is no school because of severe cold. On Thursday, January 20, there is another newspaper display, the front page of the Sunday *Chicago Tribune*, its headline also proclaiming "Brrrrrrrrr!" over a picture in the center of the page of a woman bundled up in a warm cap and scarf. From now on, Brrrrr, with varying numbers of rs, appears frequently among Words for Today.

THE FIRST STUDENT WRITER OF WORDS FOR TODAY

On Monday, February 21st, the 105th day of school, Erin is the helper for the weather report. Mrs. Poremba says, "Boys and girls, our friend Erin is ready to start when you show her that *you're* ready. Eyes right up here, Jeff."

"Is it sunny?" asks Erin. She surveys children's thumbs-up or thumbs-down votes and slides the *Yes/No* card so that the *Yes* shows.

"Is it cloudy?" The decision is *No*. "Is it windy?" *Yes*. "Is it rainy?" *No*. "Is it snowy?" As is usually the case, Erin would like to say that it is a snowy day, even though it isn't. She posts a *Yes*, and some children giggle while others say "Yay" with quiet voices. Erin looks at Mrs. Poremba, but she is stonefaced as if nothing untoward is happening. Erin quickly makes it official by reporting the number sentence, "Two *no*s and three *yes*es make five altogether."

"Erin, I was wondering: Would you like to come up and do the Words for Today with us?"

"Oh my—!" says Tara G., but Erin is game. She calls on Tara J., who suggests *cold* for the first word. "What?" asks Erin.

"Cold," repeats Tara.

Mrs. Poremba asks, "Is there something we need to add, put on the Words for Today, before we start?"

With her classmates' help and with the calendar as a model, Erin writes the date at the top of the Words for Today sheet. Then she proceeds to writing the first word for today, which Tara G. had already suggested, *cold*. She writes a backwards c (see figure 5.1).

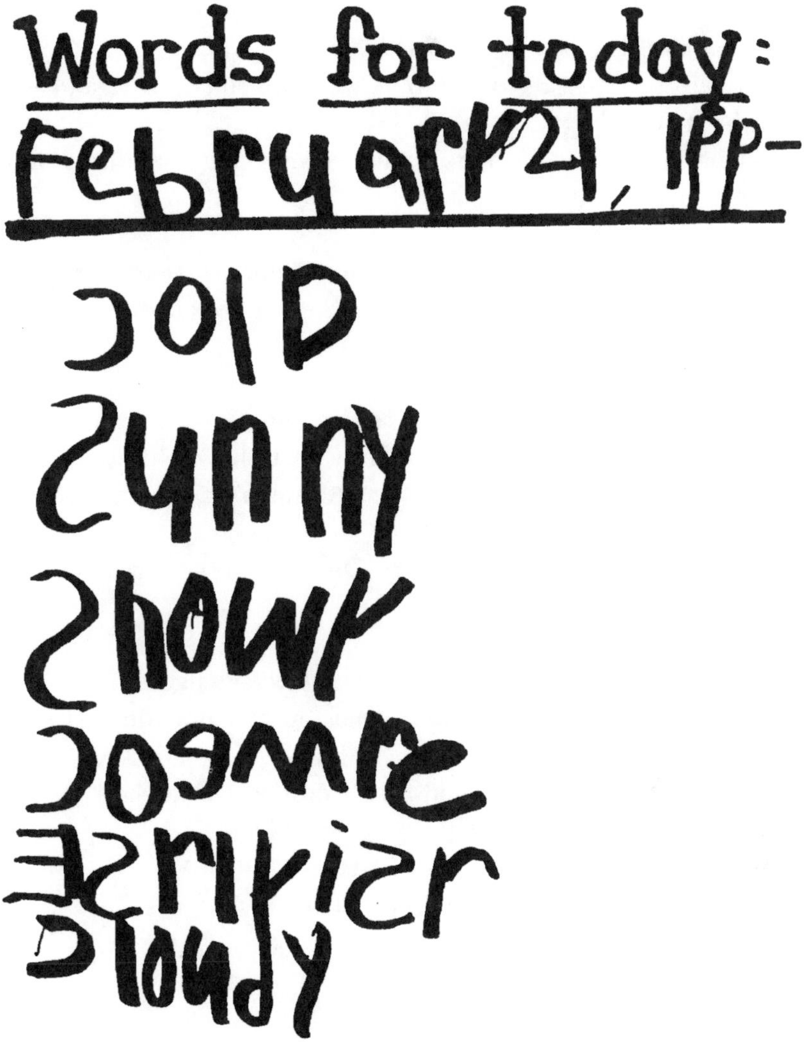

Figure 5.1. Erin's February 21 Words for Today

"What word are you working on, Erin?" asks Mrs. Poremba.

"*Cold*," Erin replies.

"*Cold*," several kindergartners echo.

"*Cold*? Okay. You might want to ask friends to help you."

"*C-O-*" suggests Jason. "*O-*" he repeats.

"*C-O-*" "*C*" "*O*" "*L*" say several kindergartners.

"*C-O-L-D*," spells Ian.

"*L*" "*D*" say others.

"*Cooooohlllld*," says a kindergartner. Erin's finished writing is **colD**, with a backwards **c** (see figure 5.1).

Erin calls on Meagan for the next word for today. Meagan can't decide what to offer.

"Maybe Meagan needs more thinking time," suggests Mrs. Poremba.

"Sarah."

"Sunny."

Erin immediately begins copying *sunny* from the weather chart while Sarah begins prompting her also from the weather chart but with a different word, *snowy*, for her model: "*S*—"

"*U*" prompts Freddy.

"*N-O*" continues Sarah. She stops when Tara G. leans over and begins whispering to her. A discussion follows that shows that writing these words is a meaningful activity for Mrs. Poremba's kindergartners, not an empty exercise.

"She's looking up there!" reports Deborah about Erin's use of the weather chart model.

"*Y*!" prompts Freddy.

Erin has written **sunny** with a backwards **s** (see figure 5.1).

"What just happened? Sarah, what just happened?" asks Mrs. Poremba.

"She was working on *snowy* at first," interjects Tara G.

"I meant *snowy*," says Sarah.

"She meant *snowy*," says a classmate.

"What did you say?" asks Mrs. Poremba.

"*Sunny*," answers Sarah.

"It's not snowy out," says a kindergartner.

"You said *sunny*. What did Erin write?"

"*Snowy*," answers Sarah, nodding her head.

"No—*sunny*," asserts Deborah.

"I meant—"

Erin has been standing by. Now, she points to Sarah with the marker and says, "You said *sunny*."

"I meant *snowy*," says Sarah.

"It's not snowy," shouts Deborah. "It's going to be snowy tomorrow."

"Yeah, but she can *say* it," replies Tara G.

"Maybe Sarah's thinking about the snow she heard about for tomorrow," suggests Mrs. Poremba.

Erin begins to write *snowy*.

"Is that what you were thinking about, Sarah?"

Sarah nods.

"Okay, Sarah, can you help Erin with the spelling?"

"She already wrote—that's funny," muses Freddy.

Erin begins copying from the weather chart, but when Sarah and classmates begin telling her the spelling, she follows them. She writes snowy, with a backwards s and y (see figure 5.1).

Erin calls on Jeff for the next word.

"Crummy," says Jeff.

Erin is uncertain.

"Did you hear what he said?" asks Mrs. Poremba.

Erin nods and says, "*Crummy*."

"*Crummy*," echoes Mrs. Poremba. "Can you help Erin out with the spelling on that, Jeff?"

Erin waits on Jeff's suggestions, which are not automatic. They get through coe together.

"Anything else you think we need for *crummmmy*?" asks Mrs. Poremba.

"*M*," suggests Freddy immediately. "*R*," he adds.

Erin adds Mr.

"*R*," echoes Jeff.

"She just put an *R*. Did you want two *R*s, Jeff?" asks Mrs. Poremba.

Jeff shakes his head. "Just one."

"*E*," suggests Erin, looking to Mrs. Poremba for approval. "How about a *E*?"

"A *E* on the end?" asks Mrs. Poremba.

Erin adds e. Now, she has coeMre with the c and the first e backwards (see figure 5.1).

"Erin, I just noticed something," says Freddy as he gets up and approaches Erin. He points to the two es, the first one backwards and the second one correct. He says, "*E* and then *E*. That's the right one—"

Erin interrupts, pointing to the two cs in her colD and coeMre and the two ss in her sunny and snowy. "Look-at—two *C*s and two *S*s."

"Erin, no. That's not what I mean. See, this *E*'s the wrong way; this *E*'s the right way."

"That's okay," suggests Erin.

"That's okay," agrees Freddy.

Kaitlynn, who has otherwise written only wavy lines of mock-cursive scribble writing on her sign-in sheet, now writes coeMre in the *Today is* line, with the c backwards.

Erin calls on Ian.

"*Easter*," suggests Ian. Children laugh as if this is a challenge.

"Ian, what do you know about *Easter*?" asks Mrs. Poremba.

"*E*—"

"Um, Erin, you'd better make it a capital *E* because Easter is a holiday, and you always write holidays beginning with a capital letter. So start it with a capital *E*."

"*S-R-L*—" continues Ian confidently suggesting each next letter immediately after Erin has written its preceding one.

Some children are sounding out, "*EEEEaster*." "*Easterrr*."

"What?" asks Erin about Ian's *L* suggestion.

"*L*," repeats Ian.

"Where do you hear the *L* in *EEassterr*, Ian?" asks Mrs. Poremba. "*EEEassterrr*."

"I don't hear it," says a kindergartner.

"There is no *L*," asserts Deborah.

"I just thought it would be a little letter," answers Ian. He knows there are little sounds in words, fillers, that are not as predictable as the big sounds.

"There is no *L*," repeats Deborah.

"I just wondered. I was just wondering where you heard it," says Mrs. Poremba.

"What, Ian? What's the next?" asks Erin.

Ian appears stumped.

"Why don't you look at what Erin has written so far?" suggests Mrs. Poremba.

After a pause, Ian says, "*Y-I-S-R*."

Erin writes exactly what Ian suggested, ending up with Esrlyisr, with backwards E, s, and y (see figure 5.1).

"You know what, Erin? I think we can take one more word. Then we'll have enough for today, or we'll have our sheet all filled up."

Erin calls on Zack, but he can't decide.

"I think Zack needs some more thinking time. Does anybody else have a word that they're all ready with?" says Mrs. Poremba.

Jason's hand is up, and Tara G. says, "Jason does."

"Go ahead, Erin. You're in charge," says Mrs. Poremba. Erin calls on Jason.

"Cloudy," says Jason.

Erin immediately and confidently begins copying from the weather chart.

"I can't really see because they're too close together," says Jason about Erin's beginning to write *cloudy* close to the word above it because of the small amount of space left at the bottom of the paper.

"Now this word has a *L*," notes Deborah.

"Very good point, Deborah," says Mrs. Poremba.

One kindergartner is stretching out each sound in *cloudy* as he writes it on his sign-in sheet.

"Can you hear the *L* in *clllloudy*?" asks Mrs. Poremba.

Erin finishes with cloudy, with a backwards c (see figure 5.1).

"Thank you very much. Erin, could you read the words that we wrote up today, so everybody knows?"

Erin begins confidently, pointing and reading, "'Cloudy [for cold], sunny, snowy —'" She stops at coeMre, her spelling for *crummy*.

"What starts with a *C*—kuh, kuh?" asks Kaitlynn.

"*Cloudy*?" asks Erin uncertainly.

"*Crummy*," answers Kaitlynn.

"No, it's *cloudy*," asserts Deborah.

"No, it isn't. It isn't *cloudy*," argues a classmate.

"Yes it is!" says Deborah.

"I think that might have been Jeff's word," hints Mrs. Poremba.

"It's *crummy*," says Kaitlynn.

"No, we already had *crummy*," argues Deborah.

"She wasn't—" starts Mrs. Poremba.

But Erin is satisfied and continues pointing and reading, beginning now with coeMre: "'Crummy, and Easter, and —'"

"'Cloudy,'" a classmate reads.

"'Cloudy,'" finishes Erin, and she is tall enough to place the marker easily back atop the cupboard. She is comfortable, satisfied, and pleased with her work.

"Thank you very much, Erin. Erin, you did a great job on our words today! My goodness!"

MORE STUDENT WRITERS OF WORDS FOR TODAY

The next day, Tuesday, February 22, day 106, Elise becomes the second kindergartner to lead Words for Today. The first seven items are *cold, muddy, wet, snow storm, snowy, cloudy,* and *windy* (see figure 5.2).

Then Zack suggests the word *brrrrr.* Both newspaper pages that inspired the popularity of this word over a month ago are still attached to the wall work bulletin board immediately below the Words for Today sheet.

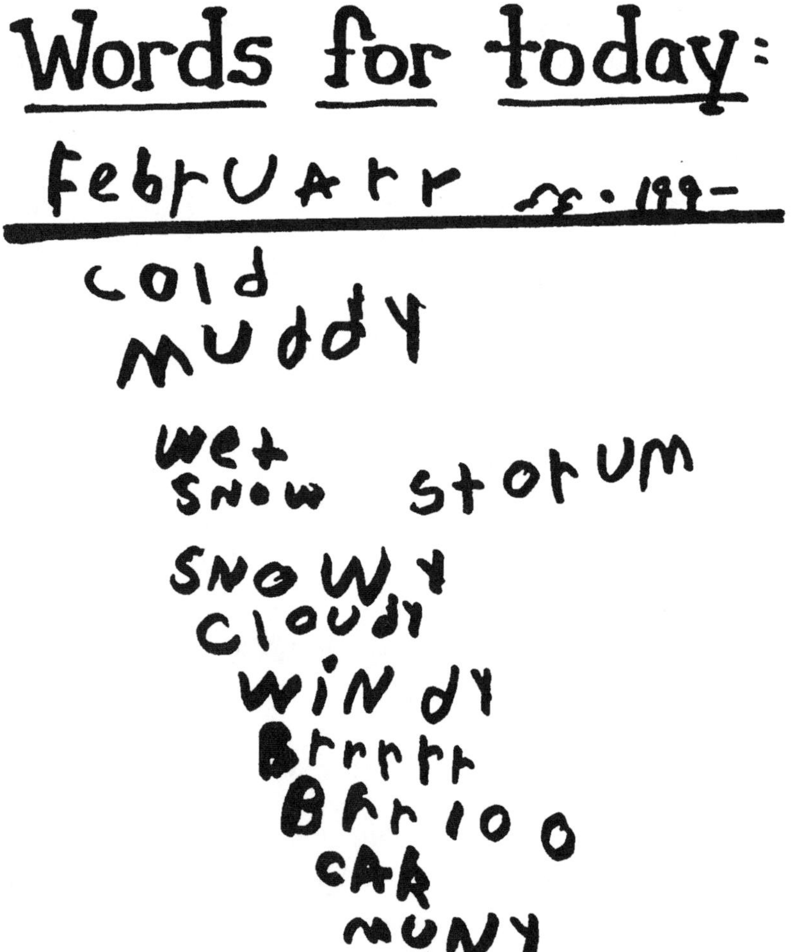

Figure 5.2. Elise's February 22 Words for Today

"Elise, you'd better ask him how many *Rs* he wants," directs Mrs. Poremba.

"How many *Rs* do you want?"

"Five."

Elise begins writing, and several children react with their own ideas. "I would have said fifty thousand," says Jeff.

"No, I want five," says Zack.

Elise writes Brrrrr.

"Zachary, did you check your *brrrrr* up there—and make sure she had all the *Rs* you needed?"

Zack studies Elise's work from his place on the carpet. "Yes."

"Yes? Okay," says Mrs. Poremba.

"Jason," Elise calls next.

"Brrrrr," says Jason proudly. He plans to challenge Elise with what he knows will come next.

Elise laughs.

"He's going to waste all our time," moans a kindergartner.

Jason says something to Mrs. Poremba that can't be heard but is probably a hint for Elise to ask how many. "You need to tell Elise; she's your writer for today," responds Mrs. Poremba.

Elise picks up on this, "How many *Rs* do you want?" she asks.

"A hundred!" answers Jason mischievously.

The children react. "Oh!!" "Oh!!"

"I want twenty. I want twenty," says Ian.

"Um, Jason, I think you'd better think of another number," says Mrs. Poremba. "That would be too long."

"I know how I'm going to do it," says Jason.

"How are you going to?"

"Write *brrrrr* with three *Rs* and then write one hundred."

Meanwhile, Ian is saying, "*Brrrrrrrrrrrrrrrrrrrrrrrrrrrrrrr*."

"Jason, show me that on your sign-in sheet," says Mrs. Poremba. Jason kneels and leans over his sign-in sheet on the floor in front of him, and Mrs. Poremba explains, "Elise, Jason has an idea for how to write *brrrrr* with a hundred *Rs*."

Jason writes Brr100 on his sign-in sheet.

"Okay," says Mrs. Poremba. "Do you have your idea? Okay, Jason, go up and show Elise that idea."

Jason takes his clipboard to Elise. "Write it like that?" Jason asks.

Elise nods and turns to write.

"I couldn't see it," says Tara G.

"Watch. Elise is going to write his idea up there. I think you'll be interested in how Jason thinks Elise could write *brrrrr* with one hundred *R*s. He took a short cut."

"I want to see her short cut," says Jeff.

Elise stands aside to show her Brr100. She laughs gleefully.

"Ohhhhh!" says Tara, and other kindergartners also react with appreciation. After wall work, Jason adds cAR and Freddy MUNy (for *money*) to Elise's list (see again Figure 5.2).

The next day, February 23, I am unable to come to school because of a snowstorm. On February 24, I look at the Words for Today sheet from the 23rd. The date is written as FebruAry23 and the year. The words are FrezziNG COlD, SNOWy, MybirthDAy, wind, DiNOSAurs (with a backwards s), and WLReSNOW. Deborah is nearby, writing on her sign-in sheet. She jumps up and comes to me. "I did that yesterday," she explains.

"That's a good job. What all did you write here?"

Deborah demonstrates that Words for Today is a reading project as well as a writing project. She is able to read her words one day after writing them. "'Freezing cold —'"

"Mmm hmm."

"'Snowy,'"

"Mmm hmm."

"I can't read—"

"'My —'" I prompt.

"'My birthday!' reads Deborah excitedly. "That was—"

"Whose idea was that?"

"That was Elise's. Her birthday was yesterday."

"Right. I remember that. How about this word that starts, wi—

"'Windy. Wind.'"

"Uh huh. There's a word everybody's—"

"'Dinosaurs.'"

"—writing these days!"

"'Dinosaurs,'" Deborah reads a second time.

"Mmm hmm. What about this one?"

"Um." A pause.

"This part of it is *snow*."

"Yeah." A pause. "'Really deep snow.' Only I didn't write *deep* anywhere."

"You just wrote *really snow*."

"'Really snow.'"

"Really snow?"

"Yeah."

"That's very good."

"It—And also it's going to snow today."

"I heard that."

"Two more inches!"

"Really?"

"I know!"

"That's going to be a lot. Thank you, Deborah."

During wall work today, February 24, Jason does the weather report. It is *Yes* for sunny and *No* for cloudy, windy, and rainy. Then he asks, "Is it snowy?" The children hold up hand signals for *yes* and *no*. Jason moves the strip so that *No* shows, then slides it the other way so that *Yes* shows, then repeats this tease amidst "Aw"s and "Yay"s, finally settling on *Yes*. He smiles and hooks his thumbs on the waistband of his pants on his way back to his place.

But Mrs. Poremba stops him, "Jason? Would you like to write our more words today?"

"Yeah!" he answers immediately, nodding his head and pinching his lower lip with the fingers of his right hand.

"It's up to you."

"Yeah!"

"Do you want to do it?"

"Yeah."

"Okay."

Jason's Words for Today demonstrate the variety of strategies for word writing available to Mrs. Poremba's kindergartners. His performance of this task opens it up for others to follow, who, like him, are not as fluent writers as the three girls who first accepted the challenge of writing Words for Today.

Jeff suggests *sunny* for the first word, and Jason copies it confidently, without hesitation, from the weather chart (see figure 5.3).

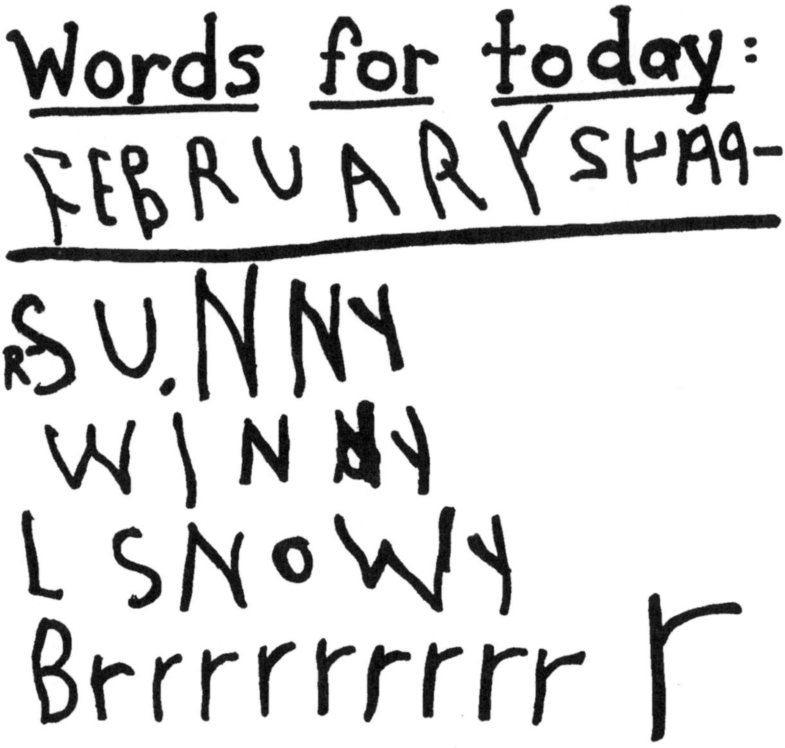

Figure 5.3. Jason's February 24 Words for Today

Tara G. suggests the next word, *windy*.

Again Jason copies from the weather chart.

"Jason seems to know where to look to find those words," comments Mrs. Poremba.

But Jason writes WINN, sees his mistake, tries to rub out the second N, finally writes a d over it, and ends with a y (see figure 5.3).

Next, Ian suggests *really sunny*.

"How do you spell *really*, Ian?" asks Jason

"The same way we did yesterday." (Yesterday, Deborah wrote *really snow*.)

Jason bows his head, his chin on his chest, a perplexed look on his face. "I think he needs some help with it, Ian," suggests Mrs. Poremba. "Can you give him some ideas for the word *really—rrrrrrr-ealy*?"

"It would be like *real*," says Tara G.

"*W*," says another kindergartner. "*R*," says still another.

"You're right," says Mrs. Poremba.

"I mean *R*," amends the *W* sayer.

Jason writes R- before his already written SUNNy (see figure 5.3). He points with his marker to his R and reads "'Really'" and to SUNNy and reads "'sunny.'" Then he takes a puff on the end of the marker.

When Nathan suggests *lot of snow*, Jason immediately turns to the wall and writes L, and then, leaving a space, he copies SNoWy from the weather chart (see figure 5.3).

"Look at how he's writing *lots of snow*," comments Mrs. Poremba when Jason is at the *W*. "He puts an *L* for *Lots*, and then he puts the *snowy* word."

Next, Zack suggests *brrrrr*. Jason immediately begins writing B. "Ask him how many *R*s he wants," directs Jeff.

Jason turns to the class and asks Zack, "How many *R*s?"

"A thousand!" answers Zack.

But Jason is spared by the arrival of the kindergartners' third-grade buddies and Zack's mercifully amending his order to ten *R*s.

Not every kindergartner is ready yet to write Words for Today. On Tuesday, March 1, the 111th day of school, I am the teacher for wall work, and Kaitlynn is the weather report helper. After her weather report, she says, "I want to do the"—she points to the Words for Today sheet—"thing."

"Eric should be able to do it," says a kindergartner, because Eric C. is the other helper.

"I don't want to do it," Eric says immediately and definitely. He will be ready for the challenge a month later, when on April 7, his Words for Today will be windy, DAP (for *damp*), MDEDY (for *muddy*), and Br-rrrrrrrrrrrrrrrrrr.

Today, Tara G. suggests *freezing cold* and Kaitlynn begins writing. The class is silent. "Did you all hear Tara's word, *freezing cold*?" I ask. "Really, that's two words isn't it: *Frrreeeeeezing—cold*."

"She's writing it in kindergarten writing," observes a kindergartner. And indeed, Kaitlynn is inventing a spelling on her own, by attending to sounds and using her knowledge of letter–sound relations. She writes Firezzn with the n backwards. Then she writes colD quickly, from memory. And that is all we have time for.

THE WORLD IS OUR HOME.

On Thursday, May 5, the 152nd day of school, Words for Today shows just how far such a routine can evolve, what literate potential it can unlock in a group of kindergartners whose teacher has been patient and supportive in her providing models and opportunities over the course of a school year. Ian is the helper for the now coveted job of recording Words for Today. Eric C. offers the word *breeze*, and Ian immediately begins writing. Meanwhile, Mrs. Poremba emphasizes the sounds at the beginning and middle of *breeze*; she says, "*Breeze*? Oh, *b-b-reeeeze*."

Deborah picks up on part of this, "It starts out like *brrrrr*."

But Ian is past that part of the word in his spelling and has omitted the *R*. He ends up with BeZA, with a backwards Z (see figure 5.4).

Ian calls on Jason, who says "Tri-City Soccer."

Ian seems stunned by this. Usually the Words for Today helper only has one or two words to write at a time. He leans toward Jason and asks, "What?!"

Jason repeats in level tones, "Tri-City Soccer."

Looking at Mrs. Poremba with widened eyes, Ian echoes this unprecedented offering, "Tri-City Soccer," and he even takes a step back.

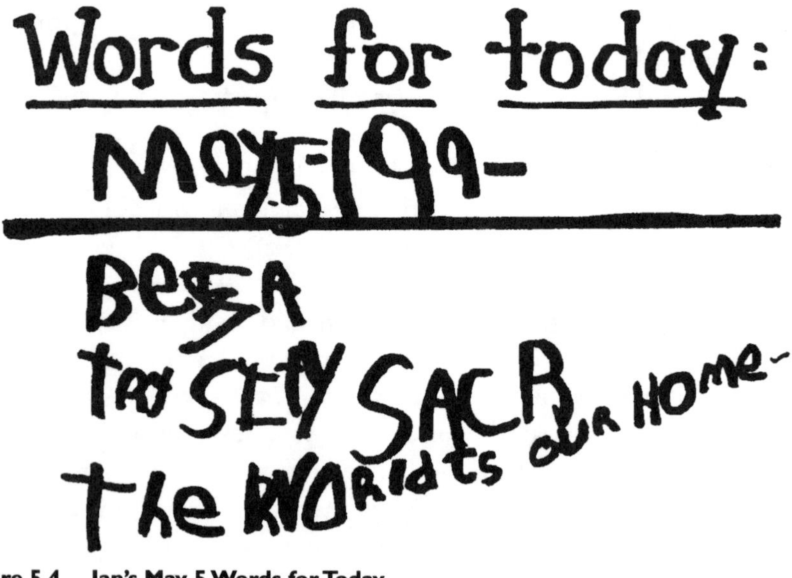

Figure 5.4. Ian's May 5 Words for Today

Mrs. Poremba says, "Tri City Soccer—hmmmm."

Mrs. Poremba suggests, "Ian, why don't we work on the *tri* part first?" Ian immediately writes t, and Lauren suggests, "*T-R-Y*." Lauren repeats her suggested spelling several times as Ian finishes writing tRy.

Jason has a suggestion that may help his buddy with the challenge he has posed him. He asks, "Mrs. Poremba, should I go get the dictionary?"

Lauren continues offering Ian guidance: "*S-I-T-Y*."

And Ian again follows her lead up to a point. He writes SI but seems to ignore her repeating "*T-Y*."

When Jason returns with a picture dictionary, he declares, "I found *city*!" He points to a picture of a city scene.

Mrs. Poremba comments, "Underneath it, it says *street car*." Jason points to the *S*-word that seemed to confirm his guess that he had found *city*, and Mrs. Poremba says, "That says *street*."

Now Lauren suggests, "*City* would be in the *S*s." But when Mrs. Poremba offers that it could be a different letter, Lauren immediately says, "*City* could be in the *C*s."

As Jason pages to the *C*s, Lauren spots the word and spells it, "*C-I-T-Y*."

"There it is!" confirms Mrs. Poremba.

Jason shows the dictionary entry to Ian and spells the word aloud as Ian returns to the Words for Today paper and finishes writing *city* by adding a ty to his earlier SI.

Now Jason wants to use the dictionary for *soccer*, but Ian says, "It starts with *S*. I know that." Then Mrs. Poremba helps Ian and the class to listen to the remaining sounds in soccer, and he ends up with SACR (see figure 5.4). "All done!" he announces.

Ian calls on Lauren for the next word for today, but she is not now going to be content with a mere one-word contribution. "The world is our home," she says. This was a theme of the class's environment unit.

Again Ian is astounded at what he's being asked to write: "What?!"

Lauren calmly repeats her sentence, and so does Jeff, who counts with his fingers as he does so.

"What do you know about that, Jeff?" asks Mrs. Poremba.

"Five words," answers Jeff. Mrs. Poremba confirms that, counting on her fingers as she repeats the sentence one word at a time. Sarah counts along on her fingers.

Steven announces the spelling of the first word—"*T-H-E!*"—and Ian writes it.

World is more difficult. Mrs. Poremba asks, "Does anybody know anything about the word—"

Ian says, "Well, I know. *I* know. I know something about that."

"You know something about it? Okay."

"It's a long word."

"*World* is a long word," echoes Mrs. Poremba.

Jason, Eric C., Erin, and Lauren begin pouring over picture dictionaries, but Freddy has a different idea. "I know, I know, I know *world*!!" he shouts. He goes to a big, display-size atlas, *It's a Big, Big World Atlas* (Rahaniotis and Brierley 1994), which is leaning against a cupboard to the right of the wall work bulletin board. He points to its cover.

Lauren says, "World!"

"Wait a second," says Ian. "Yuck! It's *not* a long word!"

Freddy holds up the big book as Ian copies **WORld**. For the next word, Ian says, "Oh, I know how to spell *is*." He says, "*I-S*" as he quickly writes **Is**. Lauren chimes in with that spelling and then dictates the spelling of *our*.

Mrs. Poremba reads what Ian has written so far. "Now we need to work on *huh-home*."

Ian responds immediately to this clue. He says, "*H*" and writes that letter. He then puts the cap on his marker and crouches down to join Jason, Erin, and Eric C. as they look for *home* in their dictionary.

Eric says, "Yeah, that's it."

Jason announces "I found it!" Jason is looking at the entry for *house*, which is accompanied by a drawing of the wooden frame of an unfinished house. On the previous and opposite page is the entry for *home*, which is accompanied by a picture of a ranch-style house!

Three children voice their skepticism about this discovery: "House?" "House?" "House?"

Lauren reminds her classmates of what she had said, "Home."

Mrs. Poremba reinforces this by asking Lauren, "Did you say 'The world is our house?'"

"No—home."

"You said, 'The world is our *home*.'"

One student repeats, "The world is our house!" and laughs at the unacceptable wording of the class's familiar slogan.

Lauren is looking over Erin's shoulder at the entry for *home*. She says, "*H-O-M-E*" several times, but Ian is not looking to her for help.

Pointing to the entry for *house*, Jason asks, "What does this say?"

Lauren tells him "House" but goes on spelling *home* for Ian: "*H-O-M-E*."

This misleads Ian. "That would be *house*," he says to Lauren and rejects that by demonstrating that it is nonsense: "The world is our *house*? I don't think so."

Now Lauren and Ian are standing, facing each other, Ian with his marker in hand, Lauren using her hands to mark the rhythm both of her patient but methodical repetition of the sentence that, after all, was her contribution to Words for Today and of her confident spelling of the currently disputed word: "The world is our home. *H-O-M-E*."

"But this doesn't spell *home*," protests Ian, pointing with his foot to Jason's dictionary.

"*This* does," argues Lauren. She bends over the dictionary and this time points directly to the entry for *home* and again says "*H-O-M-E*."

As she does this, Ian continues to argue: "That would spell *hou*—" But he interrupts himself with a revelation, "No, wait, that IS *home*."

Jason has called for Mrs. Poremba's intervention, but she responds instead to Ian's conversion. "How do you know it's *home*, Ian?" she asks.

"Because—" He pauses and puts the marker to his mouth, deep in thought as he sorts out how to explain his discovery. And then he ventures an explanation, as much to himself as to Mrs. Poremba, "—because *house* doesn't have an *M* in it."

Mrs. Poremba responds, "That's absolutely correct."

Ian then directs his assistant, "Okay, turn back, Jason." He crouches down and examines the word *home* in the dictionary and then stands and without pause completes his writing HOMe (see figure 5.4). Lauren keeps close watch until he finishes, then returns to her place on the carpet.

Mrs. Poremba signals the end of the activity: "Okay, boys and girls, Ian is going to read our list today."

Ian reads back the three entries for Words for Today, pointing to each word in each entry as he reads. "Nice job!" says Mrs. Poremba. Ian's businesslike facial expression is betrayed by his hands. They show satisfaction with, even self-congratulation for, a challenge well met. He grips the marker in one hand and raps its end several times with the open palm of his other hand before stretching to put the marker in its place atop the cabinet. Then he takes his place with his classmates for the next activity.

FROM MRS. POREMBA

The Words for Today routine promotes valuable elements of balanced writing instruction: writing to, with, and by children. It begins early in the year with the teacher acting as the scribe while practicing the effective technique of modeling. This is when the foundation is poured. Children learn to think, analyze, question, problem solve, draw conclusions, make connections, and take risks right along with the teacher as these processes are modeled. Later, when they lead the Words for Today routine, they will apply what they have seen and participated in so many times.

As Words for Today becomes student led, it is essential that the efforts of every child be held in the highest regard. Every student's thinking and writing must be respected and celebrated regardless of where that student is on the path of literacy.

I believe that we must emphasize the content of children's writing and the processes they go through as they communicate on paper. Handwriting mechanics (such as polished letter formation) are insignificant compared to the higher levels of thinking we want our young writers to be engaged in.

Teachers must be ready, willing, and able to embrace their roles as facilitator, supporter, and interested observer during literacy routines. It is very important for the baton to be handed over, but it will be transferred at different times for different children, depending on the readiness and interest of individual students. Teachers must be patient as they gently nudge! They must always be on the lookout for those awesome moments when yet another student reaches for the baton.

6

ONE GREAT BIG BUNDLE OF ONE HUNDRED

Numbers are a big part of what happens in Mrs. Poremba's kindergarten. Children match numbers on storage jars and storage shelves in order to return supplies to their places on the math tool cart. They count drinking straws that represent the number of days they have been at school and add that number to a number line each day. They construct each month's calendar by adding a number each day for the date. They study the clock face and discuss what its numbers tell about time remaining in free-choice time. They count words on posters and book pages and labels to know how many words to say when they read. This word counting helps them to develop what the experts call "concept of word" or "one-to-one correspondence" in reading—an important literacy prerequisite that cannot be taken for granted in kindergartners (Downing & Oliver 1973–1974; Ehri 1975; Roberts 1992). They read a number displayed at the snack table each day and count the corresponding number of snacks they are allowed to eat. All of these are functional uses of numbers and math knowledge; they are embedded in everyday, meaningful classroom activities (Baratta-Lorton 1995; Burton 1992; Cobb 1991).

SETS OF THREE

The first two weeks of school include work dedicated to learning what to name numbers and how to form the numerals *1* to *10*. On the third day of school, the children have brought bags containing sets of three things. The class sits in a big circle on the carpet, and each kindergartner has a turn to reveal the set of three brought from home and to count the objects in it.

Many sets elicit comments from classmates. "They're nice ones!" declares a kindergartner about Nathan's three shiny stones. Others agree.

"I think a lot of people like your rocks!" notes Mrs. Poremba. Nathan beams.

Earlier, Elise had already shown Mrs. Poremba what is in her bag. "Wait until you see this!" says Mrs. Poremba.

Elise shows a photograph of three babies, her siblings. "My triplets," she says.

Mrs. Poremba asks, "Elise, what are triplets?"

"Three babies who were born at the same time," says Elise proudly.

Next, Mrs. Poremba reads a big book about buses, *The Bus Ride* (McLean 1989). She invites the children to speculate about what the book is about. Alyssa and Meagan use the picture on the cover to guess that the book is about buses. Steven remembers the book about buses the class had read on the first day of school, and he guesses that this book is going to be about the same topic.

"If I look at the cover of the book," says Mrs. Poremba, "I see the picture of the bus right here. But I also see some things up here. What are these called?"

"Words!" shout several kindergartners, led by Zack.

"Words! Good for you. How many words do we have? One, two, three," counts Mrs. Poremba, and she is accompanied by a few kindergartners.

"There's that number *3* again! Three words on this title! Let me read those three words for you: '*The Bus Ride*.'" Mrs. Poremba makes sure everyone is looking at the book cover and repeats this demonstration. "Let's count those three words, shall we?"

This time she is accompanied by almost all the kindergartners: "One, two, three."

"'*The Bus Ride*,'" reads Mrs. Poremba.

Then she reads again, slowly and pointing to each word as she reads it, this time joined in her reading by several kindergartners: "'The, Bus, Ride.'"

"Three words," says Mrs. Poremba.

NUMBER POEMS

By September 8, the seventh day of school, Mrs. Poremba's kindergartners have had many routine, functional experiences with numbers. Each day, they have placed a new straw in the *ones* cup in the straw cup display; there are six straws there now for the number of days of kindergarten before today. They have changed the label on that cup every day so that it records the number of straws in the cup. They have watched Mrs. Poremba add a new numeral each day to the number line on a strip of paper over the bulletin board; it now shows the numerals *1* through *6*. And they have constructed a September calendar, so far showing dates *1* through *7*.

As the children gather on the carpet after signing in, Kaitlynn predicts that today she will see a *7* "because after six comes seven." Mrs. Poremba gets out the number poem book. This is a book she has made, with a page for each new number the class learns. The page has a large numeral written with marker and traced with glue. Students can easily trace this numeral with their fingers, getting to know its shape by feel as well as by sight. Mrs. Poremba has been talking about the five senses and emphasizing opportunities for using as many senses as possible to learn. Also on the page is a simple, two-line poem that tells how to make that numeral.

Today, Mrs. Poremba reads the *7* poem, and the children ask for each previous poem in order, all the way back to the *1* poem. Then they call for the *zero* poem.

"We don't have a *zero* poem," says Mrs. Poremba. "What could we say—"

"Around and around goes *zero*!" suggests Tara G.

"Oh, we could say, 'Around and around goes a *zero*.' That's a good poem. What else could we say about the *zero*?"

"I've got another poem," says Ian. "Around and around/And make a hoop/Number *zero* rolls on a hoola hoop." Ian has borrowed this hoola hoop image from the *6* poem.

Mrs. Poremba laughs, "That's a great one, Ian! What's your idea, Eric?"

Eric C. is ready to make a connection with another frequent kindergarten topic from these early days of the school year. "The bus goes around the block," he says.

"'The bus goes around the block'?" Mrs. Poremba elaborates to make the number tie-in explicit, "That's the way you make a—"

"—*zero*," finish several kindergartners.

"You're thinking about buses, aren't you?"

"And to go to school," says Eric.

"We read a lot of bus books last week, didn't we?"

Five more kindergartners offer *zero* poems.

Kaitlynn's is almost identical to Ian's: "Around and around/And you make a hoop/Number *zero* rolls on a hoola hoop!"

"Oh, I like that one!" says Mrs. Poremba.

Already in this young school year, Mrs. Poremba's kindergartners have often heard her defuse complaints about classmates' copying or stealing their ideas. Now, Ian uses the language Mrs. Poremba has modeled on those occasions. "She agrees with me," he says about Kaitlynn's poem.

Mrs. Poremba laughs. "She agrees with Ian. Ian, I think you're right!"

Mrs. Poremba leads the class through their straw cup work.

Then Jeff says, "Mrs. Poremba, I have another idea for *zero*."

"Do you have another poem? Okay, let's hear one more *zero* poem."

"Around and around the clock/And that's the way the *zero* goes."

"So when you look at a clock—" and Mrs. Poremba repeats Jeff's new poem. "Jeff, that's great."

On Monday, September 20, the fifteenth day of school, children who have completed their signing in are gathering at the wall work bulletin board. Several of them are reading the number poem book. By the time they are at the *8* page, one kindergartner is the leader, calling out the number, and the others answer by reciting the appropriate poem in unison.

Mrs. Poremba comments, "I think it's really great that you are working so hard on tracing the numbers with your fingers and saying the poem. Do you know, if you ever want to write numbers and just practice doing that, there's lots of paper in the Writing Center for you. And that might be a good thing to do some day. Say, 'Hey, you know, today during my choice time, I think I'm going to take out some paper, and I'm going to try to write some numbers.' If you want to get the number poem book to take back to the Writing Center with you, so you'll have some ideas on how to write numbers, you can—"

Erin asks, "Can we write the poems?"

"You're welcome to write the poems as well, Erin. If you'd like to do that. Yes! Today, a little bit later, I want to talk about the words that we should write for our *zero* poem. . . . Then if you want, if you'd like to check this book out and take a turn taking it home and reading it with your family, you may."

But it is not until two days later, on September 22, the seventeenth day of school, that there is an opportunity for writing a *zero* poem in the number poem book. The children's interest in the number poem book, however, has not diminished. They frequently read it during free-choice times and consult it when writing numbers.

After reminding the kindergartners of their usual free-choice options, Mrs. Poremba says, "There's lots and lots of things to do. Also, during your choice time, if you have an idea for a poem for our *zero* page, today I'd like to get this done, where we write our poem into our *zero* page."

"I know, I know, I know," announces one kindergartner.

"If you have an idea, come to me during your choice time, and I'll write your idea down." Zack, Jeff, Tara G., and Eric D. do so. After free-choice time, the children go to gym class, and Mrs. Poremba writes on large paper the four poems. She is finishing with this as the children return from gym class. They enter the room so quietly that Mrs. Poremba seems not to notice them—until they begin to giggle and then laugh out loud with delight at their stealth.

Then Mrs. Poremba leads a discussion that teaches about *zero*, about group decision-making processes, and about the uses of writing. She begins, "Today during choice time, four kindergartners came up and gave me ideas for the *zero* poem. In our number poem book, we have the number, but we don't have the words for a poem yet." Mrs. Poremba names the four poets. "And what we are going to do right now is, we are going to read their suggestions—I tried to write them very quickly—and we can decide which one we will write in the book. Before we decide that, though, you need to all understand that each idea is a really good one. Each is a really good idea, but we'll be able to pick one for our book."

Mrs. Poremba points to the large sheet of paper on which she has written the suggested *zero* poems. "I'll start at the top right up here. Does anybody know whose name that is?"

"Zack!" "Zack!" answer several kindergartners.

"That says *Zack*. The words next to his name are his idea. And they say this: 'Round and round you make a loop/That's the way you make a zero.' I'll read Zack's poem again: 'Round and round you make a loop/That's the way you make a zero.' Now, I'll read this poem next."

"Jeff!" says Erin. Meagan reaches over her neighbor Erin to pat Jeff.

"That says *Jeff*. And, Erin, you could read his name, couldn't you? So the words next to Jeff's name are Jeff's ideas, and they say this: 'Around the clock/Around the clock/That's the way you make a zero.' And Jeff had an idea when you look at a clock—tell me what you thought about, Jeff."

"It's a circle."

"It's in the shape of a circle, like a *zero*. So that's why he said that. I'll read his words again so you can remember them."

This time, several kindergartners join Mrs. Poremba's reading of Jeff's poem: "'Around the clock/Around the clock/That's the way you make a zero.'"

Now Mrs. Poremba points to the third poem. "And anybody know whose that name is?"

Several kindergartners indicate Tara G.

Mrs. Poremba confirms this and adds, "And I'll read—the words next to her name are her ideas. And I'll read them to you: 'Zero goes round and round/Like a hoola hoop.' I'll read them again: 'Zero goes round and round/Like a hoola hoop.'"

A kindergartner identifies Eric D. as the next poet.

Mrs. Poremba confirms this and adds, "The words next to his name tell what his idea was. He says, 'Make a circle/That's the way you make a zero!' I'll read them again, 'Make a circle/That's the way you make a zero!'"

"I didn't hear that one," says Jason.

"You didn't hear Eric's? Okay, 'Make a circle/That's the way you make a zero!' Now, you need to start thinking about which idea was most appealing to you. That means the one that you thought you liked the best."

"I liked that one!" "I liked that!" shout several children. The kindergartners give Zack's poem two votes, Jeff's eight, Tara's five, and Eric's two. Mrs. Poremba records the votes.

Zack points out to Eric that they got the same number of votes.

"Two, two!" comments one kindergartner about Eric's and Zack's identical vote counts.

"Oh, you noticed that two people liked Eric's, and two people voted here."

"We're gonna do Jeff's," comments a kindergartner.

"Why did you say that we're going to do Jeff's?"

"Because that's 8."

"Well, eight people voted for Jeff's, and that seemed to have more than the others. Is eight more than two?" Mrs. Poremba points to Jeff's vote count and Eric's.

"Yeah!" answer several kindergartners.

"Is eight more than five?" pointing to Tara's vote count.

"Yeah!"

"Is eight more than two?" pointing to Zack's tally.

"Yeah."

"Okay. So it looks as though that our poem that's going to go in our book right here—"

"Two plus two makes four," Jeff declares.

"That's absolutely right."

"I know."

"—is going to be 'Around the clock/Around the clock/That's the way you make a zero.' And I'll write that down."

As Mrs. Poremba writes the new poem in the number book, some children continue to discuss their preferences. And then Jeff declares, "All of them are good."

Mrs. Poremba responds, "You know, Jeff, you bring up a very good point. Could you say that again?"

"All of them are good."

"Is he right about that?"

"Yeah," answer several kindergartners.

"He sure is. But because our book needs one poem, we had to do some voting here. Let me show you how our *zero* page turned out. We have *zero* written at the top. And there's our *zero* that you can touch and feel. And the words say—"

Some kindergartners join Mrs. Poremba in reading, "'Around the clock/Around the clock/That's the way you make a zero.'"

THE TENTH DAY OF SCHOOL

September 13 is a momentous day, one of keen number awareness in Mrs. Poremba's room. Even before Mrs. Poremba and her students document its being the tenth day of school, the children have a variety of experiences of numbers and their usefulness.

It's a rainy day, so the children wait indoors for school to start. The kindergartners sit in a line along the wall in the hallway outside Mrs. Poremba's room. The line is a crazy rainbow of the bright colors of their raincoats and book bags. It's a long line, each kindergartner needing extra space for those coats and book bags. The children wait patiently. Already only ten days into the school year, they have learned many of the rules and routines of going to school. Sometimes these include waiting in line.

Mrs. Poremba comes into the hallway to greet the children. She counts aloud; there are sixteen children in the line. "We have eighteen children in our class. How many more do we need?" she asks.

A few kindergartners are able to figure out the answer. "Two." "Two."

Inside, after hanging his coat and book bag in his locker, Ian goes to the straw cup display. Soon he is joined by several classmates as he removes the straws and counts them. *Plink*, *plink* go the straws as Ian drops them one by one back into the *ones* cup. "One, two, three, four, five, six, seven, eight, nine," they count.

Meanwhile, there is a crowd on the floor around the number poem book. Erin, Kaitlynn, Zack, Alyssa, Nathan, Meagan, and Jeff are reciting the poem for each number in turn as they page through the book.

Alyssa is one of the two helpers for today. When it is time for the straw cup routine, Mrs. Poremba says, "We need our helper Alyssa to come up. Alyssa, we need to do something with our straw cups, don't we?"

The blue *tens* cup and the red *hundreds* cup are empty. Pointing to the yellow cup, which contains the nine straws that Ian and his classmates had counted earlier this morning, Mrs. Poremba asks, "Alyssa, what do we need to do with that straw cup there?"

"Put it in the blue cup," answers Alyssa.

Jason says, "Teacher, teacher, we have to add them."

Mrs. Poremba responds, "We'll get to that in just a minute, Jason. You're thinking ahead. Let's look at our cups. Alyssa, have we been in school one more day?"

"Yes."

"So how many straws do we need to put in today?"

"One."

"One more. Can you take out a straw—" Alyssa takes a straw from the large cup to the side that contains extra straws for this purpose—"and put it in the—"

Alyssa puts the new straw in the blue cup, the *tens* cup.

"Interesting," comments Mrs. Poremba in a neutral voice.

"I was right yesterday," comments Tara G.

Today is Monday, but on the previous school day, Friday, during the straw cup routine, Tara had called out excitedly, "Mrs. Poremba, nine's the only one in there. Nine's the last picture that's in there." She was referring to the tiny flip cards that show how many straws are in a cup. There are ten cards, bearing numerals *0* to *9*; each time a straw is added, the next card is flipped from the inside to the outside of the cup so that the newly revealed numeral tells how many straws the cup contains (see figure 1.2, chapter 1).

Tara had elaborated, "There's only one more picture. We're going to use it up today, and we're going to start on the blue one tomorrow."

Mrs. Poremba had commented, "Tara is making a prediction about what she thinks will happen tomorrow. She thinks that tomorrow—actually tomorrow we won't be in school, it's Saturday—but the next time we're in school, she thinks we're going to start using our blue cup. We'll have to check that out."

Now, on Monday, Tara has reminded everyone of her correct prediction, "I was right yesterday."

"There's no more," says a classmate, recalling Tara's explanation for needing to use the *tens* cup. All the flip cards for the *ones* cup were used up on Friday.

"I'm interested in why you put it in the blue cup," Mrs. Poremba asks Alyssa.

Zack speaks up, "There's no more numbers in the yellow cup."

Mrs. Poremba repeats, "I'm interested in why she put it in there."

"Because there's no, no more letters in the yellow cup," someone answers.

Tara G. elaborates, "Because it only goes up to 9."

Mrs. Poremba responds, "Oh, the numbers in our yellow cup only went up to 9. Are there any more numbers in there, Alyssa?"

"No." "No," answer Alyssa and several of her classmates.

"No, she said there's no more numbers in there."

"*N-O*, no," chants a classmate, and several classmates pick up the chant.

"You can spell *no*, can't you?" comments Mrs. Poremba, amid the hubbub that now also includes "*Y-E-S*. I can—"

"One, two, three, kindergarten check time," intones Mrs. Poremba, and silence and attention are restored with no further ado.

"Well, I have something really special to show you today," continues Mrs. Poremba. "Today is the very first day of kindergarten that we are going to take those nine straws and that one more that Alyssa took out," she says as she takes the nine old straws in one hand and the new one in her other hand. "So we have nine, and now, we have—"

"One more," says a kindergartner.

"Nine plus one more. Should we count to see how many we have altogether?"

"Ten!" "Ten!" predict two kindergartners.

"Let's count them."

As Mrs. Poremba separates the straws, she and the class count in unison, "One, two, three, four—"

"Four plus four!" Jason shouts, repeating what he had said at this point in the counting of the straws on the eighth day, when there had been two groups of four straws.

"Five, six, seven, eight, nine, ten."

"We have our ten," concludes Mrs. Poremba. "Watch what we are going to do with our ten. You're going to like this." She puts a rubber band around the handful of ten straws and holds it up for all to see.

"A pile, right?" asks a kindergartner.

"A pile," repeats Mrs. Poremba. "That's a word you could use to describe this. What else could you use?"

"Haystack," says another kindergartner about this fistful of yellow straws.

"Does this look like a haystack?" Mrs. Poremba replies in an accepting way. "When you take things and put them together and hold them tight together, what does it make?"

Zack shouts, "A tower!"

Mrs. Poremba continues, "Let me tell you the math word that we are going to call this. An important math word. Jeff, the math word for this is—ready, Jason?—*bundle*."

"Bundle," repeats one kindergartner.

Mrs. Porema continues, "A bundle of—"

"Hay!" finishes one kindergartner and many others echo this.

"How many straw pieces do we have?" asks Mrs. Porema.

"Ten," answer several children.

"A bundle of ten. That's an important math word. Let me show you the cup. Let me show you where we put bundles. Bundles of ten go in the blue cup. It's time to use the blue cup. Our bundle—and that's an important math word, you're going to be using that word a lot in kindergarten and in first grade—our bundles go in the blue cup. But there have to be ten straws in the bundle. When we counted them, we know that there are ten there now. Now, I want you to take this one bundle, and I want you to put it in the blue cup, Alyssa."

Alyssa complies, dropping the one bundle with one clearly audible clink into the blue cup, labeled *Tens*.

Mrs. Poremba asks "How many bundles do we have?"

"Ten!" comes the immediate reply from nearly the whole class.

"Are there ten bundles?" Mrs. Poremba asks.

"Yeah," answers one kindergartner with confidence.

"Well, there's ten straws. Certainly," replies Mrs. Poremba.

"But there's *one* bundle," adds Ian with confidence.

"Yes. But ten straws put *together* make one bundle. There's just one bundle here, made up of ten straws. So, Alyssa, we need you to flip over the *1* on the blue cup because we have one bundle."

Observing that this makes a *1* in the *tens* place and yesterday's *9* is still in the *ones* place, Ian says, with considerably less confidence than with his previous comment, "We're almost gonna have like—we're gonna have *19*."

Mrs. Poremba continues, "Now, let's look at what's going on, on our straws now. Does anything else—I want you to pay close attention to the yellow cup. What's funny about that, Jason?"

"It don't match," answers Jason.

"What do you mean?" asks Mrs. Poremba.

"There's 9 in the *tens* cup and *1* on the *ones* cup."

Mrs. Poremba accepts but clarifies, "Hmmm. There's a *1* right here," pointing to the *tens* cup.

"'Nineteen,'" reads a classmate.

"Look in the yellow cup, Alyssa. Can you look in the yellow cup? How many straws are in there?"

"Zero," Alyssa answers immediately.

"Zero," echoes Mrs. Poremba. "So what number do we need to have on our cup?"

The children answer, "Zero."

"Zero, because there are zero straws in the cup," continues Mrs. Poremba. "If we flip all those numbers back, we could find a *zero*. Do you want to try that, Alyssa—put them all back?"

"Start again!" observes Jason.

"It's time to start again. That's right!" answers Mrs. Poremba.

"Do we keep going back and forth?" asks Tara G.

"You know, Tara, that is very good thinking on your part. We'll have to check to see if we'll keep going back and forth. What do you mean by 'going back and forth'?"

Tara explains, "We'll go to the blue, then the red, then the yellow again."

"What do you think? You think when what? When which one?"

"The blue one."

"When the blue one is full, what do you think will happen?"

"Then go back to the yellow," says another kindergartner.

"No—red!" declares Tara, and a debate begins among a small group of kindergartners.

"We'll have to wait and see," concludes Mrs. Poremba. "Hmmm. I want you to pay close attention to the number on the blue cup and the number on the yellow cup. We have a—"

Tara finishes, "—*10, 10*. Today's the tenth day and it's *10*."

"One," begins another.

"Yeah, did you notice that *1* and that *zero* right there?"

"How come there's the red cup?" asks a kindergartner.

Mrs. Poremba replies, "Hmmm. We haven't used the red cup—"

"What's on the red cup?!" demands Jason.

"The word on the red cup? That word says 'Hundreds.' The word on the blue cup says 'Tens,' and the word on the yellow cup says 'Ones.' And you're going to learn lots and lots about *hundreds* and *tens* and *ones*. And today's the very first day we used our *tens* cup. Now, we have one bundle of ten."

Freddy explains his now defunct hypothesis. "I thought we'd keep all the straws in there," pointing to the *ones* cup.

"What's that?" asks Mrs. Poremba.

"I thought we would keep all the straws in there—"

"Ahh."

"—until it's full, and then we'd go on to the other one."

"We'll watch, Freddy, to see if your idea is what really happens. We'll keep an eye on it and see. Now, we need to write a new number up on our number line to tell us how many days—"

"Ten! Ten!" shout many kindergartners.

"—we've been in school. It's a *10*. I'm going to get our number poems, and I'm going to go to *10*, and I'm going to read what the words say here." Now, Mrs. Poremba makes a comment that teaches the children about the utility of print. "I don't always remember the poems, but it helps me that they're written down, and I can look at them to read and remember the number poem. Okay, so on Friday, Jason put up a 9, and after nine comes—"

"Ten! Ten!" the children again shout out.

Mrs. Poremba reads the *10* poem, and the whole class joins her for the final line.

Children begin talking to Mrs. Poremba about their favorite numerals. "I like the *6* and *7*," says one kindergartner.

"That's your favorite?"

"And *8*!"

For the first several days of school, Mrs. Poremba wrote the numbers on the number line. But already now, the children are doing this job. It's

Jason's turn, as the other of today's two helpers, to perform this task. "Let's look at that *10* poem," coaches Mrs. Poremba, "and when you make your *10*, Jason, start at the top of the *1*, right where our sticker is." Mrs. Poremba reads the poem as Jason writes, and the class joins Mrs. Poremba again for the final line of the poem.

Mrs. Poremba comments, "Good for you! Ten days of kindergarten, but, you know, I want to have a special way of remembering that we put that bundle of ten in the blue cup, so—"

Tara G. points out, "There's our number again!" She notices a *10*, the last numeral on the calendar, for Friday, September 10, the previous school day.

"—I want us to be able to remember that that bundle of ten went in the blue cup. So I'm going to take my blue marker—"

"You're going to color it in," predicts Ian.

"—and I'm going to make a blue circle around the *10* so we'll always know that that's a bundle number, and we put the bundle in the—"

Several kindergartners join Mrs. Poremba, "—blue cup."

Mrs. Poremba continues, "Put that bundle of ten. We'll be doing lots of this in kindergarten."

Freddy announces, "I have something—"

"Freddy?"

"We got ten straws, and we got *10* there [pointing to the number line], and *10* [pointing to the calendar]."

"Did you notice the *10* on the calendar from Friday? Do you remember when we put that *10* up on Friday? Okay."

A LETTER FROM AUNT EDITH

Another opportunity for number work comes a little later, when the whole class is seated on the carpet in a big circle for Headline News. Each person gets a turn to tell a bit of news, perhaps something that happened during the weekend. The rule is to keep it short—like a headline—not to tell an entire long story. Mrs. Poremba's turn is last. She says, "Today when I came into class, I was looking at Aunt Edith and Uncle Wally, and Aunt Edith had a big envelope in her hand." Aunt Edith and Uncle Wally are large, floppy stuffed-cloth dolls. They are as big as kindergartners. Mrs. Poremba shows the envelope, on which is written Headline News. "And I looked at the envelope, and there were some words on the envelope."

Elise guesses, "Happy New Year. Happy Birthday."

Another kindergartner guesses, "Dear Edith."

Mrs. Poremba continues, "Aunt Edith had this, and it said, 'Headline'—"

The children join in finishing, "'—News.'"

Mrs. Poremba continues, "I think Aunt Edith wants a turn for Headline News."

The children giggle.

"Should I open this envelope up?"

"Yes." "Yeah," answer the children.

"Thank you, Aunt Edith," says one kindergartner.

"Why don't you turn around and scoot up by the easel, and we'll look at what this is?" directs Mrs. Poremba as she posts the letter (see figure 6.1) on the easel.

Dear Kindergartners,

Uncle Wally and I went

to Hawaii for 10 days. We saw

10 whales and 10 sea turtles

in the ocean. We love Hawaii.

Love,

Aunt Edith

Figure 6.1. A Letter from Aunt Edith

Several children immediately notice and comment on the *10*s: "A *10*!" "*10*!"

Mrs. Poremba replies, "Another *10*? Oh my goodness. Do you notice anything else about this?"

"*S*!" "*C*!" "*S*!"

Mrs. Poremba replies, "You notice an *S*."

Jeff says, "Another *10*!"

Mrs. Poremba confirms, "Another *10*."

"Another one!"

Mrs. Poremba asks, "What could we do to know what this means?"

"Read it!"

The children and Mrs. Poremba read and talk about the letter from Aunt Edith. Many children identify alphabet letters. Sarah points out an *S* in the letter and says, "It starts in my name."

Jason brings them back to number work. "There's a *10*," he points out.

Mrs. Poremba elaborates, "There's a *10* in our letter—"

Several children join this: "And there's a *10* right there!" "And a *10* here!"

Mrs. Poremba confirms, "And there's a *10* there. And a *10* on our number line."

One kindergartner suggests, "Let's go *10* hunting!"

The class had gone on a *9* hunt in the classroom on the ninth day of school, but Mrs. Poremba wants to stay with the letter. "Let's keep working here," she says. "There might even be some more *10*s right here in the letter."

Later, Jeff gets a chance to report on his personal *10* hunt. "There's a *10* on that clock and a *10* on that clock," he announces, pointing to the clock on the wall and a large clock made of pressed board, with plastic, movable hands and large, colorful numerals. It's a demonstration clock for teaching how to tell time.

Mrs. Poremba observes, "Jeff noticed the *10*s on the clocks and the *10*s in our letter. Good for you, Jeff."

Jeff repeats, "And on that one!"

"Yes, you are right."

Another kindergartner points out another *10*, and Mrs. Poremba comments, "Absolutely! *10*s all over the place! Are you ready for me to read this?"

The children immediately and enthusiastically reply, "Yeah!"

Mrs. Poremba says, "Listen carefully. Okay, Aunt Edith, we're going to read your letter now. It says, 'Dear Kindergartners.'"

Some children giggle.

Mrs. Poremba asks, "Who is this letter for?"

The children answer, "Us!"

Mrs. Poremba confirms, "It's for *you*! It says, 'Dear Kindergartners.' It's for you. 'Uncle Wally and I . . .'" Mrs. Poremba points and reads, pausing to allow the kindergartners to fill in when she comes to a *10* and to **ocean**.

TEN LITTLE BEARS

At the end of the day, the class gathers before Mrs. Poremba's blue chair again. Now, on the easel is a big-book version of *Ten Little Bears* (Ruwe 1989). The children will enjoy this story of ten bears losing one of their group at a time to go on rides—in a car, in a truck, in a helicopter, and so on—until only one is left at home. This is a pattern book. Every page has the same text except for the new vehicle and the reduced number of bears. The children will be able to read the book once they learn the pattern, and they will get practice recognizing numbers and counting.

After reading the title, Mrs. Poremba asks, "I wonder why I would pick a story called *Ten Little Bears*?"

"The tenth day!" answers Meagan.

"Because today's the day we have ten" "Ten!" "Ten today!" answer several kindergartners.

"Yes, to remember all the—the tenth day of school," confirms Mrs. Poremba. She begins reading, "'Ten little bears were sitting at home—'"

"Let's count 'em!" suggests Freddy. He remembers counting school buses during a big-book reading on the first day of school.

"'—They wanted something to do,'" finishes Mrs. Poremba.

"Write it down," suggests Nathan. He remembers Mrs. Poremba's recording the results of the school bus counting.

Mrs. Poremba asks, "Should we count to make sure there are—"

"—ten," finish several kindergartners.

"Ten? Let's see," says Mrs. Poremba.

They count together, "One, two, three, four, five, six, seven, eight, nine, ten."

"There *are* ten," confirms Mrs. Poremba.

Now several children take up Nathan's suggestion: "Write it down!" "Write it down!"

Mrs. Poremba prepares to write on the small erasable-marker board, propped on the easel. "I'm going to have to take down Aunt Edith's letter here. Do you remember how to make a *10*?"

As she writes the numeral, Mrs. Poremba and several children recite the first line of the *10* poem, and the whole class joins in the last line.

Mrs. Poremba and the kindergartners count the declining number of bears on successive pages, led by Freddy's repeated prompt, "Let's count 'em."

At first as she reads, Mrs. Poremba pauses to let the class fill in the blanks of the pattern, "One little bear went for a ride in a _____. Then ______ little bears were left at home."

"Good reading!" responds Mrs. Poremba.

Later, kindergartners read the whole text with her. Some even attempt it on their own. For the *7* page, Freddy says in a quiet voice before Mrs. Poremba even begins reading, "'One little bear went in a ride in the truck.'"

"Good reading!" interjects Mrs. Poremba.

"'Then there was seven little bears,'" continues Freddy.

"Ooo. Freddy's thinking ahead," comments Mrs. Poremba.

Now, Mrs. Poremba reads the same page, and some kindergartners read along. Then Freddy shouts, "There's our 9!" He has noticed the page number for this page.

When Mrs. Poremba turns to the *six little bears* page, the first thing some children notice is the page number: "Ten." "There's *10*."

BUS NUMBERS

It's time to go home. On this tenth day of school, the children now know what bus they ride. They line up by bus number.

"What line is bus 1?" asks Sarah.

"Usually *ones* are over here," answers Mrs. Poremba.

"Where do I go?" asks Jason.

"What number are you?" asks Mrs. Poremba.

"He's on number 5," reports Jeff.

"He's a *five*? Jason, *fives* are on this side. *Ones* are over here."

"Where's *ones*?" "I'm *five*!" "*Ones* are here!" "I'm *five*!" "I'm *five*!" say several other kindergartners.

"Jason, I'm going to call you today. Right?" Ian says.

"You two made friends today, I noticed," comments Mrs. Poremba.

"I made a friend," says Eric C.

"Who's your new friend, Eric?" asks Mrs. Poremba.

"Zachary and—" The second part of Eric's reply is lost in the many voices of kindergartners getting ready to go home.

"Zachary and who?" asks Mrs. Poremba.

"Zachary and him."

"And Ian!" Mrs. Poremba informs. "This is Zachary and that's Ian."

"What bus do you ride, Zack?" asks Mrs. Poremba.

"I'm *five*!" "I'm *one*!" call several children.

"You ride bus 1?" Mrs. Poremba replies to Zack. "Okay."

When this day full of numbers ends and the class is finally ready to walk out to the buses, one more lesson about the utility of numbers presents itself. Jason asks, "Teacher, which side is bus 5? That side or this side?"

"I don't know which side. You'll have to just look at the number in the window, because they don't always come in the same place. They sometimes switch. So you just have to look at the number in the window, Jason, and make sure."

CALENDAR WORK AND PATTERNS

Among the many sources of number talk and number practice is the calendar. Already on September 1, the kindergartners had begun constructing a September calendar. Each day, they add the number for the day's date, noting in which day-of-the-week column it goes. On September 3, the fifth day of school, the numerals *1* and *2* already are paper clipped to an otherwise empty calendar grid. The *1* and *2* are written on an apple-shaped cutout and a bear-shaped cutout respectively.

Mrs. Poremba begins the calendar routine by saying, "Let's look at our September calendar." She points to the word *September*. "Yesterday you were telling me what you thought we would put up today," she says.

"Apple!" say some kindergartners, predicting the shape of the cutout on which today's date will appear. "Five!" predict others about the number of the date, on this fifth day of school, right after a fifth straw has been added to the straw cup and a 5 has been added to the number line.

"Eric, what do you think?" asks Mrs. Poremba.

"Um, we're gonna put up 5," Eric C. answers.

"You think we're going to put up a 5 today?" responds Mrs. Poremba. "Why?"

"Three," says Eric.

"You changed your idea," observes Mrs. Poremba.

"A 3 today."

"A 3? Why do you think it's going to be a 3 today, Eric?"

"Because it is—we've been two days, and now, we've been three days in school," says Eric.

But today is really the fifth day of school. "Three days in September," clarifies Mrs. Poremba. "We didn't start our calendar over here when we started our number line. What did we start first?"

"But those numbers are a lot more than that number," says Eric, pointing first to the number line and then to the calendar.

"You're right Eric. There are more numbers here than here. What did we start first? Did we start our number line first?"

"Yeah!" answer several kindergartners together.

"We did. We started this first," says Mrs. Poremba, pointing to the number line. "So we have more up here. We didn't start this the same day," continues Mrs. Poremba, pointing now to the calendar. "So we have a little bit less. Eric says he thinks a 3 is going to go here. Let's check."

As Mrs. Poremba points to and reads the two numerals already on the calendar, several kindergartners join her, "'One-two –'"

"—three," predict some kindergartners as Mrs. Poremba points to the blank calendar space after the 2.

"Apple," says Jason.

"Jason, what were you just saying?" asks Mrs. Poremba.

"Apple."

"Do you think a *3* is going to be written on an apple? Why?"

"Because it goes apple, then bear, then apple," predicts Jason.

"So you think it's going to go apple, bear—" Mrs. Poremba repeats, pointing to the two shapes already displayed with their numerals *1* and *2*. "—apple?" she continues, pointing to the blank calendar space after the numeral *2* on a bear. Mrs. Poremba asks for other opinions. Eric D., Eric C., Jeff, Zack, Kaitlynn, Steven, Meagan, and Elise each get a turn to predict, and all think the pattern will be apple, bear, apple, bear, and so on. "So you agree with Jason," Mrs. Poremba remarks after each child's prediction.

"Well, let's take a peek," says Mrs. Poremba. She takes today's date's cutout from the envelope that holds all the cutouts for the September calendar and shows it to the class.

"I knew it," says one kindergartner.

"Me, too," says another.

"'Three!'" read several kindergartners together.

"It was a *3* on an apple. It was!" confirms Mrs. Poremba. "I wonder where this apple with a *3* should go. I wonder."

Steven places it correctly.

"Right underneath the *Friday* word. Look at that," says Mrs. Poremba. "He put the *3* right there, after the *2*. Let's look up from the *3*." She points to the word *Friday* at the top of the sixth column of the calendar grid.

"'Friday,'" a few kindergartners read.

"Let's go back and say the days of the week and see if that word up there above the *3* is really *Friday*. Ready?"

"'Sunday, Monday, Tuesday, Wednesday, Thursday,'" reads Mrs. Poremba as she points, and she is joined by more and more kindergartners, "'Friday!'"

"It *is* Friday today!" confirms Mrs. Poremba.

"Saturday," finishes Jason.

"Saturday's coming. There's Saturday," Mrs. Poremba acknowledges, pointing to the last day-of-the-week label. "I won't see you tomorrow, though."

"Four," announces a kindergartner who is thinking about Saturday's date.

AN EYE COLOR GRAPH

Nearly three weeks later on Thursday, September 23, the eighteenth day of school, the number of dates on the calendar has surpassed the number of numerals on the number line. The kindergartners in Mrs. Poremba's class, however, are becoming quite fluent in their talking about numbers and dates.

Every few days, Mrs. Poremba sends home a "home-link" note that describes an activity for children to complete with their parents' help and return to school. Today, the children bring drawings of two large eyes which they were to have colored at home with their own eye colors.

"What's the red thing for?" asks Zack, pointing to a red poster paper chart on the wall work bulletin board. The chart is headed, *What color are my eyes?* and has columns for *blue*, *green*, *brown*, and *hazel*.

"It's eyes," says one kindergartner.

"Teacher, what's the red thing for?" asks Jason.

"That is for something we are going to be doing a little bit later. Did you bring in your eyes today?"

"I did!" answer several kindergartners.

"Did you, Kaitlynn?" asks Tara G. Kaitlynn hasn't. "She forgot," explains Tara.

Later, during free-choice time, the class builds a graph about eye colors from the red poster paper chart. Mrs. Poremba announces, "Today, during choice time, I want you to come up, and I want you to get your eye, and I want you to cut your eye out. One of your teachers will be right over here by this eye graph, and we are going to put your eye with its color underneath the eye that it matches. You might have brought a blue eye today because your eyes are blue, or green, or brown, or hazel. So today during choice time, make sure you get your eye put up on the graph."

After choice time and art class with the art teacher, Mrs. Poremba directs, "I want to make sure that you come by and take a peek at the eye graph before you sit down. Do your thinking about what you notice."

"There's a lot here," observes Kaitlynn.

"There *is* a lot there," confirms Mrs. Poremba. "I wonder how many there are."

Kaitlynn had colored an eye brown during choice time, to make up for having left hers at home.

Ian observes, "The blue line is the longest."

"There are more blue eyes because this row is the longest," confirms Mrs. Poremba.

The kindergartners also talk about which color is least represented in the class. "This is shortest," says Erin.

"No, *this* is shortest," says Ian, pointing to the hazel column.

"That one has only one. You're right," confirms Mrs. Poremba.

Ian counts, "One, two, three—" all the way to seventeen. "We've got seventeen eyes altogether," he declares.

"Ah," responds Mrs. Poremba. "Well, I have one right here that didn't get cut out. Jeff accidentally cut out the wrong eye."

Ian says, "That would make eighteen." But he is puzzled. He's the expert on the number of children in this class. Earlier today, when the class had read a recipe together and made Brown Bear Bread, he had wondered whether there would be enough bread for all the kindergartners.

"Five bears," he had said, misinterpreting step 5 in the recipe, "for eight—" He had corrected himself: "—nineteen kids?"

Jeff had disagreed: "Eighteen." He knew that Mrs. Poremba's class had begun the year with eighteen students.

Ian had needed only one word to explain his self-correction: "Deborah!" Deborah had become the nineteenth member of Mrs. Poremba's class just two days ago.

Now Ian knows the total number of eyes should be nineteen. But then he remembers that *he* hasn't colored and posted an eye. "I wasn't here. Mrs. Poremba, I didn't make one of these."

"Okay, you were gone that day. Maybe you'd like to make one tomorrow."

All the children sit before the eye chart. Mrs. Poremba comments, "I was glad to see that so many of you visited the eye graph that we made today. We'll do some more talking about it tomorrow, but I heard children talking about what they noticed when they saw the eye graph. And that was good to see. I heard words like *most*; I heard words like *least*. I saw children counting eyes. Ian, you counted all the eyes, and what did you notice? What did you come up with?"

"There's nineteen eyes," says Ian, his belief in that number stronger than his memory of what he counted.

"You got nineteen? Think," says Mrs. Poremba.

"About twenty eyes," Ian now estimates.

"I'm going to be adding mine, also," says Mrs. Poremba. "And we'll have Dr. Richgels and Mrs. Roloff add theirs."

The Brown Bear Bread is ready to eat. As Mrs. Poremba begins cutting it, the children clamor for specific pieces. "I want a raisin part!" "I *don't* want a raisin part!"

"I'll eat the whole bear!" one child says jokingly.

"It doesn't matter what piece you get, you just need a piece," says Jeff.

Mrs. Poremba has Jeff repeat this suggestion. Then she adds, "Yesterday, I remember, Jeff, when we put all of the *zero* poems up on the chart, and people were saying, 'That one's best' and 'That one's best,' you said something good then, too. Jeff said—"

"They're both good," remembers a kindergartner.

"He said, 'They're all good,'" says Mrs. Poremba. "I think Jeff's got some good ideas about how to get along in a group."

"I *was* going to say that!" declares one kindergartner.

WEIGHERS

Four days later, on Monday, September 27, the twentieth day of school, Mayra joins Mrs. Poremba's class. Actually, Mayra has been in Mrs. Poremba's afternoon class since the beginning of the school year. Starting today, she will be in both the morning and afternoon classes. Mrs. Poremba has encouraged this double attendance in order to give Mayra more opportunities to participate in kindergarten activities and especially to use language in the classroom. Mayra is almost a full year older than her classmates and taller than most. She speaks almost no English; her first language is Spanish. She is a very friendly, affectionate girl. She comes to school every day in colorful, coordinated outfits and with her long, black hair carefully done, usually in braids. She is eager to participate. Her wide set dark eyes light up with her frequent smile.

At each table, Mrs. Poremba has set up a balance scale. As the children arrive, she announces, "When you get to your tables today, there's something at your tables that I want you to look at. And I want you to talk to each other about it."

"Weighers," declares Erin when she arrives at her table. She immediately places four glue sticks from the supply tray at her table onto the scales, two in each pan. "They balance," she announces.

Soon others are putting supplies from their tables onto their scales. "Cool!" "Let me try it!"

Mrs. Poremba guides a group of kindergartners: "Which one's heavy? Which one's light? Is there something you can put into the light side to make it balance?"

"Did you come up with a name for yours yet?" Mrs. Poremba asks Zack's group.

"A weigher."

"A weigher?" Mrs. Poremba echoes.

"I made it balance!" announces Erin.

"What made it balance, Erin?" asks Mrs. Poremba. "That's a good word, *balance*."

TWENTY KINDERGARTNERS

Meanwhile, children are also attending to the routine first activity of their day. "Sign in!" one kindergartner reminds everyone. The kindergartners have not yet begun using individual sign-in sheets. Ian bargains with his tablemate Jason: "You know what? I got a new idea. Everyday, we both get to—everyday—like one day I got to do a lot of writing, and one day you got to do a lot of writing."

Jason agrees, "Today will be my day to write a lot."

"No," disputes Ian. "It was my idea, so today is my day. You can, like, write straight lines."

Other children talk about the scales, but Ian and Jason continue vying for the sign-in sheet at their table. "Jason, it isn't your day to write!" declares Ian.

"Yeah, it is," answers Jason.

"Okay, fine. We're having your day."

"Good!"

Ian seems content just to coach Jason. "Then you got to erase that . . . Jason you usually put a space."

Eric D. is talking with his tablemates, "Now we got twenty."

Mrs. Poremba rings a bell. "Thank you. We just noticed."

Eric interrupts, "Now we got twenty kids—instead of eighteen."

Mrs. Poremba continues, "We started out with eighteen children—"

"Now we have twenty," Tara G. interjects.

"—Then we had Deborah," Mrs. Poremba continues.

"Now, we got more than Mrs. Meanger's class," notes Eric.

". . . new kid . . . " another kindergartner says.

"There's more boys," says Ian.

"Boys and girls," Mrs. Poremba continues. "We have a brand new friend to introduce you to this morning. We're very lucky in our class—"

Another kindergartner interjects, "Now we have twenty."

"—because we have Deborah who's new, and now, she's our kindergarten friend. And I'd like you to meet Mayra. Mayra will be coming to kindergarten in the morning. And she'll be our new friend. And Eric D. noticed something about what's happening to our class. Eric, what did you notice about the numbers?"

Ian is still talking to Jason about their signing in: ". . . going to write, Jason."

Jason's reply is lost as Mrs. Poremba tells Eric, "Say it so Jason and Ian can hear you."

Several kindergartners join Eric in speaking about the number of students in the class. "More than Mrs. Meanger's class." "Mrs. Meanger's class only has—" "We have twenty." "Mrs. Meanger's class has seventeen."

Jason and Ian's argument continues, but in voices too low to decipher. Then Ian reneges on his earlier agreement with Jason. He erupts, "It is *not* your day to write. It's both of our day to write."

Mrs. Poremba says, "I actually think Mrs. Meanger's class has nineteen."

"Nine?" a kindergartner asks.

"Nine*teen*," Mrs. Poremba replies.

Ian joins in, "We got twenty!"

"Should we count to see how many we have?" asks Mrs. Poremba.

"Yeah!" answer several kindergartners.

But Ian amends his count, "We got twenty-three."

"Ian, how did you figure that out?" asks Mrs. Poremba. "How did you do your thinking?"

"We got twenty-three, including you guys," answers Ian. He has included Mrs. Poremba, Mrs. Roloff, and me.

"Oh, did you count teachers when you counted twenty-three?"

But Ian is not losing track of his squabble with Jason. "Jason, it's not your day to write."

"It's my day," asserts Jason.

"Jason, I *need* it," Ian says about their sign-in sheet. "I want to write my name!"

Some children are counting. "Five, six, seven, eight, nine, ten, eleven, twelve, fourteen, fifteen, sixteen, seventeen," counts one kindergartner.

"Twenty-three. You're exactly right. Twenty-three, Ian," says another.

TWO BUNDLES OF TEN

When it's time for wall work, Elise is one of the helpers. When she adds today's straw to the *ones* cup, there are ten straws there.

Some kindergartners recognize the need to make a second bundle, like the one they made on the tenth day of school.

"And now, we'll have two bundles of ten," predicts Eric D.

"Two bundles because ten and ten makes twenty," says Ian.

"It's time to make a bundle?" asks Mrs. Poremba.

"You got to put in one bundle with that bundle," replies Eric pointing to "that bundle" already in the *tens* cup from the first ten days of school. "You'll have two bundles."

"Ooo! Time for a bundle!" reponds Mrs. Poremba. "We have our ten. Elise, would you get a rubber band from right up there? Oh, Elise, did you know you were going to be a helper on a bundle day? Wow!"

Tara G. reports, "Well, I guess my dad was right when I said no—no more bundles."

"And what did Dad say?" asks Mrs. Poremba.

Tara nods.

"He thought there *were* going to be bundles?"

Tara nods again.

"Ah. Where will you put that bundle, Elise?"

Elise puts the new bundle in the blue, *tens* cup.

"Oh! In the bundle cup!" responds Mrs. Poremba.

"Two bundles!" notes Eric D., and he is echoed by several other kindergartners.

Mrs. Poremba directs Elise to flip the *2* card so that it shows in front of the *tens* cup, "Elise, we need a *2* now because Eric said we have two bundles."

"Two and two make twenty," comments one kindergartner.

"And then, then when we put one more in, then we'll have three bundles," predicts Eric.

Ian directs Elise, "Now you have to put all those numbers—you've got to put the yellow cup all the way back to *zero*."

"How many straws in the yellow cup now?" asks Mrs. Poremba.

"Zero!" "None!" call out several kindergartners.

"Zero straws!" echoes Mrs. Poremba, and she repeats Ian's directive to Elise to flip the number cards on the yellow cup back to *zero*.

"And then that will be twenty!" notes Ian.

Tara G. observes, "Mrs. Poremba, twenty people!"

"No, there's twenty-three people, because including the teachers," says Ian.

"Look at our straws. Look at how many straws we have," directs Mrs. Poremba. "You did some really good thinking about *tens*. We only have two bundles today, two bundles since we started school, and you've already figured out that it needed to be a bundle. And when you count bundles, you count in a very special way. It's called counting by *tens*. Remember how many straws were in this bundle?"

"Ten," answer several children.

"I talked about this last night with my mom," reports Ian.

"Did you?" responds Mrs. Poremba. And then she begins to ask about the other bundle of ten: "Do you remember how many were in—"

"Ten!" interrupt several kindergartners.

"When you count by *tens*, this is the way you count: ten—now we have twenty. After we have more days of kindergarten—"

"You forgot to draw numbers up there!" prompts Ian, pointing to the number line.

"We're going to do that. After we've had more days of kindergarten, you're going to learn a lot more of counting by *tens*. It will become much more clear to you as we have more days of school, but I notice that you've already learned a lot about bundles."

THE THIRTIETH DAY OF SCHOOL

After bundling ten more straws on October 12, the thirtieth day of school, Mrs. Poremba says, "A 3 is for those three—" She removes the three bundles from the blue cup and holds them in a fanlike display.

"—bundles," say Mrs. Poremba and the kindergartners together.

"If you count our three bundles by tens—because there's ten in the first bundle—we have ten—"

Mrs. Poremba puts the bundles back in the *tens* cup as she counts, and the kindergartners join her, "—twenty, thirty!"

"There it is," says Mrs. Poremba pointing to the numerals *3* and *0* on the cups, "our *30*, for our three bundles of ten."

Kaitlynn has been following this from her table, where she is taking extra time for sign-in writing. Now, she twists in her chair, her writing hand resting on her sign-in sheet on the table but her face to the wall work, and says, "And I was right! And this is the last day of school! This is the last day!"

"Why do you think it's the last day today?"

"Because on the thirtieth, it's the last—a week—because it's when, when because I, I just know it because the thirtieth, I know because I've been counting for long—"

"Well, I have some good news for you, Kaitlynn. Today *isn't* the last day of school. We're going to spend many more days together! Isn't that good news?"

"Yeah," answers Kaitlynn, and she turns back to her sign-in sheet.

"Yeah." "Even on Christmas!" respond two other kindergartners.

"Take your eyes and put them up on our number line. I want you to think about how to write a *30*. Turn and tell a friend how to write a *30*."

The kindergartners whisper to one another.

Mrs. Poremba crouches down beside Steven who has no partner and pats him on the back. They whisper together. Her last words as she nods to him are "A *3* first and then the *zero*?"

"Okay," says Mrs. Poremba returning to the number line, "can you tell me—what number do I get to write first?"

"Three! Three!" shout all the kindergartners.

"The *3* comes first," confirms Mrs. Poremba. "Remember how to write a *3*?"

Mrs. Poremba and the kindergartners recite the *3* poem together as she writes on the number line.

"What other number do I need?"

"Zero," call out the kindergartners. But one of them says, "*Oh*!"

"Well, if it's a number, we call it something different than an *oh*."

"Zero!" shouts Kaitlynn from her table, and she is echoed by the other kindergartners.

"It's called a *zero*. That's right," says Mrs. Poremba as she writes on the number line.

"And we're going to circle it," predicts Kaitlynn, "because it's a bundle today."

PUMPKIN SEEDS

As part of their Halloween party on October 29, the children count pumpkin seeds they have dried after making a jack-o'-lantern. First, during free-choice time, they bunch seeds by *tens*. Individually or in small groups, kindergartners count out ten seeds and place them in little paper pill cups. Later, the class sits in a big circle on the carpet. They watch intently as Mrs. Poremba displays a tray full of their paper pill cups, each containing ten pumpkin seeds.

"Everybody helped to put ten seeds in each cup. The longer you've been in kindergarten, the more you'll understand this, because we're going to be doing lots and lots of counting by *tens*. When we count our bundles, we count by *tens*. We're going to do lots of counting by *tens* today. Today, we're going to put our seeds into groups of ten that will make a hundred. Let me show you what I mean. Just watch. You can even help me out. There are ten seeds here," says Mrs. Poremba, picking up one cup and setting it on the carpet in front of the tray. "So we have—"

"Ten—" count several kindergartners and Mrs. Poremba together. Then as she places each additional cup on the carpet, making a row of ten cups, they continue, "—twenty, thirty, forty, fifty, sixty—"

"Eighty," says one kindergartner.

But the class and Mrs. Poremba continue, "seventy, eighty, ninety, one hundred!"

"There's one hundred seeds right there," Mrs. Poremba summarizes. But the tray is not empty. "But there's more left to count. Let's make another group of one hundred. Are you ready?"

Mrs. Poremba places a second row of cups behind the first, as she and the class count again by *tens* to one hundred, "Ten, twenty, thirty, forty, fifty, sixty, seventy, eighty, ninety, one hundred!" With each count, Eric

D. nods his head, and Sarah waves the magic wand that is part of her Halloween costume.

"How many groups of a hundred do we have?"

"Two," answers one kindergartner.

"Now there's two," answers another.

"Now there's two groups of one hundred. We have two hundred. Guess what—more seeds," says Mrs. Poremba, pointing to her still not empty tray.

"Maybe four hundred!" predicts Tara J.

"Should we count up another group of a hundred?"

"Yeah."

"All right guys. Ready?"

"Ten, twenty, thirty, forty, fifty, sixty, seventy, eighty, ninety, one hundred!"

"Now we have three," says Tara G.

"Now we have one, two, three hundred now," says Mrs. Poremba.

"Three hundred!" says a kindergartner.

"There's more seeds left," says Mrs. Poremba. "I think we need to make another group of one hundred."

"Yeah, nine hundred!" says Sarah.

"There's more left here," says Mrs. Poremba. "Do you think we'll have enough to make another group of one hundred? Let's see."

"Ten, twenty, thirty, forty, fifty, sixty, seventy, eighty, ninety, one hundred!"

"Now we have one hundred, two hundred, three hundred, four hundred," says Mrs. Poremba pointing to a row of ten cups for each hundred and quickly joined by the kindergartners in her counting. "But there's more seeds!"

"We have enough still!" declares Ian.

"Oh! Let's see if we have enough to make another group of a hundred. You ready? Help me count."

"Ten, twenty, thirty, forty, fifty, sixty, seventy, eighty, ninety!" They run out of cups at ninety.

"You only have ninety!" observes Erin.

"Ninety more *hundreds*," says Freddy.

"Watch this. Watch this," directs Mrs. Poremba as she gets out the small erasable-marker board.

"Write *90*," suggests Freddy.

"Watch, watch. *90*'s going to be part of the number I'm going to write. Watch what I'm going to do." Mrs. Poremba points again and counts, row by row, and several kindergartners join her, "One hundred, two hundred, three hundred, four hundred and—"

"Five hundred," says one kindergartner.

"—ninety," finishes Mrs. Poremba. "Watch this. You won't believe how to write a *490*. What do you think you might see in a *490*?"

"A *4*," says Tara G.

"Probably a *4*," acknowledges Mrs. Poremba.

"And a *9*!" says Freddy.

"Probably a *9*."

"And a *zero*," says Eric C.

"And a *zero*! Wow!"

"One!" says another kindergartner.

"Watch this." Mrs. Poremba writes 490 on the erasable board. The children are silent, and every eye is on the number. "Four hundred and ninety is written with a *4*—that's for the four *hundreds*."

"And a *9*," predicts a kindergartner.

"And a *90*," says Mrs. Poremba. "That's for the ninety in the last row. Look at how you write *490*."

The class erupts with comments. "I know. The next one would be a hundred. It will be five hundred," says Eric D.

"Write nine hundred!" says Ian.

"Four hundred and ninety seeds in that pumpkin that we picked," says Mrs. Poremba.

"That was close, cause I had five hundred," says Jeff.

"Five hundred is very close to 490," confirms Mrs. Poremba.

"We need one more cup until it had that much," says Eric D.

"One more cup and we would have had five hundred," agrees Mrs. Poremba.

"Maybe I'll bring ten seeds, and we'll have—" says Freddy.

"If you bring ten seeds, we will have five hundred," says Mrs. Poremba.

"Well, Dr. Richgels," says Ian turning to me as I videotape this activity, "it was close!"

"Next time I'll bring all my seeds," offers Freddy.

"Woah! That's great," says Mrs. Poremba.

ONE THOUSAND OR ONE THOUSAND AND ONE

On January 10, the eightieth day of school, during free-choice time, Freddy, Steven, Eric C., Nathan, Jeff, Erin, Kaitlynn, Deborah, and Meagan are playing with the math cubes. These multicolored, one-inch plastic cubes can be joined to one another, end to end. They are stored in big, clear plastic canisters on the math tools cart. The children make a snake that stretches two-thirds of the length of the room, from the wall work bulletin board, across the open carpet area, under tables, to the end wall of the room (see figure 2.1, chapter 2).

As they near the end wall, they comment about their creation. "This is going to be humungous!" "This is going to be bigger than a house!" "Bigger than the Sears Tower!"

"It already is bigger than the Sears Tower," declares Jeff as he walks by, on his way to the Reading Center with a book.

But Ian is not interested in such hyperbolic speculation. He is determined to count exactly how many cubes are in the snake. He crawls along the floor, all by himself at the beginning of the snake, while his classmates collaborate noisily on the growing end. He points and counts, very serious, very deliberate. Part way along, he has to start over. He gives up his second try after about seven feet. "I got to 149," he reports, and then he joins the prediction game, but in terms of math cubes, not houses or skyscrapers. "It's probably like one thousand or one thousand and one."

Several kindergartners, impressed by this accomplishment, want to join the fun. They begin to build a second snake.

"It was Freddy's idea anyway," says Jeff.

"No. It was not my idea, 'cause it was already—" says Freddy.

"Who's idea *was* it?" asks Jeff.

"Zack and hers," replies Freddy.

"It's the mind's idea. Put your mind to it, it's not hard," says Nathan.

Mrs. Poremba observes, "Oh, Erin. You know a lot about A-B patterns, I see. Red-green, red-green."

"I'm making mine even longer, Freddy," says Jeff.

After a short time when the children are making their own segments for the second snake, one says, "Put 'em together."

As they work to combine segments, Ian adds, "It was my idea to start—"

"—blue now," says Erin.

"Freddy doesn't make the rules of this second one," says Ian. "I do, 'cause I started it."

"Not long compared to *that*," says a kindergartner comparing the second snake to the first.

"Red, blue," says Erin. And then as she finds and adds each new cube following this new pattern, she says, "Red—blue. Red—blue. Red, red—blue. Red—blue. Red—blue."

"Erin, can I take this one?" a kindergartner asks.

"You can take this part. Now, I'm making red, green, white, red. White-blue! No, white-yellow!"

More time passes, and Erin has announced still more new patterns, before a classmate says, "This is how long we did ours."

And another kindergartner says, "Hey you guys, look how long these are!"

The second, parallel snake ends up being considerably shorter than the first. "The second one is one thousand and five," declares Ian. But when I ask him for an explanation, he corrects himself, "The other one [the first one] was probably a thousand and five. This one was about a thousand—because we didn't finish it."

ESTIMATING

The class has been leading up all year to the one hundredth day of school with their daily straw cup and number line activities. A party is planned for the one hundredth day of school. Children bring *100* Projects all during the week leading to the one hundredth day. Each child has assembled a display, usually on a large piece of poster board, of one hundred objects, grouped in *tens*. Every day that week, several children display and report about their *100* Projects. Today is Monday, February 7, the ninety-sixth day of school, and six children have brought their projects and put them on the orange and red tables, which are adjacent to the wall work area. Eric C.'s project is one hundred nails hammered into a two-feet-by-six-inch board, Zack's is a night scene on black poster board with one hundred stars in the sky, Jeff's is one hundred stickers (through sixty) and stampings (sixty-one to one hundred), Tara G.'s is one hundred pieces of candy, Alyssa's is one hundred pieces of food (cookies, noodles, cereal pieces, raisins), and Steven's is one hundred chocolate kisses.

The children are gathering around the table as they arrive at school, Deborah still wearing her coat. "That's a lot of a hundreds!" declares Nathan, surveying the whole tabletop of projects.

"Okay, let's count. One, two, three, four, five, six, seven, eight—" Jason begins counting Eric's nails by *ones*. He gets to thirty-nine with dispatch, but he has a tendency to repeat the *thirties*: "Thirty-nine, thirty, thirty-one, thirty-two . . . fifty-nine, thirty, thirty-one, thirty-two."

"Who did this!?" asks Zack, impressed with Eric's one hundred nails.

Jeff tells that Eric C. did.

"This is his—"

"Yeah."

"—*hundreds* thing?"

Jason says, "A hundred nails. See: ten, twenty—"

"Just leave this thing alone," says Jeff.

"A hundred. There's supposed to be a hundred," says Jason.

"We know there's a hundred," answers Jeff.

"Just leave it alone. It's not even ours. It's Eric's," says Ian.

"How do we know for sure?" asks Jason. Then he reads, "'Eric, hundred'—What is this?" Written across the top of Eric's nail board is Eric's 100 Nails.

"Now we don't have to write estimating anymore," says a kindergartner when whole-group time begins. For many days, the sign-in sheets have had a drawing of a jar, labeled "Estimating Jar." On the table when the kindergartners arrived each day was a big clear plastic jar, in which were several objects, different ones each day (one day they were small plastic dinosaurs). As part of the sign-in routine, kindergartners wrote their estimate of the number of objects. Then during wall work time, one of the helpers counted the objects. Today, with the *100* Projects to view when they arrive, there is no estimating jar on the table, but there still is a drawing of one on the sign-in sheet (see figure 6.2).

"What you could do, though—this might be kind of interesting," says Mrs. Poremba. "I want you to keep your eyes right up on me. I want you to think about how many *100* Projects are on the orange table and the red table. Do not turn around and peek. Don't peek. Make a guess how

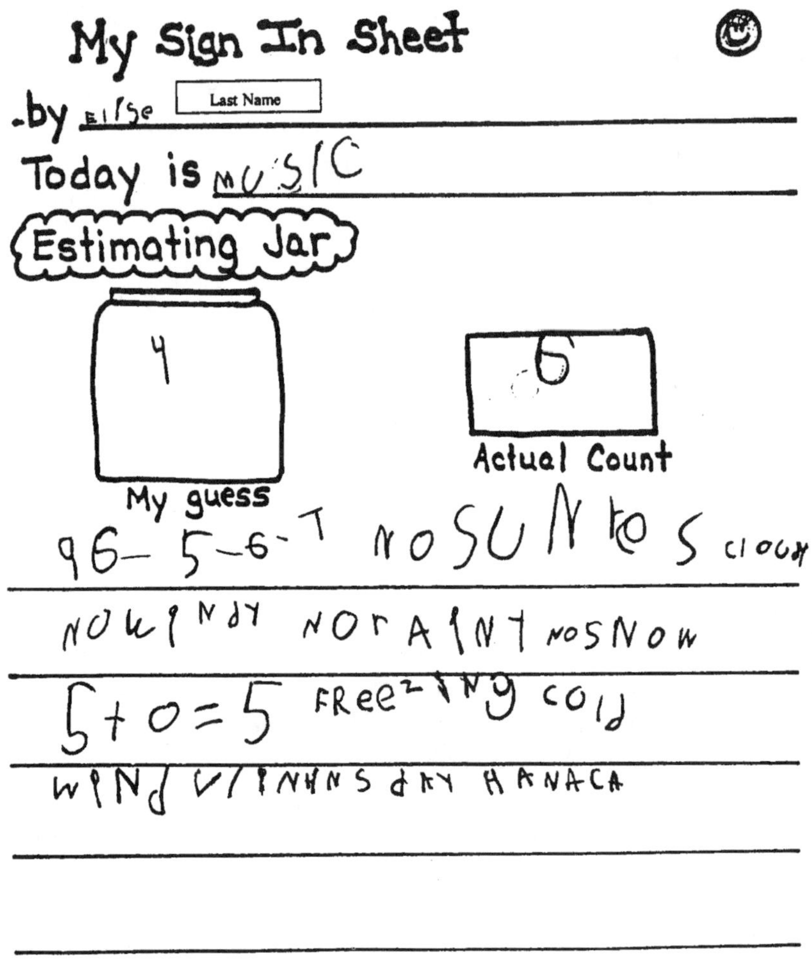

Figure 6.2. Elise's Febreuary 7 Sign-in Sheet

many you think are out there, and write it in the estimating jar."

"How many what?" asks Jason.

"How many *100* Projects are on the orange table and red table. You can't turn around and peek. Take a guess, and write it in your estimating jar."

"Hmmm," says Jason.

"Well, we're going to guess how many friends brought in a *100* Project."

"I guessed ten!"

"And you wrote it in the estimating jar? . . . Think of the orange table and the red table. Think of how many different *100* Projects there are."

"Just make a guess," says a kindergartner.

"Just make a guess. We're just making an estimate," says Mrs. Poremba. "Okay, did you make your estimates?"

"Yeah!"

"You can turn around. Let's take a moment to—oooo, we got some wonderful things in today—please sit down. Okay, we're going to start right over here on the left—it's always good to start on the left—and we can count the projects." They count six projects.

"I got five!" declares Deborah.

"Well, that's very close to six," says Mrs. Poremba.

"I got four," says a kindergartner.

"I got twelve," says Tara G.

"I got five!" shouts Jeff.

"Then, Jeffrey, in the rectangle—" There is a rectangle next to the drawing of the estimating jar on the sign-in sheets. "—you need to write a *6*, because today we had six. Five is very close to six."

Elise's estimate was four. She follows directions and writes 6 on her sign-in sheet for the *Actual Count* (see figure 6.2). Elise's other sign-in writing shown in figure 6.2 includes the name of the special class for today, Music, the number of days of school so far, 96, a weather report, a number sentence, and her version of Words for Today. Elise's weather report differed from what Freddy, the helper, gave. His, inexplicably, was all *Nos*, which produced the number sentence 5 + 0 = 5 for "five *nos* plus zero *yes*es equals five altogether," which Elise faithfully recorded. Figure 6.2 shows that Elise made some changes when recording the Words for Today, which Mrs. Poremba had written as freezing cold / wind / Vlntins / Day / Hknk. Mrs. Poremba had demonstrated spelling only the easy-to-hear sounds in *Valentine's,* and Jason had directed her spelling of the knk part of Hknk for *Hanukkah*. Elise improved on both spellings by including additional vowels.

There are more declarations of estimates. Someone must have changed an estimate to six in order to be right (this is a common temptation) because one kindergartner is heard saying, "You cheater!"

Mrs. Poremba concludes, "We have six friends who will be telling us about their projects a little bit later."

100 PROJECTS

The next day, Tuesday, February 8, is the ninety-seventh day of school. There is no estimating jar on today's sign-in sheet. Instead, Mrs. Poremba has written Eric D. is coming on 100 Day! (She has spelled out Eric's last name.) Eric D. has not been in Mrs. Poremba's class since he moved to a neighboring community in December.

"Did you see the note that's on your sign-in sheet that I want you to read?" asks Mrs. Poremba as the children arrive.

Kaitlynn says, "I know—it says, 'Eric D. is coming on the one hundredth day party—on the one hundredth day.'" (She and the others in this exchange say Eric's full last name where I indicate here only his initial.)

"Wooo! You can read that!" says Mrs. Poremba.

"We have new sign-in sheets, Elise," declares Tara G.

"You know what that says: 'Eric D. is coming on the one hundredth day,'" reads Kaitlynn.

"It doesn't say *the*—it doesn't say *the*," Tara asserts.

"What?"

"It doesn't say *the*."

"'On one hundredth day,'" Kaitlynn corrects herself.

"'Eric D. is coming on one hundredth day,'" read Kaitlynn, Erin, and Tara together.

"I'll make *the*," says Erin, but she is distracted and doesn't amend the message on her sign-in sheet.

Later, Mrs. Poremba explains, "Would you like to know how I found out that he's coming? His mother called me at my house and said, 'Eric wants to tell you something.' And I talked to Eric, and he said he got the invitation from the mailman and they read it, and he *will* be able to come on our one hundredth day party."

But now, at the beginning of the day when the kindergartners are looking at a second batch of *100* projects, Mrs. Poremba reads from Nathan's project, "'Nathan's one hundred barn tacks!' Wow!"

"Can I see?" asks a classmate.

"What is a barn tack?" asks Mrs. Poremba.

"You use it to build barns with," answers Nathan.

"Oh, is it like a nail?" asks Mrs. Poremba. "Oh."

"My mom used to have a barn, but her dad died and then they had to have a house."

"Oh, my goodness."

Several kindergartners near Nathan's project count, "Ten, twenty, thirty, forty, fifty, sixty, seventy, eighty, ninety—a hundred."

"Oh, you counted those groups of ten very well," says Mrs. Poremba. "I think people are going to enjoy your barn tacks, Nathan. That is such an original idea! Whose is this?"

"Sarah's."

"There's a lot of stickers there," observes Mrs. Poremba.

Sarah begins counting the stickers in her project, by *ones*: "One, two, three, four, five, six, seven—" She counts quickly and without skipping a number until she gets to the thirtieth sticker. "Twenty-thirty," she says and then continues without hesitation, "thirty-one, thirty-two, thirty-four, thirty-one, thirty-two, thirty-six, thirty-four, thirty-five, thirty-six, thirty-seven, thirty-eight, thirty-nine," and then she hesitates but recovers when she gets to the end of the decade, "thirt—forty." Then she continues, "Forty-one, forty-two, forty-three, forty-five, forty-four, forty, forty-five, forty-six, forty-seven, forty-eight, forty-nine," and she hesitates again at the end of that decade, "fort—"

"What were you on?" asks Meagan. "What is this? What is that one?"

"Forty-nine."

"Forty-nine, fifty!" Meagan helps.

"Fifty!"

And now, the two girls count together. "Fifty-one, fifty-two, fifty-three—" They make it past sixty.

At sixty-four, another classmate interjects, "Is this yours? Meagan, is this yours?"

But Meagan and Sarah continue to count—until the end of the *seventies*. "Seventy-eight, seventy-nine, ninety! Ninety-one—"

"Ope—you've got eighty," notes Mrs. Poremba.

"Oh," and the girls are stymied.

"Eighty," coaches Mrs. Poremba.

The girls echo, "Eighty," and then as Mrs. Poremba begins to say eighty-one ("eighty-"), they pick up the count, "Eighty-one, eighty-two, eighty-three, eighty-four, eighty-five, eighty-six, eighty-seven, eighty-eight, eighty-nine." They hesitate again at the end of this decade.

"Ninety," coaches Mrs. Poremba.

And again the girls echo this and pick up the count, Mrs. Poremba with them for the first few numbers of this decade and they on their own for the rest, finishing with "ninety-seven, ninety-eight, one hundred."

"Well, you must have skipped one some place, because there's a hundred altogether. Did you do your number writing, Sarah?"

"Yes."

"Sarah, you did such a good job."

"This is Sarah's?" asks a kindergartner.

"Well, look at the name on it," suggests Mrs. Poremba. "Who did the writing up there?"

"I did," asserts Sarah.

"Sarah, you did such a good job!"

Several kindergartners gather around today's *100* Projects.

Jeff counts Freddy's shells, by *tens*, "Ten, twenty, thirty, forty, fifty, sixty, seventy, eighty, ninety, one hundred."

"That's a lot of shells," observes Mrs. Poremba.

"It looks more like a thousand!" answers Jeff. He then counts the shells by *ones*, quickly, urgently, and without mistakes, all the way to one hundred.

"One, two, three, four, five, six, seven, eight, nine, ten," begins Jason at a more deliberate pace.

"I can count faster than that!" brags Jeff.

Jason begins counting Sarah's stickers by *ones*, "One, two, three, four, five, six, seven—" He's counting faster and louder than earlier when Jeff out-counted him. He counts flawlessly and quickly all the way to "fifty-seven, fifty-eight, fifty-nine." Then he pauses and repeats, "fifty-nine—" He decides the next number is forty.

"No, fifty-nine, fifty-nine, sixty!" says a classmate. "Sixty-one, sixty-two, sixty-three, sixty-four—"

They continue together, helping one another with the decade numbers all the way to the end, "ninety-eight, ninety-nine, one hundred! Whew!" Then they count the stickers again, by *tens*.

Later today, Mrs. Poremba displays Sarah's project on the easel. She says, "Would the person who made this project please come up?" Sarah's one hundred stickers are arranged on black poster board in ten neat rows, with the decade number written at the end of each row on a piece of white paper. At the top, on three white, cut out shapes, is written SARAH'S 100 StiCKErS. Mrs. Poremba hands Sarah a twelve-inch ruler to use as a pointer and waits in silence, looking expectantly at Sarah.

The children whisper their admiration, "Ooo" "Wow" "Wow, I love it!"

Sarah begins, pointing to the first three rows of stickers, "I put ten of each, and I put—" Sarah points to the writing at the top, "and I spelled this all by myself."

"Wow!" says Mrs. Poremba looking at the class. She turns to Sarah, "Can you read your words that you wrote?"

Sarah points and reads, "'Sarah's one hundred stickers.'"

Mrs. Poremba nods and says, "Very nice."

"They look like stamps," says Kaitlynn.

"They are," responds Sarah very quietly, standing sideways to the easel and the class, nodding her head, and turning the ruler-pointer in her hands.

"You just writed *stickers* instead?" asks Kaitlynn.

Sarah nods.

"I like all the projects—tons," says Ian from the back.

"Different ideas for each one, isn't it, Ian?" confirms Mrs. Poremba.

"I know. I like a ton of—I like all of them—" continues Ian.

"Yeah, that's a nice thing to say," says Mrs. Poremba.

"—all of them I saw," continues Ian.

"Sarah, are you ready to count your groups for us?"

Sarah nods.

"Okay."

Sarah points to the numerals at the ends of her rows and counts, "Ten, twenty, thirty, forty, fifty, sixty, seventy, eighty, ninety, one hundred."

"How many do you have altogether, Sarah?"

"One hundred."

"She did a fine job! That's a lot of stamps, or stickers. Look at what a hundred stickers looks like. I wonder how many are in that row right there," says Mrs. Poremba pointing to the first row.

"Ten," answers Kaitlynn.

"Ten," repeats Sarah.

"Ten in a row," confirms Mrs. Poremba. "So these are like bundles—only are they held together with a rubber band?"

"No," answer several kindergartners.

"No—a little different than our—" says Mrs. Poremba, but Kaitlynn is up at the easel counting repeated occurrences of the same sticker ("Some of these are the same"), and Mrs. Poremba has to remind her to stay seated, "Kaitlynn, your bottom needs to stay down. Sarah, thank you very much." During this week before the one hundredth day of school, all kindergartners will have turns sharing their *100* Projects with the whole class in this way.

THE ONE HUNDREDTH DAY OF SCHOOL

On Monday, February 14, the one hundredth day of school, Mrs. Poremba begins the straw cup routine for the one hundredth time. "Boys and girls, the big day is here. We are going to put one more straw in our cup to make one hundred straws!" She calls on the class's special guest, Eric D. In striped, railroad-style bib overalls and a long-sleeved, red turtleneck shirt, he comes up to the straw cups. Mrs. Poremba asks, "Eric, do you know the number that's made with nine bundles and nine loose straws?"

"Ninety-nine."

"Eric, are we still in school ninety-nine days?"

"Uh-uh."

"Eric, what do you need to do?"

"He needs to add a straw," says Erin.

"There he goes!"

His left hand in his pocket, Eric grabs with his right hand a straw from the supply cup and plops it into the yellow *ones* cup.

"Right in the yellow cup—one of—straw," observes Mrs. Poremba. "Eric, how many straws do we have in the yellow cup now?"

Eric puts his hand to his mouth.

Mrs. Poremba holds the 9 flip card on the *ones* cup so that Eric can see it. "There used to be nine," she says.

"Ten," says Eric.

"Now there's ten. What do we do when we have ten straws?" asks Mrs. Poremba.

"Flip the number," answers Eric, already reaching to flip the number cards on the *ones* cup.

"Flip the number. Go right ahead," says Mrs. Poremba.

Eric flips all the cards on the ring back into the cup and then reaches into the cup to flip the first card, the *zero* card, back out, so that it is now the label for the *ones* cup.

"What are you going to do with all those straws right there?" asks Mrs. Poremba about the ten loose straws in the *ones* cup.

Eric has his left hand back in his pocket and is reaching into his turtleneck with his right hand. Then he remembers, "Make a bundle." He takes the straws out of the *ones* cup and gets a rubber band from the bulletin board.

"You need some help with that?" Mrs. Poremba helps Eric put the rubber band around the straws to make a new bundle of ten straws. "Okay, Eric, we need you to take that bundle and to add it to the nine bundles we have in that cup." She points to the *tens* cup.

Eric does so and then puts both hands in his pockets.

"Eric, there used to be nine bundles in that cup. You added one more. Nine plus one more makes—"

"Ten," says Eric immediately and confidently.

Mrs. Poremba indicates the flip cards in the *tens* cup. "Want to flip that over?"

Eric examines the cards.

"What are you doing, Eric?" asks Mrs. Poremba. "Is there a *10* in there for you to flip over?"

"No," says a kindergartner.

"No," says Eric.

"Oh, oh," says Mrs. Poremba.

"What are we going to do then?" asks Tara G.

"What are we going to do?" echoes Mrs. Poremba.

Eric is still looking at the flip cards on the *tens* cup.

"Put it in the red cup," suggests a kindergartner.

"Time for the red cup!" says Mrs. Poremba. "We're finally getting to use it!"

Eric gathers the ten bundles of ten straws in his hands. Mrs. Poremba helps him to take them out of the cup and then holds them before the class. "Eric, we're going to take those ten bundles—the first thing we need to do is to count them to be sure."

Eric fingers the flip cards on the *tens* cup one more time, finally leaving them all outside the cup with the 9 card still showing, and puts his hands back in his pocket.

"By *tens*!" suggests Freddy.

"We'll count by *tens*. We've been doing lots of practicing." Mrs. Poremba refers to the counting by *tens* that has been part of the children's sharing their *100* Projects with the class. "We need to make sure we know how many are right here. Are you ready, Nathan? Okay, hang on there, Eric. You ready? Here we go."

She places the bundles of ten in the *hundreds* cup as everyone counts together. "Ten, twenty, thirty, forty, fifty, sixty, seventy, eighty, ninety, one hundred!" Everyone cheers and claps.

"But you know what, Eric? We are going to take—"

"One hundred!" exclaims a kindergartner.

"—those ten bundles of ten, and we are going to do something really special to them. Could you get me that large, blue rubber band, Eric?"

"Oh, I—my dad was right!" exclaims Tara G. "What he said was right."

Eric holds out the rubber band to Mrs. Poremba. "All together," he says. Mrs. Poremba makes a look of surprise and holds the big handful of ten bundles out to Eric. He puts the large, blue rubber band around it.

"My dad was right!" repeats Tara. And others say they knew it would be like this.

"What do you mean, your dad was right, Tara?" asks Mrs. Poremba.

"He made a pledge that it was going to be like this."

Eric is having trouble getting the rubber band around the straws. "A whole big bundle," he says.

"One great big bundle of—" says Mrs. Poremba.

"Ten!" say several kindergartners.

"One hundred," says one kindergartner.

"One hundred altogether," says Mrs. Poremba. "This is such a big bundle, it's hard to get the rubber band around it."

Eric finally succeeds.

"I want to show you what a hundred straws look like when they're together in one bundle," says Mrs. Poremba. She holds the one-hundred bundle so that the class sees it end-on.

The children exclaim. One says, "It looks like a beehive!"

"Does it look like a beehive?"

"Yes, it does," agrees another kindergartner.

"Eric, I have one big bundle of a hundred. One group of a hundred. You need to flip over the number on the red cup that shows us one big bundle."

Eric does so.

"And now, we have to flip over the blue cup," suggests Tara G.

"Can you put that one big bundle right there?" asks Mrs. Poremba. She helps Eric to lower the hundred bundle into the red *hundreds* cup.

"You forgot to flip over the blue cup," notes Tara.

"It just barely fits," says Mrs. Poremba. "Eric, how many straws do we have left in the blue cup?"

"Zero," say Eric and several other kindergartners.

"Better flip it over then."

"Go bye-bye," says Eric flipping all but the *zero* card back into the blue cup.

As the numerals on the front of the cups are revealed to be *1-0-0*, Eric and the class exclaim together, "One hundred!"

Eric stands aside, puts his hands in his pockets, and says with relief, "Whew!"

Mrs. Poremba points to the flip cards on the cups, "Look at the *100* on our cups now! We've been planning for this and talking about it!"

Kaitlynn has run to a *110* chart farther down the wall work bulletin board. This shows the numerals *1* through *110*, arranged in eleven lines of ten each. "But it's already circled!" she exclaims, pointing to the *100* at the end of the tenth line of the chart.

Mrs. Poremba nods. "That's because—we've had that circled so we know—so we could count the days."

It's time to write on the number line, but Jason asks, "Are we going to go past a hundred?"

Mrs. Poremba sits back down. "Jason asked a very important question. Jason, go ahead and ask."

Jason repeats, "Are we going to go past a hundred?"

"Why don't you think about that?" suggests Mrs. Poremba.

"Yeah." "Yeah." "Yeah," say several kindergartners.

"We're going to be here until summertime," says Jeff.

"This is my last year of kindergarten!" says Tara G. (It's also her first!)

"It sure is. I know. Jason, as a matter of fact, tomorrow you'll come back, and tomorrow won't be one hundred. Tomorrow will be one hundred and—"

"Two," say several kindergartners.

"One," say many others.

"One," says Mrs. Poremba. "So when we go back—"

"A hundred and one dalmatians!" says Tara G.

"So will we go past? Like a hundred and one dalmatians—right," says Mrs. Poremba. "Are we ready for the number line?"

"Yeah!"

"Can I have a drumroll, please?" and Mrs. Poremba leads the class in making the motions and sound of a drumroll. "Drumroll is when something really exciting is going to happen." She stands and takes from the cupboard top a red paper heart outlined in glitter and with the number *100* on it in glitter. She sits and holds it before the class.

"One hundred," say the kindergartners.

"This will help us to remember that the one hundredth day of school was on Valentine's Day."

"And we just—I just noticed that we already brought in our *100* Projects," notes Kaitlynn.

"Yes, and that helped us to learn more about the number *100*. That's great. So let's take that number *100*—" Mrs. Poremba stands, gets a glue stick, and glues the heart to the number line after *99*. "I wonder why I chose a red heart for the *100*."

Children suggest that it is because of Valentine's Day. Mrs. Poremba agrees but adds, "There could be another reason that I chose a *red* heart." The heart begins to slip from the number line.

"Oh! Oh!" exclaims Freddy, pointing.

"Oh, it's kind of falling over, isn't it?" says Mrs. Poremba. "Maybe if I push on it and count by *tens* to one hundred, it will stick. Ten—"

"Twenty, thirty, forty, fifty, sixty, seventy, eighty, ninety, one hundred," count the kindergartners.

"Boys and girls, what cup did we use today for the first time?"

"Red!"

"What color is the heart that our *100* is on?"

"Red!"

"That's why you choosed red!" says a kindergartner.

BUT WHAT DOES ANOTHER BUNDLE MAKE?

It is Friday, February 18, the 104th day of school.

Elizabeth is the straw cup helper, and she is adding one more loose straw to the *ones* cup to mark 104 days of school.

"There she goes," says Mrs. Poremba. "She flipped over the brand new number. We used to have a hundred and three days, but we added one more—"

"A hundred and—" "One hundred and four!" say two kindergartners.

"One hundred and three plus one more equals a hundred and four," says Mrs. Poremba. "That's absolutely right!"

"But what does another bundle make?" asks Erin.

"What do you mean?"

"Like when we have a hundred, and then we have another bundle," explains Erin.

"What could we do to figure that out, Erin?"

Several children talk at once.

"You think—a bundle where?" asks Mrs. Poremba. "What bundle are you—"

"Like a bundle—"

"Are you thinking of a bundle of ten or a bundle of one hundred?"

"A bundle of ten."

"A bundle of ten, when we use this cup right here?" Mrs. Poremba indicates the middle cup, the blue *tens* cup.

"Yeah."

"Erin asks a very good question," notes Mrs. Poremba. "Erin wonders what will happen when we start putting bundles—if we add one more bundle to the blue cup. She's thinking ahead today. Do you have an idea?"

"No." "No," say two kindergartners. Kaitlynn raises her hand.

"Kaitlynn, you raised your hand without shouting out. That's wonderful."

Kaitlynn approaches the *110* chart. She points to *110*. "This is going to be the number, and then that yellow cup is not going to be—with a wuh, with a *4* on it anymore. It's going to be just like that."

"Did you see how Kaitlynn used the number chart," Mrs. Poremba asks the class, "to do her thinking? Kaitlynn, that was very interesting the way you explained your thinking."

"The number chart doesn't go on after that—and so, so, so we'll have to get a new number chart out," predicts a kindergartner, referring to the *110* chart.

"That's an idea," says Mrs. Poremba. "You think numbers will go on even when we're finished using this number chart?"

"Yeah," say several kindergartners.

"They'll keep going on?"

"It goes a hundred ele—a hundred and eleven," says a kindergartner.

Zack says, "School's—school's not over until um—"

"A thousand," says Jason.

"—summer," finishes Zack.

"I know," responds a classmate. "Yeah," says another.

"That's right," affirms Mrs. Poremba. "That's right."

"And then I'm going to be going all day," predicts Kaitlynn.

"I wonder how many—I wonder how many days of school we'll have when it's summertime," says Mrs. Poremba.

Several kindergartners respond at once: "I'm not—" "One."

"How many—I wonder how many days we'll have up on our number line when summertime comes."

"A thousand," says Jason.

"You think a thousand?" responds Mrs. Poremba.

Several kindergartners shout out suggestions, and Mrs. Poremba repeats them, "Two hundred and sixty-four? A thousand? Nine hundred and fifty-six."

"Infinity," suggests a kindergartner.

"We talked about infinity once before, didn't we?" responds Mrs. Poremba.

The children shout out many more suggestions all at once.

"Ten hundred and sixty," says one kindergartner.

"Possibly," says Mrs. Poremba.

"A hundred and sixty."

"Ah, that's interesting. You're getting very close."

"A hundred and four," says Sarah.

"A hundred and four? That's an interesting idea, Sarah. Can you give your friend the quiet sign, please? And make sure your eyes are right up here."

They proceed to writing *104* on the number line.

FROM MRS. POREMBA

We live mathematics, plain and simple. It's part of our lives from the moment we wake, squint at the clock, and hit the snooze button for nine more minutes of rest. It is unlikely we'd go through a day when concepts of number, counting, measurement, geometry, computation, and estimation were not used. Cooking, driving, shopping, banking, and even using the remote control are mathematical in nature. It's impossible to imagine a day without mathematical applications!

Mathematical applications in everyday kindergarten life are just as prevalent. There are abundant opportunities to make numbers come alive in ways that are meaningful and relevant to children. Consider the simple routine of keeping track of the days of school using a number line and counting straws. Children practice number recognition, sequencing, place value, number formation, ordinal numbers, patterns, and the passage of time relative to number. ("The one hundredth day of school is in February." "My birthday was the third day of school." "We will go to the farm on the 164th day of school.") The thinking a child does in these applications is deeper than any worksheet could ever stimulate.

One doesn't need to look far to see the natural integration of math into all areas of the curriculum. This integration helps children to make connections in their learning and deepens their understanding in all the disciplines. Reading a trade book about a child who doesn't feel good could be the catalyst for studying the numbers on thermometers and taking body temperatures. In this example, language arts, science, and math are integrated. This interconnectedness is what we experience in real life, and real life is what is pertinent to young children.

7

ONCE UPON A TIME THERE WAS A DINOSAUR. HE WAS MEAN.

In this chapter, we see how Mrs. Poremba promoted the reading and writing of informational texts (Richgels 2002). An ongoing unit of study, in this case a unit about dinosaurs, provided a productive context for students' learning not only about the unit's topic, but also about forms and functions of written language (Robb 1994). The kindergartners read storybooks and wrote their own imaginative texts about dinosaurs, but they also learned uses of nonfiction books and wrote their own factual texts about dinosaurs.

It's Wednesday, February 16, the 102nd day of school. Yesterday began a unit of study about dinosaurs. Mrs. Poremba invited the kindergartners to bring dinosaur books and toys to school. Today, I am immediately asked, upon arriving late because I had been attending a function at my daughter's school, to inflate a large *Tyrannosaurus rex* that Jason has brought. The reading center is all dinosaur books. Today, there is no signing in. Instead, children engage in two other routines, partner reading (Dixon-Krauss 1995) of dinosaur books and Headline News.

THINK OF SOMETHING YOU KNOW.

At the beginning of Headline News, Mrs. Poremba says, "I want you to think of something you know about dinosaurs." Thus begins her use of a technique known as K-W-L (Ogle 1986). When students begin reading an informational text or studying a new topic, they write down what they already *K*now and what they *W*ant to know. At the end of their study, they write what they have *L*earned. Mrs. Poremba adapts this for kindergartners by being the writer of what they already know and by modeling writing what she herself wants to know. She also uses this group writing activity to emphasize the recording function of written language (McGee & Richgels 2000).

She continues, "Maybe you want to tell us about something you know because you read books about dinosaurs. Maybe you want to tell us about something you have that has to do with dinosaurs. I'm going to remember—I want to remember what you say. So I'm going to be writing down what you know about dinosaurs. That's the way I can remember best what you have to say. So when it's Sarah's turn and she tells us something she knows about dinosaurs, I'm going to write that down, Sarah, because it's so important to me and I want to remember. I'm going to give you a few minutes to think." Mrs. Poremba reminds the kindergartners of the partner reading they just completed. Then she says, "You might want to think about those things right now that you saw in the book. That might be what you want to share. Put your hands down. And I want you to think if you're ready. If you're ready, you can give me the thumbs up; if you need more thinking time, you can give me the thumbs down." After a short pause, Mrs. Poremba calls on Kaitlynn to begin.

Kaitlynn says without hesitation, but speaking slower than usual, as if she understands the demands of Mrs. Poremba's being a scribe, "Some dinosaurs are big."

Mrs. Poremba begins writing on a notepad in her lap, "Okay, 'Some—dino—dinosaurs are big.' Did I get that, Kaitlynn—'Some dinosaurs are big'?"

"Yes."

"Thank you, Kaitlynn."

When it's Jason's turn, he says, "Okay. Okay. I know—it's just I can't remember." There's a quiet, five-second pause. "Oh yeah. If you don't make noise, a meat eater can't see you—if you don't make noise."

"Okay, Jason, let me see if I got that: 'If you don't make noise, a meat eater can't see you'?"

"Yeah, an aminal. Whatever. Aminals."

DINOSAURS HAVE BEEN LIVING MANY YEARS THAN US.

Eric C.'s turn is next. He says, "Dinosaurs have been living many years than us."

"Let me see if I've got that, Eric," Mrs. Poremba responds. "'Dinosaurs have been living many years—'?"

"Than us."

"'Than us.'"

"That's true, Eric," notes Zack.

Mrs. Poremba asks, "Um, Eric, could you tell me a little bit more about what you mean by 'Dinosaurs have been living many years than us'? What, what—could you tell me more about that? I'm not quite sure what you mean."

"Than when they were living many years than us, they knew that we weren't here."

"Oh, so dinosaurs were living—"

"Many years than us."

"So, um, when we weren't here? Is that what you said? Okay, that's important. Let me see if I got that, Eric. You said, 'Dinosaurs have been living many years than us, and we weren't here.' Did I get that right? Okay. Freddy."

"Raptors are meat eaters."

"'Raptors are meat eaters.' Did I get that right, Freddy? Okay."

"What's a raptor?" asks a kindergartner in a quiet voice.

"A raptor is—" begins Freddy.

"—didn't get a turn," says a classmate.

Mrs. Poremba says, "We'll come back—thank you, Freddy. Uh, we need to show Nathan that we are ready to listen to him. Okay, Nathan."

"The dinosaurs extincted—ex—extincted. They died from a big rock swoopted down from the air."

"Okay, let me see if I've got that, Nathan—"

Jason asks Nathan, "You mean like a comet?"

Mrs. Poremba continues, "'The dinosaurs are extinct. They died from a big rock that—'"

"Has swoopted down from the air."

"Swooped down—did you say 'from the air'? Okay—"

Jason is talking quietly to Nathan, "—from space."

Mrs. Poremba continues, "'from—the—air.' Nathan, can I read this back to see if I've got your idea? Did you say—" Mrs. Poremba pauses until Jason stops talking. "Did you say, 'Di—The dinosaurs are extinct. They died from a big rock that swooped down from the air'?"

"Yeah."

"Thank you, Nathan."

"I heard that at my grandma's house."

"It sounds important," Mrs. Poremba responds.

THAT'S A LOT OF WORDS!

Next, Mrs. Poremba asks, "Zachary, what would you like us to know about dinosaurs?"

"Well, meat eaters, um, they don't care if babies are still in their egg. They eat the egg. And if their mom's there, then the mom will, and then if *Tyrannosaurus* is doing that, then—" Zack speaks rapidly, and it is difficult to distinguish his words. "—fight, the Tyranna will just run, and then he'll eat the eggs."

Mrs. Poremba says, "Okay. Boy!"

Kaitlynn says, "That's a lot of words!"

Mrs. Poremba agrees, "That's a lot to write, guys. It's going to take me a minute to get that all down. Zack, this is the part I've gotten so far: 'Meat eaters don't care if babies are in eggs. They'll eat the egg even if the mom is there—'"

"No. No. They will, they'll keep the, they'll fight, the mom will fight the *Tyrannosaurus*, and, um, but the Tyranna will destroy 'em, and then he'll eat the eggs."

There is a pause while Mrs. Poremba writes. "Wow. Lots to say there. Zack, can I try it this time and see if I've got it? Okay: 'Meat eaters don't care if babies are in eggs. They'll eat the eggs. The mom will fight the *Tyrannosaurus rex*, but the *Tyrannosaurus rex* will win and eat the egg.' Did I get it?"

"No, he can't eat the eggs," says Jason.

"Thank you, Zack."

Zack agrees with Jason: "Not eat the egg—the baby in the egg."

Mrs. Poremba asks, "Will eat the egg?"

"He would—and the baby."

"And the baby. Okay."

"He'll break the egg. He won't eat the egg, but he'll break it. And then he'll get in and eat the baby."

"Thank you very much, Zack. That sounds important."

"—will be junk," says Jason about the egg.

COULD I SEE YOUR WRITING?

Mrs. Poremba calls, "Jeffrey."

"Dinosaurs were alive, um—"

"A thousand years ago," Jason finishes for Jeff.

"Shhh. Jeff's turn. Go ahead, Jeff."

"A thousand years ago," says Jeff.

"'Dinosaurs were alive one thousand—'"

"Ten thousand," Jeff amends.

"Ten thousand years ago? Okay. 'Ten thousand years ago.' Jeff, let's see if I've got that: 'Dinosaurs were alive ten thousand years ago.'"

Jeff wants to amend it still more: "I think longer than that."

"Oh. 'I think longer than that.' Jeff, let's see if I've got that: 'Dinosaurs were alive ten thousand years ago. I think longer than that.' Mrs. Roloff?"

But Nicole asks, "Could I see your writing?"

"Yes." Mrs. Poremba displays what she has written so far on her tablet.

"Whoah!" "Wow!" say the kindergartners.

"There's a lot there."

"My mom can write fast," says Freddy.

When it is Elizabeth's turn, she and Mrs. Roloff confer. After a pause, Elizabeth says, "Dinosaurs got sharp teeth."

Mrs. Poremba says, "'Dinosaurs—'"

"Have sharp teeth," prompts Kaitlynn.

"'Have sharp tee'—ooo, that is important," says Mrs. Poremba.

"Yes, that is really important," says Kaitlynn.

"I know how sharp they are," says Freddy.

"Okay, Elizabeth, let's see if I've got this. Did you say, 'Dinosaurs have sharp teeth'? Thank you."

"I know how sharp they are," repeats Freddy.

WHAT I WANT TO KNOW

Mrs. Poremba continues recording ideas. Some kindergartners have nothing to contribute; they say, "Pass." Mrs. Poremba is last in this special Headline News. She explains, "What I think I'm going to do is I'm going to tell you a question I have about dinosaurs that I would like to figure out."

Mayra says, "Kaitlynn's turn."

"No, I already went, Mayra," says Kaitlynn.

Here is where Mrs. Poremba models the *W* in K-W-L. "I want to know," continues Mrs. Poremba, "I want to know if dinosaurs hatched from eggs."

"Yeah," say several kindergartners together.

"I want to find that out. So I'm going to write my question down because it's something I want to learn about."

"Yes they do," says Zack, whose contribution earlier was about *Tyrannosaurus rex's* eating babies right out of their eggs. And others agree.

"Zachary, how do you know?"

"Well, if the eggs get luck—if the eggs get lucky, then—if the mom leaves the eggs in a really good hiding place, where no dinosaurs can find 'em, then they'll hatch."

"But how do you know they hatch eggs? How do you know?"

"You told—" begins one kindergartner.

"Because we saw a real dinosaur egg," answers Zack.

"Oh! Where did you see it?"

"At this one—"

"Museum," finishes Freddy.

"At a museum with dinosaur bones," Zack concludes.

"Well, that would be one way to prove that dinosaurs hatched from eggs. How else—"

"And Jurassic Park," suggests a kindergartner. And others take up this idea.

"—could we find out?" asks Mrs. Poremba. "Nathan?"

"I saw a movie about, about, um, dinosaurs."

"Yes?"

"Say they hatched from eggs."

"Oh!"

Kaitlynn asserts, "*All* dinosaurs hatch, hatch from eggs!"

"But how do you know?"

There is some debate in the background: "—true—" "—not all dinosaurs!"

Jason says, "Like dogs don't hatch from eggs."

Over this can be heard Kaitlynn's loud explanation: "Because, when, every single thing that . . . hatches from eggs and dinosaurs—"

The kindergartners never mention books as a possible resource for answering Mrs. Poremba's question. Mrs. Poremba does not impose that idea on them, doesn't require that they take up the "kindergarten-style research" that so consumed the previous year's class. "Well, we're going to do some more thinking on this," she says. "We have some great ideas about dinosaurs."

READING THE *WHAT WE KNOW ABOUT DINOSAURS!* POSTER

The next day, Mrs. Poremba has taped to the chalkboard a huge poster that she has made on green bulletin board backing paper. In the middle of it, she has drawn a big outline of a *Brontosaurus.* In the *Brontosaurus* are the words *What we know about Dinosaurs!* and on one of its feet *Mrs. Poremba's AM*. Around the *Brontosaurus* is a record of the kindergartners' and their teachers' ideas (see figure 7.1).

During free-choice time, Mrs. Poremba announces, "Up on the chalkboard, you will find the important things we know about dinosaurs that you told me about yesterday. So if you would like to go up there and

What we know about Dinosaurs!

Allyssa - "Some dinosaurs have spikes that really hurt people."

Elise - "Dinosaurs eat leaves off trees and dinosaur teeth are stones now."

Tara G. - "Dinosaurs lived long, long ago."

Nicole - "If a meat eater bites behind a 3-Horn's plates he wouldn't like the taste because there's poison back there. Some terodactyls look like eagles with bald heads and catch fish."

Mayra - "Dinosaurs have sharp claws."

Mrs. Poremba - "Do dinosaurs hatch from eggs? I think they do."

Kaitlynn - "Some dinosaurs are big."

Dr. Richgels - "There is a museum in Chicago with dinosaur skeletons."

Jason - "If you don't make noise, a meat-eater can't see you."

Eric - "Dinosaurs have been living many more years than us. We weren't here."

Freddy - "Raptors are meat eaters."

Nathan - "Dinosaurs are extinct. They died from a big rock that swooped down from the air."

Zack - "Meat eaters don't care if babies are in eggs. The mom will fight the Tyrannosaurus Rex but the Tyrannosaurus will win and eat the egg and the baby."

Jeff - "Dinosaurs were alive 10,000 years ago. I think even longer than that."

Mrs. Roloff - "There was a dinosaur who could fly. It was teradactyl."

Elizabeth - "Dinosaurs have sharp teeth."

Erin - "Tyrannosaurus was the king of all the dinosaurs."

Figure 7.1. What We Know about Dinosaurs!

find your name, you can see the words that you told me that I wrote down."

Several kindergartners run to the chalkboard.

"'Eric D.,'" reads Jeff. (He and others in this exchange say Eric's full last name where I use here only his initial.) And although Eric D. moved away months ago and was only back for the One Hundredth Day party, it's true that the first words of Eric C.'s entry look like Eric D.'s first and last names: *Eric - "Dinosaurs . . ."* (see figure 7.1).

"It's a pattern, guys! What are you talking about?" says Freddy. And it's true that the children's names and ideas are written in alternating colors of ink, black and red.

"Mine's over here." "There's mine." "There's mine." "This is mine," say the kindergartners.

Deborah says, "Freddy, I'm looking for yours."

"There's mine," says Freddy.

"Eric D.," says a kindergartner, now mistaking Erin's entry for Eric's.

"No, it's Erin," asserts Tara G.

"I'll look for yours, Eric," a classmate says to Eric C.

"Not down there."

"No, 'Dinosaurs'!" reads Deborah, correcting the still current misreading of the first word of Eric C.'s entry. "That says 'Dinosaurs'."

"Eric, I don't think your name's up here."

"It is."

"It *is*," asserts Deborah. "Eric!" she calls to him. "'Eric'—right—"

"'Eric D.,'" Jeff persists.

"Eric!" Deborah repeats. "No that says, 'Dinosaur.'"

"Uh uh."

"That's from yesterday," explains Deborah. "Yesterday he—"

"Wasn't here," completes a classmate.

"—he was here," continues Deborah, perhaps remembering Eric D.'s presence *three* days earlier for the One Hundredth Day party, "and he wouldn't stay."

Eric says, "Wait. Dr. Richgels?" And he summons me.

"Which one?" I ask. "Oh, *your* words, down here. Okay. It says 'Eric' and it says, 'Dinosaurs have been living,'" I read slowly, pointing to the words as I read. "'Dinosaurs have been living—'" I repeat. "Do you remember what you said?"

"'Many . . .'" Eric says two more words, but they are inaudible.

"'Many more years,'" I point and read.

"'Than us,'" Eric finishes.

"'Than us!'" I repeat. "There's the *than us* part. You remembered. And then, Eric, there's a little bit more here: 'We weren't—'"

Eric doesn't finish this part, so I do, "'here.' Do you remember saying that?"

"We *weren't*," repeats a classmate.

"'We weren't here,'" I read again.

"Can you read those words?" asks Zack about his entry.

"Those are your words, Zack, aren't they? You were telling about—" And I point and read, "'Meat eaters. Meat eaters don't care—'" I pause.

"'Some dinosaurs are big,'" Kaitlynn reads from her entry.

I repeat, "'Meat eaters don't care if babies are—'" I pause.

"'In eggs,'" Zack finishes.

"'In eggs,'" I repeat. "'The—'" I pause. "'M—'"

"'Mom will,'" says Zack. He continues reading his long contribution, but in too soft a voice to hear on the tape recording.

"'*Tyrannosaurus*,'" I prompt.

"'. . . will win,'" Zack reads.

"'Will win,'" I repeat. "Here's the *will win* part. 'And eat the—'" I point to *egg*.

"'Baby,'" says another kindergartner.

I try again, "'Eat the—'"

"'Baby.'"

I go along with that: "'Baby.'"

"This is mine," declares Kaitlynn. And she reads, "'Some dinosaurs are big.'"

"That's right, Kaitlynn."

BECAUSE THERE'S A *S* AT THE END

Later, after wall work, the kindergartners gather before Mrs. Poremba, who is in the blue chair. She is ready to read the factual picture book, *Story of Dinosaurs* (Eastman 1989). "My goodness, when I look at the cover of this book, I see a word that we just learned to spell today." One of today's Words for Today was *dinosaurs*.

The kindergartners read, "'Dinosaurs.'"

"I see the word *dinosaurs*. There's the *di-no-saurs* part. I wonder if this book is about one dinosaur or lots of dinosaurs."

A chorus of kindergartners answer, "Lots of dinosaurs."

And one kindergartner shouts, "Lots!"

"Deborah, how do you know for sure?"

"Because there's a *S* at the end."

"Ah!"

Tara G. comments, "Like in your last name." Deborah's last name begins with *S*.

Kaitlynn reads, drawing out the last syllable in "'Dinosauuuuuurrrs.'"

Another child tells about a book about one dinosaur, "Yeah, it was one dino*saur*."

And Deborah explains, "Like that if the *S* wasn't on it—"

"Uhm hmm."

"—that would be *dinosaur*."

Mrs. Poremba pursues this opportunity. "If we took the *S* off, would the book be about one dinosaur or lots of dinosaurs?"

"One dinosaur," answer several kindergartners.

"Just one; we need that *S*," confirms Mrs. Poremba.

"Yeah, because it's about dino*saurs*," adds Deborah.

"Ah ha! So we'll probably be reading about lots of dinosaurs. The name of the book is *Story of Dinosaurs*."

Deborah asks, "Why is it called that?"

"I wonder why."

Tara G. asserts, "It should be *THE Story of Dinosaurs*."

CONNECTIONS: THE BOOK AND THE POSTER

After Nathan and Ian tell what dinosaur resources they would like to bring in, Mrs. Poremba returns the class's attention to this book. "The book goes like this, 'Dinosaurs lived a long time ago.' Dr. Richgels what are you looking at?"

I have gone to the large green dinosaur poster taped to the chalkboard at the other end of the room, the poster that contains quotations from the previous day's discussion. I say, "I'm looking at something that Tara said yesterday."

Mrs. Poremba says, "Well, let me read this again: 'Dinosaurs lived a long time ago.' Tara, do you—"

I return to the group, bringing the poster with me, and I hang it on the big bulletin board next to the carpet where the children are sitting. "I thought that sounded familiar!" I explain.

One child says about Tara G.'s entry on the chart, "I'll find it, too."

"It's got to be there, guys," answers Mrs. Poremba.

Tara G. vows, "*I*'ll find it."

The kindergartners gather around the poster, competing to be the first to find Tara's words: "Right here." "Right here." "Hey, I found it right here."

Jeff says, "I found it first."

Mrs. Poremba summons them back to their places on the carpet. "Tara, would you like to go up to our dinosaur words up there and read what you said?"

"'Dinosaurs lived long, long ago.'"

"My goodness, that's almost like what our book just said. I wonder if there'll be anything else up there that's in the book. Let's keep reading."

But Tara has an observation, "There was just one—I said two *longs*. I said two *longs* and the book said one *long*."

"Listen to this page: 'Most dinosaurs were very big.'"

Kaitlynn gasps. Not only does Deborah immediately spot Kaitlynn's entry on the chart, but she also sees how it differs from the book's text: "*Some* dinosaurs."

Kaitlynn goes to the chart and reads her entry, "'Some dinosaurs are big.'"

"Wow. That's a lot like what the book says here," responds Mrs. Poremba.

Tara G. again notes the details: "It didn't have *very* in it."

"Let me keep reading."

The children are engaged now in a matching game. Nearly every sentence that Mrs. Poremba reads prompts a comparison with the class's ideas on the poster. There are many matches. When Mrs. Poremba reads about a turtlelike dinosaur with sharp points on its sides, Jason erupts, "We've got some—I know somebody might have—I think somebody said they have those stuff to protect themselves."

As the children hunt down this possible match, Mrs. Poremba watches and listens intently.

Tara G. says, "I think Freddy was it. Look-at."

"No," says Freddy. From his place right next to the bulletin board, he points and says, "*This* is what I said. This is what I said." He asks Mrs. Roloff, "Can you read it for me?"

"Somebody said like they have prickers on their tails to protect themselves with," continues Jason.

"Yeah, somebody," agrees Tara.

"Spike tail," comments Jeff.

"Spike tail," agrees another kindergartner.

"I think so, but I can't remember," adds Tara G.

Mrs. Roloff points to Alyssa's entry on the chart, which is "Some dinosaurs have spikes that really hurt people."

Two kindergartners read her name: "'Alyssa.'" "'Alyssa.'"

Mrs. Poremba looks from the chart to Alyssa, and Alyssa nods her head. Mrs. Poremba nods, too, "Alyssa is sitting over here doing this, guys. She's shaking her head yes. Alyssa, could you go up to our dinosaur facts?"

"She's the first one," comments another child, noting the position of Alyssa's entry at the top of the chart.

Alyssa just points to her entry. Mrs. Roloff points and reads the first word, "'Some —'"

Then Alyssa reads the rest as "'dinosaurs have big spikes what can hurt some people.'"

CONNECTIONS: THE BOOK AND TOYS

Mrs. Poremba and the kindergartners move on to talk about the *Stegosaurus* pictured on the page opposite the turtlelike dinosaur. Freddy, however, has more to say about the turtlelike one: "Mrs. Poremba. Mrs. Poremba, I see something." He directs Mrs. Poremba, "Stay on this page, I saw something." He goes to the dinosaur corner with its display of dinosaur toys and models and returns with two six-inch models of the turtlelike dinosaur. He holds them up and uses one to point to the book, "Someone brought these—the same thing as that."

"Well, Freddy, I think you found—" But she doesn't know the name of this turtlelike dinosaur.

"What's it called? What's it called?" asks Tara G.

"Does anybody know the name of that dinosaur?" asks Mrs. Poremba.

Several kindergartners respond, "No. No."

"What could we do to figure that out?"

One kindergartner refers to the spikes on its side: "With things like that, I would call it Pointy."

Tara G. says, "I would call it Spikey."

Ian counters with another suggestion, "I would call him Steggy." He must be looking at the *Stegosaurus* page in the book.

"Where could we found out the name of that dinosaur?" asks Mrs. Poremba.

Jason and Kaitlynn, who had followed Freddy to the toy corner, return with *Brontosaurus* and *Stegosaurus* models. "Ta dah!" they announce.

But Freddy is not distracted from Mrs. Poremba's challenge to find a source for the turtlelike dinosaur's name. He consults a recognized dinosaur expert. "Jason, do you know what these are called?"

Jason suggests, doubtfully, "Hmmm—*Stegosaurus*?"

Consistent with his having suggested "Steggy" in the nickname contest a minute ago, Ian confidently seconds Jason, "*Stegosaurus*."

Kaitlynn repeats this. But she and Ian are on the wrong page; they are looking at the *Stegosaurus* picture, opposite the turtlelike dinosaur's page. Jason has sorted this out. Standing right before the book that Mrs. Poremba holds, with its two very different dinosaurs, one that he knows is *Stegosaurus* and the other, the turtlelike one, that can't therefore be *Stegosaurus*, he renounces his tentative *Stegosaurus* identification. "No," he says. And then after a short pause to think, "I know where to look. Hold it."

FREDDY AND JASON HAVE A REPORT TO GIVE YOU.

Jason thrusts his toys into Mrs. Poremba's lap and heads for the dinosaur book display.

Mrs. Poremba explains, "Jason says he knows where to find out the name of Freddy's dinosaur that Freddy's holding right now."

"'*A to Z Dinosaurs*,'" reads Jason, identifying the book he has brought to the group.

"Will that dinosaur be in your book?" asks Mrs. Poremba.

"I don't know."

"Okay, Jason and Freddy, I'm going to give you both a job. Your job is to come right back over here and to see if you can find out the name of that dinosaur together. Okay? See if you can figure it out."

"I'll keep holding these," says Freddy, taking his toy turtlelike, spike-sided dinsosaurs along as he and Jason go to a neighboring table.

"It's A to Z," explains Jason as they begin paging through his book, *Dinosaurs: An A-Z Guide* (Benton 1988).

Mrs. Poremba turns a page in *Story of Dinosaurs* and continues reading about a dinosaur with a sail-like fin on its back.

Nathan gets up, "Stay on that page." He and Eric run to the dinosaur corner, and Nathan returns with toys that match this sail-backed dinosaur. Now, many kindergartners run to the dinosaur toys with each new page of the book.

Meanwhile, Freddy tells Jason, "There it is, there it is."

"Is that it?" asks Jason.

"Yeah." Then in a loud voice, "*H-Y*—Here, we found it."

Jason seconds that, "We found it." He and Freddy return to the group.

"Okay. Show them," Mrs. Poremba directs.

Jason begins to share his find, "It is *H-Y-L-A*—" But he stops, uncertain, and asks, "Who is this? Pree-to-saurus?"

Mrs. Poremba tries, "Okay. 'HAL-eo-saurus'?"

Jason is doubtful, "*Haleosaurus*. I never knew his name was *Haleosaurus*."

Nathan jokes, "Hal." Several children join in, in this vein.

Erin says, "Haleosaurs?"

Jeff says, "Harold!"

And Mrs. Poremba tries a different pronunciation, "'Hy-LAY-asaurus.'" But it turns out that Jason's and Freddy's *H-Y-L-A* word is for a different picture than the one that matches their turtlelike dinosaur. Mrs. Poremba points to the correct picture. "Is it that one?" she asks.

"Yeah," answers Jason.

"Oh, in that case, it's 'Ankleosaurus,'" Mrs. Poremba explains, misreading *Ankylosaurus*.

Erin asks, "Ankleosaurus?"

And Ian declares, "Oh, I know Ankleosuarus! I know him."

Mrs. Poremba announces, "Boys and girls, Freddy and Jason have a report to give you. Freddy and Jason could you come out and give us the report on the name of that dinosaur, please?"

Their report is short but to the point. Each simply says, "Ankleosaurus."

Mrs. Poremba nods to the group. "Okay?"

Eric responds, "Oh, I heard that name before."

Both games, finding ideas on the class's poster to match ideas in *Story of Dinosaurs* and finding toys from the dinosaur center to match pictures in the book, continue for several minutes.

The kindergartners can't resist playing with the dinosaur toys they have brought to the carpet before Mrs. Poremba's blue chair. Some children are making dinosaur-fighting noises, and others discuss dinosaur families. "This is the mama." "This is the dad." "That's the boy-dad."

Mrs. Poremba comments, "Okay, I think we're going to be ready to start playing dinosaurs, aren't we?" She looks ahead at how many pages remain in *Story of Dinosaurs* and then watches the children play for a minute. Then she disarms them, "Take your hands and put them in your lap," and turning to the end of the book, says, "The last words in the book are words you've heard before, 'Dinosaurs lived a long time ago.'"

"It's up there," announces Zack, remembering the first match, Tara G.'s idea on the poster.

"A long time ago," repeats Deborah, and she jumps up to the dinosaur poster where Tara's entry is **Dinosaurs lived long, long ago**. Deborah points to this and reads, "'Dinosaurs lived a long time ago.'"

Mrs. Poremba says, "Thank you for reading that, Deborah."

I COULD SEE THEY WERE THE SAME.

On Monday, February 21, day 105, Mrs. Poremba displays a commercially published dinosaur poster.

"Teacher, what is that?" asks Jason.

"A great big poster, and you're supposed to cut it apart and put it together. I've only got one, but maybe you can look at it and figure this out." More kindergartners gather around the poster. She opens it and spreads in on a table. "We can think about whether we want to try this later. It could be pretty neat."

"Where'd you get it?"

"Um, it was sent to me from a company that has lots of things about dinosaurs. . . . I think when you put it together—'A-pat-o-saurus. *Apatosaurus.*' I wonder what *Apatosaurus* looks like." Mrs. Poremba asks Jason, "Do you think it's in your dinosaur dictionary? Why don't you go and look?"

"What does it start with?" asks Jason. "A?"

"It starts with an *A*," Mrs. Poremba confirms.

Jason gets his *Dinosaurs: An A-Z Guide* book. He pages through the *A* pages, checking the second letters of the dinosaur names at the top of each page, the guide words. He stops at *Apatosaurus*, noting the *Ap*. "Is that it?" he asks me.

"Check all the letters," I suggest. "Are they all the same?"

He looks from the book to the poster over and over, pointing to the letters in sequence, one by one. He overlooks only one letter, the first *U*. "That's it! They're the same!" he exclaims. He goes to show Mrs. Poremba, who has been listening to Nathan read a snowman booklet that is a current home-link project. Jason returns to the Reading Center, but he watches, and as soon as Mrs. Poremba is free, he tells her about his find.

She says, "Jason, you wanted to show me something. What did you want to show me, my friend? You found it! '*Apatosaurus*.' Wow! Boy, he's a long neck, isn't he? He must be *Brontosaurus's* cousin. Oh, this is interesting right here. It says, '*Apatosaurus* is one of the best known dinosaurs. It has been called *Brontosaurus*, but the name *Apatosaurus* is given first.'"

Jason's response is indecipherable.

"Mmm hmm. Right over here, if you look at the map, he's found kind of over by California, in that section. I didn't know that *Brontosaurus* was really called *Apatosaurus* first. I never knew that. This dictionary has come in very handy. How did you find the name? What did you have to do?"

Jason's reply is inaudible.

"You looked on the big poster? And how did you do your thinking?"

"Mmmmm. I looked at the writing—"

"Mmm hmm."

"—and then looked in the book."

"And how did you know that that said '*Apatosaurus*?'" asks Mrs. Poremba, pointing to the word in the book.

"I could see they were the same."

"Mmm hmm. You checked each letter and made sure it was the same? That's a good way to do it. A-pat-o—*Apatosaurus*. Very, very interesting."

THIS BOOK SHOWS YOU A LOT.

The next day, Tuesday, February 22, the 106th day of school, as the children arrive, Mrs. Poremba announces, "You may have dinosaur writing or dinosaur reading—if you'd like to read a dinosaur book. . . . This is a good time to explore dinosaur books that you haven't had a chance to look at."

"I'm going to explore this book," says one kindergartner. "I'm going to explore this book." "It's mine," explains another kindergartner, taking credit for bringing the book from home.

"Oh, look at this one!" says still another kindergartner, recognizing a familiar dinosaur book.

"I know—you gave me that!" replies a kindergartner, remembering that it was a gift.

"Oh yeah—so you brought it in."

"Yeah."

"Zack!" calls Eric C.

"Look at this book," says Zack.

"No, this book is better, Zack."

"Let me see inside of it."

Eric and Zack settle at the red table, side by side, looking at dinosaur books, deciding how to use them, and writing on their sign-in sheets. Their writing shows no clear connection with the content of their books (see figures 7.2 and 7.3), but their conversation does.

"Let me see dinosaurs," says Zack. "Okay, this is the first book, and then this book, Eric. Eric, this is the first book and then this book. Okay, Eric?"

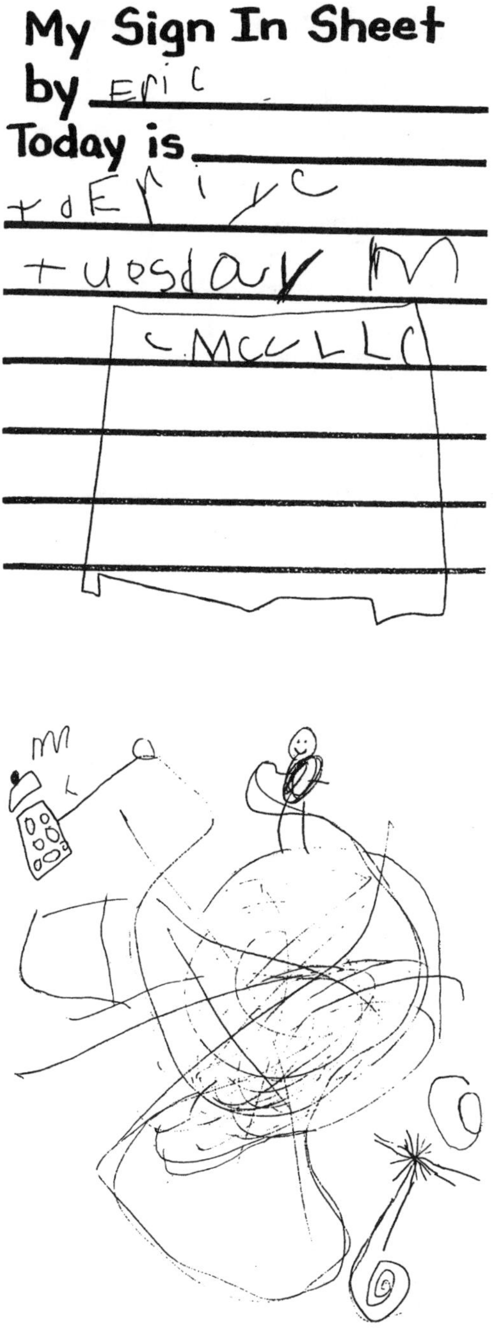

Figure 7.2. Eric C.'s February 22 Sign-in Sheet

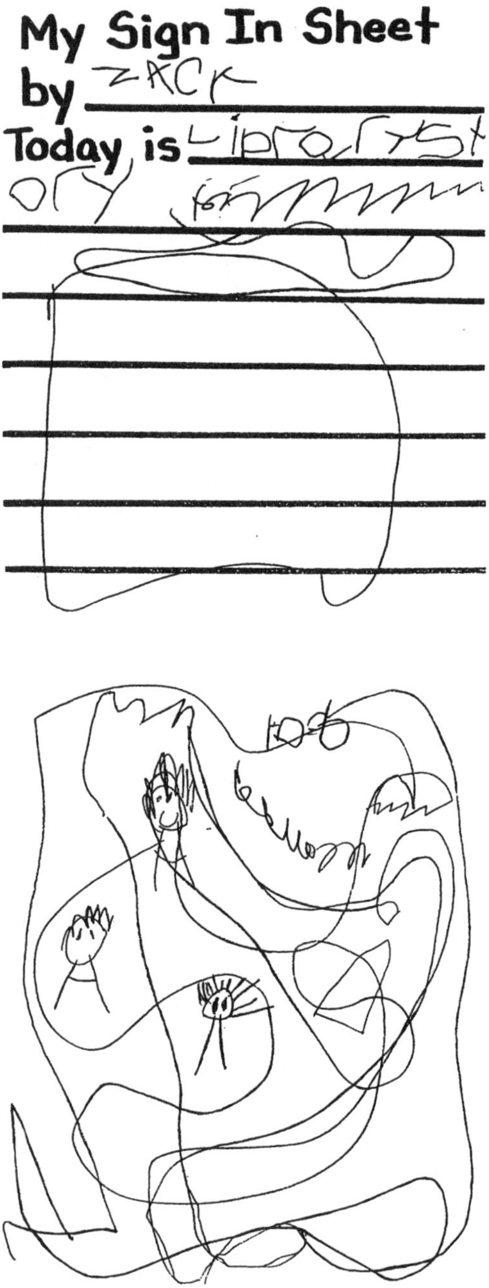

Figure 7.3. Zack's February 22 Sign-in Sheet

"No."

Zack refuses to accept Eric's abrupt reply: "Okay? Okay, Eric? Okay? Okay? Okay, Eric? Deal?" There is a pause in Eric's and Zack's talk.

"I'll be looking at these two books, okay?" says Eric.

"Fine, you can't turn the pages in these," answers Zack.

"This book shows you a lot," says Eric.

"Yeah, it does."

"We'll be finding stuff," says Eric.

There is more talk, and then Zack says, "Hey, this is an alphabet." He means an alphabet book.

"Yeah, this one isn't an alphabet," replies Eric.

After another pause, Eric reads, "'Danger claws.'" But he seems to think better of that. "No, that's not *danger*." Then he switches from a book about lizards to one about dinosaurs. "Okay, this one has a real one."

"This has real bones, Eric. Eric, this book is a lot better than that one," says Zack.

"No."

"Now what are they doing there?" Zack asks, about the people in the picture.

"They're trying to find the fish one," suggests Eric. "See?"

"They're trying to find the teeth?"

"There's bones."

"No, that's teeth," says Zack.

"Those are all rocks right there."

"No."

Now Eric agrees, "They're different kinds of teeth. See, Zack, they're really scientists. See, there they go and then—Zack, they really found bones! Zack, they really found bones! Look-at! Zack! See!"

"Stupid bones," answers Zack.

"Zack, these are real!"

"They're not fangs. They're wood."

"Uh uh."

"They're wood."

"Uh uh. These are bones, Zack."

"Those are bones, but the other ones are wood."

"No. They're all bones."

When they turn to still another book, Zack says, "Now this book, Eric. I get to do it. I'll show you a page that you're gonna like. You're gonna like something—a dinosaur is butting a *Tyrannosaurus*!" There is much page turning. "Where is he?"

"Look at that."

"Oh, yuck! Well, where is it? Here it is! See that *Tyrannosaurus*? See that dinosaur? Boom! Butting."

"Awesome."

"Isn't that awesome?!"

Meanwhile, in the wall work area, Jeff is lying on the carpet on his stomach, leaning on both elbows, copying on his sign-in sheet (see figure 7.4) from a pop-up dinosaur book open on the floor in front of him.

Mrs. Poremba stops on her way by Jeff, leans down, hands on her knees, and asks, "What are you looking up? Oh, you just did *Brontosaurus*! Wow, that's a long word! *Stegosaurus* also!" On the first line of his sign-in sheet, Jeff has written STEGOSAUS and on the second BroNToSAUrUS. He is now writing TrIcerATOPS on the third line. By the time he finishes this self-assigned copying, he also will have written, one word per line, TyrANNOSAUrUS, OrNITHOMIMUS, and BrACHIOSAUrUS.

Sarah skips between the green and red tables and on to the open, carpeted wall work area where Jeff is lying and writing. She begins copying from the cover of *Dinosaurs* by Daniel Cohen (1993). She writes DinoSAuRS on her sign-in sheet. Mrs. Poremba asks, "Sarah, do you know the word you just wrote?"

"No."

"Now, look at the cover of that book and see if you can figure it out. It starts with a *D*." Sarah's response is inaudible, but Mrs. Poremba responds, "You wrote *dinosaurs*!" Then she blocks out parts of the word, so that she can demonstrate reading it syllable by syllable: "'Di—There's the *N-O*—Di-no-saurs!'" Then, Sarah writes THE FEATHErEdDinOSAur, copied from "The Feathered Dinosaur," a heading on page 35 of *Dinosaurs*.

Now, Ian is copying from a page of *A Gallery of Dinosaurs and Other Early Reptiles* (Peters 1989). The page contains two columns of very small print. At the top of each column is a dinosaur name in larger bold print. Below these names, in italic print that is even smaller than the

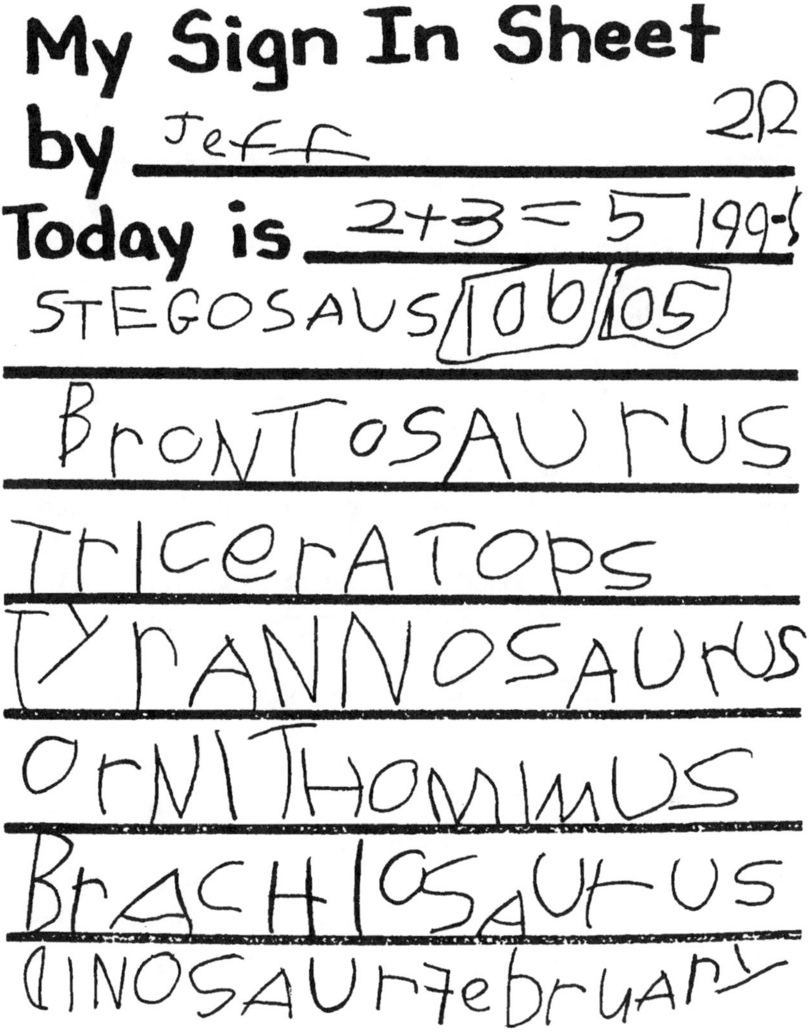

Figure 7.4. Jeff's February 22 Sign-in Sheet

print on the rest of the page, are a few lines of data: a key to the pronunciation of the dinosaur's name, its common name in quotation marks, its place in the zoological classification scheme, the geologic era in which the dinosaur lived, where it lived, and its size. From this tiny italic print, Ian copies **cup nose"** (from the common name for *Cotylorhynchus*) and **CASe** (from the classification *Pelycosauria. Caseidae*). Ian looks at the book, pointing carefully to the text, and then he sits up and writes on his sign-in sheet, back and forth. Freddy looks at the cover of Ian's book, losing Ian's place. Ian easily finds the page again.

GOOD-BYE SONG WITH *DINOSAURS! DINOSAURS!*

Two days later, at the very end of the 108th day of school, Thursday, February 24, the kindergartners, as usual, prepare to sing their Good-Bye Song (see chapter 3). Mrs. Poremba points to the song's words on a poster over the door. "Let's say good-bye to Thursday," she says as she removes the word card for *Thursday* on the face of the poster.

"'Bye Thursday!" shout all the kindergartners together.

"I wonder what day tomorrow will be?"

"Friday!" says Deborah. "Friday!" echo several kindergartners together.

"What are the first *two* sounds—the two letters in Friday?" asks Mrs. Poremba before clipping the word card for *Friday* into its place on the Good-Bye Song poster.

"*F-R*!" "Like *Freddy*!" shout kindergartners.

"*F-R*! Okay!"

"Hey, you didn't do *dinosaurs*!" says Jeff.

"Oh, that's right!" admits Mrs. Poremba. "I couldn't remember what class wanted it. *You* were the class that wanted me to change this [last line] to *Dinosaur! Dinosaur!* I thought it was the afternoon class; that's why I haven't done it yet. Jeff, I will get that done for tomorrow. Do you want to sing *Everyone! Everyone!* or do you want to sing *Dinosaur! Dinosaur!*?"

"Dinosaur!" "Dinosaur!" answer several kindergartners.

Only Deborah wants to be faithful to the current print display: "Everyone!"

"Okay."

The class and Mrs. Poremba sing together, loud and with gusto, ending with "Dinosaur! Dinosaur!"

"Jeff, do you know what you can do tomorrow for me? Could you make two *Dinosaur* cards for me?"

Jeff agrees.

"Could you do that? That way, I'll make sure it gets done."

Deborah sings again the last line, but changing it to plural: "Dinosaurs! Dinosaurs!" Then she suggests, "Mrs. Poremba, it goes 'Dinosaurs! Dinosaurs!'"

Three school days later, on Tuesday, March 1, Jeff remembers this task. During a class-writing time, when many kindergartners are writing dinosaur stories using story starter folders for the first time, Jeff makes two cards: DINOSAurS and DINOSAUrs. "I made *Dinosaur* cards," he explains to me.

"And how did you get the words? Where did you get the words?"

"From a book." He has copied the word from the front cover of *All about Dinosaurs* by Mike Benton (1991).

"Okay. And where do you want to put those cards?"

"The song."

Later, as the kindergartners are preparing to leave and lining up by the door, one kindergartner voice can be heard reading Jeff's cards, now paper clipped over *Everyone! Everyone!* at the bottom of the Good-Bye Song poster. "'Dinosaurs, dinosaurs,'" this kindergartner sings softly to herself amid the hustle and bustle of children putting on coats and snow pants, boots and mittens.

"Now boys and girls," Mrs. Poremba announces, "Jeffrey got our sign made from our new song—for our new song. Remember, we've been talking about that? So we can say good-bye to 'Tuesday —'" She removes the *Tuesday* card. "—and say hello to—" She shows the *Wednesday* card.

"'Wednesday!'" shout several kindergartners.

"And at the end, we'll sing—"

"'Dinosaurs! Dinosaurs!'" sing Mrs. Poremba and several kindergartners.

"Thank you very much, Jeffrey," says Mrs. Poremba. She and the class then sing the song together, with its new ending.

"Thank you for doing that, Jeff. It was nice to sing the song that way."

STORY FOLDERS

On Tuesday, March 1, the 111th day of school, Mrs. Poremba introduces a new writing activity, story folders. These are manila file folders with a dinosaur picture above the fold and a story starter below the fold. The story starter is *Once upon a time* written on the first line, followed by four blank lines. Mrs. Poremba and I model using these folders. We had planned the day before that we would show using "one word to tell a lot," using invented spelling, using one letter for a word or syllable, using rhebuses, using periods and exclamation marks, and finding words in familiar sources, such as the dinosaur books and posters in the room.

Mrs. Poremba shows the folders. They include pictures of a *Brontosaurus* hatching from an egg, a *Tyrranosaurus rex* towering over a cowering *Triceratops*, a *Tyrnnosaurus rex* skeleton display in a museum, a child snorkeling next to a swimming dinosaur, and two scientists working on a skeleton display. To each one, there is a chorus of reactions: "A baby!" "Cute!" "Awww." "Look at that!" "T-rex!" "Whoahh!"

"Now, Dr. Richgels, you picked a folder from the story box. Could you show us the one that you picked?"

Mine shows two *Tyrannosaurus rexes* fighting, with an erupting volcano in the background. "Ohhhhh!" say the children.

"And I picked a folder from the story box. I picked this one." Mrs. Poremba shows a boy on the back of a *Brontosaurus* hugging its neck.

"Ohhhhh!" "Long neck!" say the children.

"Our story box and our folders are a good way for children to tell wonderful stories. In this story box you saw were all folders that were about dinosaurs. What Dr. Richgels and I are going to do right now is, we're going to show you how to use a story folder to write a story about the picture in the story folder."

I begin, "I'm going to pretend that I'm a kindergartner." I model using letter–sound correspondences to spell, sometimes representing a long word with a single letter. Sometimes the kindergartners join in, as when I say "rrrrex!" and two kindergartners suggest, "*R*!"

I stop after writing on one line of the story folder 2 T Rx v f. I read, ""Two *Tyrannosaurus rexes* were out by a volcano! And there was fire coming out of the volcano.'"

BRONTOSAURUS **CAME TO SCHOOL.**

Now Mrs. Poremba begins telling about her story folder. "Now my story is going to be different from that," she says. "Because I don't have two *Tyran-*

nosaurus rexes in my story. As a matter of fact, I don't have a volcano either, and I certainly don't have fire. But I have a kindergartner right there, and that kindergartner is riding on the back of a *Brontosaurus* dinosaur."

Kindergartners respond, including "I hope he don't fall."

Mrs. Poremba continues, "I think writing *Brontosaurus* would be very important in my story, and I think I know where I could find how to write it. I just remembered something!"

As Mrs. Poremba chooses a book, there is an intake of breath by some kindergartners. "In a book," says Tara G.

"I bet you this book might tell me how to spell *Brontosaurus*."

"How about Jason's book," suggests Jeff. Jason has been using *Dinosaurs: An A-Z Guide* since the beginning of the class's dinosaur unit.

"Oh my goodness! Who'd've thought I'd be lucky—the second page I opened up. I found a dinosaur in the book that certainly looks like, a lot like, that dinosaur in my story, from the story book, and up here it says, it starts with a *B*, '*Brontosaurus*.' And I'm just going to copy that word right out of the book here. Um, 'Once upon a time,' *Brontosaurus*—*B-R-O-N-T*—"

"You should write a *A*," suggests a kindergartner.

"—*O-S-A*—"

A kindergartner laughs in appreciation of the success of the *A* prediction.

"—*U-R*—Whoah, this is a long word!—*U-S*!" Mrs. Poremba has written **Brontosaurus**. She reads, "'Once upon a time—once upon a time—*Brontosaurus*—'"

"Was riding—" suggests a kindergartner.

Mrs. Poremba has an inspiration: "—came to school!"

"Yeah!" shouts the class.

"That's what I'm going to say! Whoah—I've got the *Bronotsaurus* part."

Mrs. Poremba and Kaitlynn say together, "*Came to school*—"

"*Kuh-kuh-kuh*—*K*!" says Kaitlynn.

"*K*, okay," says Mrs. Poremba. "*Cammmmmme*."

"*M*!" say several kindergartners.

Mrs. Poremba reads her **km**: "'Came.'"

"*To*." "*T-O*!" say kindergartners amid a chorus of talk.

"*To*—" says Mrs. Poremba as she writes **to** on the next line of her folder. "Now I need to leave a space, because now I'm going to write *ssssch*—*school*."

"*S-O-O-L*," spells Lauren.

"*S-O-O-L*," repeats Mrs. Poremba as she writes that. "Okay, let's see if I've got this so far, and then I need to do more thinking. 'Once upon a time, *Brontosaurus* came to school.' And that idea is finished, so I'm going to put a period after that, because I'm done with that part of the story."

"Mrs. Poremba," I say, "you gave me an idea! You said your story starts with 'Once upon a time.'"

"So does yours!" observes Lauren.

"So does mine! So my story goes, 'Once upon a time, two *Tyrannosaurus rexes* were by a volcano with fire!'"

"Oooh!" responds a kindergartner.

"That makes it sound more like a story," I continue. "'Once upon a time'—I like that. I like your idea of a period at the end, too." I add a period to my sentence. "That was the end of my idea. But I have some more ideas now."

DINOSAURS FIGHTING

"Okay," says Mrs. Poremba.

"I've been thinking some more about my story." I begin talking excitedly and very fast: "These-*Tyrannosauruses*-were-fighting-and-their-tails-were-flying-around-and-they-were-biting-and-chewing-and-one-of-the-*Tyrannosauruses*-hit-the-other-*Tyrannosaurus*-and-it-almost-fell -down-but-then-the-other-one—"

At first the kindergartners are silent. They have never heard me talk like this before! But now there are *ohs* and laughter. I'm inspired by the fighting dinosaur play that goes on everyday in the dinosaur toy center.

"—got-the-other-*Tyrannosaurus*-between-its-front-paws-and-they-were-shaking-it-and-the-tails-were-flying—" I pause for a breath. "Oh, that's a lot to write," I say.

"That's a lot to write," agrees Mrs. Poremba.

Kindergartners react and suggest even more to write. Among the responses is "And the bones fell out." The artist has drawn part of a dinosaur skeleton in the background, as if to suggest there have been other dinosaur fights in the past at this place, but the kindergartners seem to think these bones are from the very fight they see pictured in the foreground.

I incorporate this suggestion: "—and-some-bones-fell-out!" I sigh. "What could I write for all of that? I can't write all of that."

"That's so much to write," agrees Mrs. Poremba.

"Write part of it." "Write part." "You could spell half of it!" are among the many suggestions the kindergartners shout at once.

I show the kindergartners that I can summarize all of my story with one word, *fighting*.

"*F*!" suggests a kindergartner immediately, and we listen to big sounds in the rest of the word as we decide to spell it Fitn. "'Fighting,'" I read.

YOU COULD LOOK IT UP!

Next, Mrs. Poremba says, "Well, Dr. Richgels, you just gave me a big idea."

"Oh!" say several kindergartners.

"Watch this: 'Once upon a time, *Brontosaurus* came to school'—and a boy in the kindergarten class jumped on his back."

The kindergartners react with pleased laughs and *ohs*. "I want a girl," says one kindergartner. "Me, too." "I want a boy."

"In your story, we can have a girl."

"Yeah."

"In this though—that was a lot to say—" The kindergartners are still reacting to Mrs. Poremba's story and to the dispute about whether to have a boy or girl character. "Let's have a check time: One, two, three." It is quiet. "A boy in the kindergarten class jumped on his back. Well, I know how to do the *a* part—*a boy*. I can just write the letter *A* for the *a* part."

"You can—" begins Nathan.

"I've got an idea—I'm not sure how to write *boy*—"

"*B-O-Y*!" shouts Lauren.

"Well, Lauren knows. I'll just use her idea for *boy*, but if I didn't know how to spell *boy*, I'll show you what I could do." Mrs. Poremba draws a small figure of a boy next to her word *boy*. "I could draw a picture, too." She reads, "'A boy —' Oh, *kindergartner*—that's a long word."

"You could look it up!" suggests a kindergartner.

"Write *K-P*! Write *K-P*!" suggests Jason. The kindergartners write KP on their library checkout cards to signify *Kindergarten, Poremba*.

"—on our letter," says another kindergartner, referring to the letters from imaginary Aunt Edith and Uncle Wally that the class receives from time to time and keeps in a manila envelope.

"On your letter?" asks Mrs. Poremba. She takes one of Aunt Edith's and Uncle Wally's letters from the envelope, unfolds it, holds it so that the kindergartners can see it, and asks, "Where could I find *kindergartner* on one of their letters?"

"Up there," says a kindergartner, pointing to the top of the paper.

"'Dear Kindergartners,'" reads a student. "Long name!"

"Oh, that is a good place to find—'A boy—' *kindergartner.* Boy! A long word." Mrs. Poremba begins spelling aloud and writing, "*K-I-N-D—*'

Now the class joins her, "*—E-R-G-A-R-T-E-N-E-R—*"

The class finishes triumphantly: "*S*!"

"Do I want to say *kindergartner*, or do I want to say *kindergartners*?" asks Mrs. Poremba, emphasizing the *zzz* sound at the end of *kindergartners*. They decide that no *S* is needed.

"'The boy kindergartner'—*jumped*," says Mrs. Poremba.

"*Juh, juh, juh*," says Kaitlynn.

"*G*!" suggests another kindergartner and she is joined by a chorus of others.

"I'm just going to put a *G* for that word, because I don't—that's a lot of sounds in that word. 'A boy kindergartner jumped—'"

"*On*!" shout several kindergartners.

"*O-N*," directs one kindergartner, and she is joined by many others, shouting this familiar little word.

"Okay. '—on his —' Now, I want to show that he jumped on his *back*."

"*B*!" shout several kindergartners.

"I could put a *B* for *back*. Or I could draw a picture of the dinosaur's back. I think I'll try that, too. And I'm going to put an arrow pointing to the back of the dinosaur because I'm thinking about his back. Okay. Oh, and I'm done with that idea so I need a period." Now, Mrs. Poremba's story is *Once upon a time*/Brontosaurus km / to sool. A boy (tiny picture of a boy) / kindergartener g / on b (tiny picture of a dinosaur with an arrow pointing to its back). Mrs. Poremba now points and reads, "Let's see if I've got this. 'Once upon a time, *Brontosaurus* came to school. A boy kindergartner jumped on his —'"

Several kindergartners finish with Mrs. Poremba: "'back!'"

Jeff wants Mrs. Poremba to write *Ian* for the name of the boy in her story.

"In your story, you could put *Ian*," answers Mrs. Poremba.

"You mean, Mrs. Poremba," I ask, "that you could write about this same picture and not have the same story that I did?"

"That's right, Dr. Richgels."

"Could I write about your picture and not write the same story that you wrote?"

"That's right, Dr. Richgels. My ideas might be very different than yours. And Jeff has a new idea for a story. He said he's going to put Ian in his story."

Mrs. Poremba and I model writing our names on our story folders, and she explains, "I can take my story down to the copying machine and make a copy for myself."

Finally, Mrs. Poremba demonstrates that the story folders are reusable. She wipes hers clean with a damp tissue.

STORY FOLDER WRITING

Later, during free-choice time, Mayra is among those who choose a story folder. Hers has the picture of a boy snorkeling in the water with a swimming dinosaur. "Mrs. Poremba! Mrs. Poremba. I got a idea," she says.

"You have an i—tell me about your idea, Mayra!" Mrs. Poremba answers. Several children are clamoring for her attention. "You're going to do that one? Do you know where to find the words that you need?"

Mayra stands at the green table and leans over a chair to write several lines of mock letters and scribble writing. She moves on to the red table and does some more. Later, Mrs. Roloff's substitute for today writes Mayra's ideas above her writing: **Go to the water Dinosaur. Lead me down to the hall.**

Jason and Eric C. settle side by side at the blue table with their story folders. Jason has the picture of a hatching dinosaur. Eric has the fierce

Figure 7.5. Jason's Story Folder Writing

Tyrannosaurus standing over a *Triceratops*. Each writes his name above the *Once upon a time* (see figures 7.5 and 7.6).

Mrs. Poremba suggests, "Look at your picture. Get your ideas."

"What are they—turtles?" asks Jason.

"Actually, they're um, those are baby *Brontosaurus*es, baby dinosaurs hatching from eggs."

"Oh darn! I know what I'm going to do!" says Jason urgently. He gets his *Dinosaurs: An A-Z Guide* book. "Look at this!"

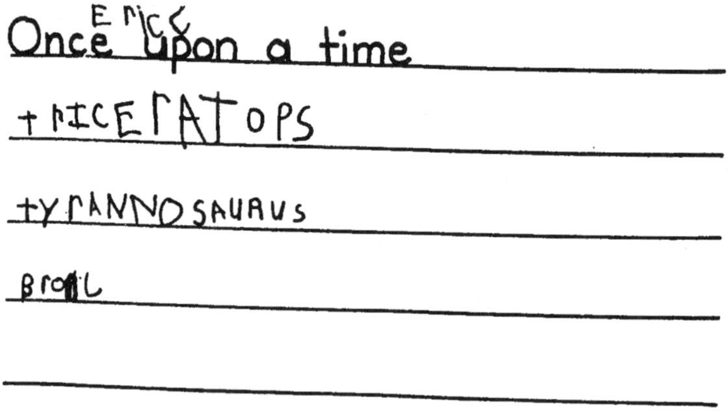

Figure 7.6. Eric C.'s Story Folder Writing

"Yeah, we could use that!" says Eric.

"Then we could write names—of the dinosaurs!"

"Let's see."

"Now what do I have to look for—baby *Brontosaurus*."

"I have to look for, um, tryna—saurus," says Eric.

"What does it start with—a *T*?"

"Tryna—saurus. No, let me see."

"*T—Tyrannosaurus*?" asks Jason. "Wait, we have to go in the *T*s—it's to be somewhere in the *T*s. And do you know why?"

Eric makes a mark on a page of *Dinosaurs: An A-Z Guide*. "Oh-oh!"

"That's okay. It's my book."

"Yeah. It's, uh."

"*T*—no. No. It could be in *T*." Jason adds something indecipherable.

"Oh yeah," replies Eric.

"*T-R*—"

"*T*? *T*?"

"I'll look at another—" says Jason, and he goes off for another book.

With Jason as his partner and with this new story folder task, Eric's writing is much different from what he did just one week ago when he and Zack had looked at dinosaur books while writing on their sign-in sheets (compare figures 7.2 and 7.6). Now, he begins copying *Triceratops*. He says, "*T-R*" and writes tr. He says, "*T-R—I*" and writes I. "*T-R-I*—one, two. If this is the wrong letter, I could just erase it," he explains to Jason, who has returned with another resource book. Eric says, "*C-E*" and writes CE. He says, "*E-R*" and writes r. "When I'm done with this letter, you look at it first. I had *R*. *A*." He writes A. But writing about *Triceratops* is not the only thing on Eric's mind. He suggests, "Jason, maybe I can ask if you can come over!"

"Maybe."

"Yeah—to stay. *A-T*." Eric writes t.

"Mrs. Poremba!" calls Jason. "I can't find *Brontosaurus* in this."

"In this one? Okay. Let's see if I can help you find that page. Did you want to find the page that I—oh, there it is."

"*O*," says Eric, almost subvocalizing as he continues to copy *Triceratops*.

"The one on top is *Brontosaurus*," says Mrs. Poremba. "Underneath it, it says *Apatosaurus*."

"*O-P-S*," finishes Eric.

"Sometimes *Brontosaures* are also called *Apatosaurus*," explains Mrs. Poremba. "So you can decide which one you want to use."

"*B-R*—" begins Jason.

"*Tyrannosaurus*!" says Eric, preparing to copy the name of the other dinosaur pictured on his story folder and getting the pronunciation correct now. He wants to be sure of the word he is copying. "Are you sure this is a *Tyrannosaurus*? Are you sure this is *Tyrannosaurus*?"

"I don't think he is."

"Let's ask Mrs. Poremba."

"He looks like one."

"Mrs. Poremba, is that a *Tyrannosaurus*?" asks Eric.

"Mrs. Poremba, this is a *Tyrannosaurus*. Look!" says Jason.

"Is this a *Tyrannosaurus*?"

"That says 'Ty-ranno-sau-rus!'" reads Mrs. Poremba.

This is enough for Eric. He begins copying it.

He and Jason talk over each other. "What does—?" asks Jason. "—I need—*T*?" says Eric.

"This says '*Tsintosaurus*,'" reads Mrs. Poremba.

"Why do they all end with *U-S*, *U-S*, *U-S*?" asks Jason.

"Lots of them do," says Mrs. Poremba, "because at the end of *Tsintosaurus*, *Tyrannosaurus*, *Alosaurus*, *Brontosaurus*, *Monocloneus*—you need *us* at the end and *us* is spelled with a *U-S*."

Eric continues writing **tYrANNOSAURUS**, looking at his source word, saying in a low voice the letters he needs, repeating each as he writes it, one letter at a time, just as he did with **trICErAtops**. Jason copies from the book, **BRONtoSAURUS)**, even copying the end parenthesis mark (see figure 7.5).

Eric finishes copying *Tyrannosaurs*: "*R-U-S*. Yes!" But he won't rest on his laurels. "Now I'll write your dinosaur's name," he tells Jason, and he begins looking for *Brontosaurus* in his book. "Look at this!"

After a bit of page turning, Jason's attention is attracted by a sequence of pictures showing the death of a dinosaur and its eventual fossilization. "Look! Look! Look! Look at this!" he says to Eric. "He was swimming, but the water dried up, so he fell to the bottom, then he turned to lava, and then he died. Isn't that cool? Look—this happened first, this happened, then this happened third, then this happened last. Look."

When Jason calls to Mrs. Poremba, she comes to his and Eric's table. "You got your story written?" she asks.

"No," answers Jason, "I don't know how to write, uh—"

"How to write what?"

"'*Brontosaurus* hatched out of a egg.' Wait, wait, I don't know—"

"You can write it the best—What does it sound like?"

Eric interrupts: "Look-at."

"*H*?" asks Jason about the first sound of *hatched*.

"Uh huh," says Mrs. Poremba.

"*Bruh, bruh, B*" says Eric, returning to his own writing of *Brontosaurus*. Then he asks Mrs. Poremba, "What's the first letter of *Brontosaurus*?"

"*Brontosaurus*? *Buh*. You've got it right there."

"*Brontosaurus* is right here," says Jason, pointing to his book.

"Here, you want to write it?" asks Mrs. Poremba.

"Right there. Not this one. The one on top," explains Jason, remembering Mrs. Poremba's earlier explanation about *Brontosaurus* and *Apatosaurus*.

"*B-R*—" begins Eric. Later, I ask Eric to read his story for me. He needs to be reminded of what he has written (see figure 7.6). When I ask him to tell me the story that goes with this, he just says, "Fighting."

Jason and Mrs. Poremba continue with *hatched*. She says the word, emphasizing individual sounds, and Jason responds with letters: She stresses the *CH* sound: "*Hat*ch*ed*."

Jason asks, "*C*?"

Then Mrs. Poremba emphasizes the last parts of the word: "*Hat*cht"

"*S*?"

Mrs. Poremba responds by especially emphasizing the *T* sound at the end: "*Hatch*-t."

"*T*?"

"Mmm hmm. *Out*."

"*Out—O*?" says Jason. He writes an *O* that looks more like a *U*.

"Mmm hmm."

"*O*."

"Ou*t*."

"*T*?"

Mrs. Poremba nods. "Then what would you put—*of*? What did you write?"

So far, Jason has BRONtoSAURUS) / HCt Ut (see figure 7.5). He reads, "'*Brontosaurus* hatched out'—*of*."

"*Of*? *Uuuuhvvv*," says Mrs. Poremba.

"*V*?"

"Uh huh."

"Looks like a *V*?"

"That's fine."

"'out of —'"

"Did you say *an egg*?" asks Mrs. Poremba.

"No."

"What?"

"*Brontosaurus* hatched out—" Jason hesitates.

"That's fine, that's right—'out of'—out of what?"

"*A egg*," answers Jason, pronouncing the article as "*ay*."

"*Ay egg*," Mrs. Poremba repeats, using Jason's pronunciation. "You know how to write *ay*, don't you?"

Jason writes *A*.

Mrs. Poremba coaches, "*Ay egggg*."

"*A*?" asks Jason for the first letter of *egg*, which is consistent with his pronunciation, "*ayg*." But when Mrs. Poremba hesitates, he suggests instead, "*E*?"

"Yes, *E*." Jason writes, and Mrs. Poremba gives the next sound, "*Guh*."

"*G*?"

"Mmm hmm. Is that the end of your idea?"

"I don't know."

Jason has written BRONtoSAURUS) / HCt Ut V A EG. Mrs. Poremba reads it to him, "'Once upon a time *Brontosaurus* hatched out of a egg.' I think it might be the end of a thought. You could put a period after the *G*. And then you can write something else."

"How do you—?"

"A period is a dot."

Jason writes a big dot.

"Do you have another idea?"

"Um—Then more dinosaurs hatched."

"Okay, you do that, and I'm going to go make a copy of this for Mayra."

After a silence from Jason, I begin helping him with a second sentence by telling him how to spell *and more*. He then duplicates those words to make AND MOREAND MORE.

"Okay, now read what you have so far," I say.

"'*Brontosaurus* hatched out of a egg. And more and more'—*hatched*."

"So now, you need to write *hatched* again."

Jason quickly writes HCt on the next line of his story folder.

"And how did you know to do that this time?"

Jason points to HCt at the beginning of the second line of his story. "I looked over there."

"That's right!"

Jason starts reading without hesitation, "'*Brontosaurus* hatched out of a egg. And more and more hatched' *out*." He copies his previous writing of *out*: Ut. Then he wants to write *The End*, so I dictate the spelling for that.

Meanwhile, Meagan has my fighting *Tyrannosaurus rexes* folder. She writes 2 Transrx Fide. n / Frt A VKnl / Ht Vknl for "Two *Tyrannosaurus rexes* fighting in front a volcano. Hot volcano." Kaitlynn has donned a dinosaur costume that a kindergartner has brought to school for the dinosaur play area. It includes a hood, legs with elastic in the bottoms, sleeves with purple spikes as cuffs. It is bright green with purple dots on the front and purple spikes from front to back of the hood, along the back, and down its tail and arms. She has Mrs. Poremba's story folder with the picture of a boy on the back of a *Brontosaurus*. After the preprinted *Once upon a time*, she writes boyONHerz B PN / THe e / THe e / krs with the s backwards. I ask her to read her story to me.

"'Once upon a time, a boy —'"

"You have to be real loud," I say.

"'Once upon a time a —' She stops, recognizing that she hasn't written the word *a*. "No. Uh—I need to write an *uh*." She names the letter she needs: "A." Then she adds A after the preprinted *Once upon a time*.

"Okay," I say.

She continues: "'—a boy jumped on his back. And the end.'" Kaitlynn hesitates over her two THe es and then just adds, "So they weren't out all day." Pointing to a little dinosaur drawing at the end of her last line of print, she explains, "And that's a little dinosaur." Kaitlynn has drawn an arrow pointing to the little dinosaur's tail, similar to Mrs. Poremba's arrow pointing to the back of her dinosaur drawing. To Mrs. Poremba, Kaitlynn explains, "I just wanted people to know that I was thinking about that." Later, Kaitlynn would read her PN / THe e as "'playing in the yard'" and her second THe e as "'the end.'" She says her first, middle, and last names when she reads her initials, krs.

Zack and Jeff are on the carpet in front of the easel, Zack drawing on a story folder, Jeff making his *Dinosaurs* cards for the Good-Bye Song. Tara G. is at a table by herself, writing in a story folder that shows a *Tyrannosaurus rex* skeleton in a museum display. She writes PePL / KaM to a MUSeyM (with a backwards y) / aNd soa boNS. The / KiNG DiNaSor boNS. / tara G.

Mrs. Poremba works with Zack, whose dinosaur story, accompanying a picture of two scientists working on a museum display of a dinosaur skeleton with spiky plates on its back, consists of three little drawings of dinosaurs, all on the first line under *Once upon a time*. Earlier, when Zack had drawn only the first two of these three dinosaurs, he had shown me his work. Pointing to the second one, he had said, "Look, a two-head dinosaur, so I'm making all these tracks." His drawing is a double circle at the end of a long oval, with eight feet (which he called "tracks"). Now, he has dictated and Mrs. Poremba has written the following: This dinosaur was alive. This dinosaur is the one with the bones. Mrs. Poremba can be heard saying, "Now this is the one that's alive. And I'll make an arrow to it." She connects the first sentence with Zack's leftmost picture. "And this is the one with the bones. And I'll make an arrow to the bones." She connects the second sentence with the middle picture. Then she writes Zack's last idea: This was the one chasing him in the museum. "And that was the one chasing him, right there?" she asks. She draws an arrow from Zack's third sentence to the rightmost drawing.

OTHER FREE-CHOICE ACTIVITIES

When free-choice time ends, Zack complains, "We hardly had any choice time." He apparently does not think of his story writing as a choice, though it was, as many children had demonstrated by doing things other than story writing. At the dinosaur toy area, Ian, Steven,

Nicole, and Sarah had staged battles among the dinosaurs. At the Housekeeping Center, Deborah and Lauren had played with a toy video camera, Deborah in a yellow satin dress over her school clothes and Lauren with a lavender scarf held on her head by a headband and a frilly, white satin dress over her school clothes. All around the room, Nathan had performed what he called a "Scotch walk"—a jerky, robotic walk.

"Pardon me?" I ask Zack.

He repeats, "We hardly had any choice time."

"Well, you had about twenty-five minutes of choice time."

In only the time it takes for Zack and me to have this exchange, Jason adds on the very bottom line of his story folder to MOM AND DAD (see figure 7.5).

"And what did you add to your story at the end?" I ask.

""To Mom and Dad,"" Jason reads.

"That's very nice. And how did you know how to write *and* this time?"

"Because it's up there," Jason explains, pointing to AND in his AND MOREAND MORE.

"You remembered! You're a quick learner, Jason. Would you like me to copy this while you're at Library Story?"

"Yeah."

FROM MRS. POREMBA

By the time children are in kindergarten, they have had a wealth of experience using the people around them as resources. Countless times each day, five year olds seek assistance for knowing and doing new things from parents, teachers, caregivers, siblings, playmates, or sometimes just any available body. Kindergartners have a high level of confidence and comfort using people to help them learn. This is usually quite natural, as it should be.

For kindergartners, an important step is making the leap to using other kinds of resources, such as print resources, for learning. With literacy as the focus, I want students to expand their comfort zone by learning about a wealth of resources such as signs, charts, books, pamphlets, magazines, posters, pictures, and technology. And that's the short list! Dinosaur study was one vehicle I thought would encourage students to seek out alternative resources. I knew there were sound possibilities here; the interest level for this topic was high. Imagine my delight when some kindergartners chose to catapult themselves, head first, into every resource they could get their hands on. In my opinion, this is the beginning of research, kindergarten-style of course!

One last thought: Kindergartners doing research? You bet! Every time a child asked a question about dinosaurs and used a book to find the answer, research occurred. Every time a child supported an idea about prehistoric creatures by pointing out evidence on a poster or a magazine, research occurred. When children discussed their thoughts as they poured over a chart, research occurred. When children put into words what they so thoughtfully gleaned from an illustration, research occurred!

8

THIS WAS THE BEST DAY!

This chapter is about play with written language in Mrs. Poremba's kindergarten. Play, especially in a classroom full of children, is usually a group activity that requires decisions about roles and props ("I'll be the mother" "This can be our car"). Many experts have noted that this is literate behavior. In fact, Wells and Chang-Wells (1992) describe literacy as social construction of meaning. Dyson (1990) emphasizes the mutually supportive use of symbols in young children's artwork, their talking, and their writing. Roskos (1991) and Paley (1990) describe the richness of opportunity for exploring written language in the context of play, especially dramatic play. All of these conceptualizations of children's play with written language (in both senses: playing with it—as when manipulating it, exploring it, experimenting with it—and including it in their other play, such as their pretend play) are evident in much that I have shared already from Mrs. Poremba's class. They were especially evident to me during two weeks in early March.

Wednesday, March 2, the 112th day of school, is an unusual day. Many of the class's routines are abandoned to make time for creating stuffed dinosaurs. Much playful talk and learning take place in this special context. But much playful talk and learning occur also on ordinary days in this class. Wednesday, Thursday, and Friday, March 9 to 11, the

116th, 117th, and 118th days of school, are just ordinary days in Mrs. Poremba's kindergarten. They are days when the kindergartners' words often make me feel what it's like for written language to be still mysterious, not obvious, something to explore. And yet Mrs. Poremba's kindergartners also make me feel what fun can be had with written language by jumping in with purpose and support.

DINOSAUR-MAKING CENTERS

On March 2, at three long tables and two big areas on the floor are five work stations. Each has an underlay of white paper, two large, identical cutouts of a dinosaur silhouette, and paint, brushes, sponges with clothespin handles (for applying paint), a pie pan full of white glue, chalk, markers, glue sticks, paper scraps, glitter, pipe cleaners, cotton balls, and other decorations. At one big table, the dinosaur cutouts are of *Stegosaurus*; at another is *Pterodactyl*; at the third is *Tyrannosaurus rex*; at one floor station is *Triceratops*; and at the other is *Brontosaurus*. Also, at each station are toy models of that station's dinosaur. Mrs. Poremba is wearing an apron, and the children have their paint shirts on over their school clothes. The children will color and otherwise decorate their cutouts. Then, Mrs. Poremba will staple the two cutouts of each dinosaur together, leaving an opening for the children to stuff their dinosaurs with crumpled newspaper. Then the opening is stapled shut, the children create signs for their dinosaurs (naming them and signing them), and the final products are hung from the ceiling.

There is no signing in and no wall work today. Mrs. Poremba calls the children to the *Brontosaurus* floor station to listen to directions for the stuffed-dinosaur project. "All dinosaur lovers, please come to the carpet right back here. Good morning."

They practice making the "Good Morning" sign and teach it to Lauren, who joined the class two days ago.

Mrs. Poremba says, "Lauren, you did it. Nice job. You're a fast learner, Lauren. I've noticed that about you."

"You already said that," notes a kindergartner. And it's true that earlier in the week, Mrs. Poremba had made the same comment.

"She really is. She really is," says Mrs. Poremba, and she directs the kindergartners' attention to the work stations. They name the five dinosaurs, and after some discussion, Mrs. Poremba gives directions. "At each center—we'll just talk about the *Brontosaurus* center right now since that's the closest to all of us—you're going to find some different things that we can use to decorate with. Um, we actually put out some *Brontosauruses*—" Mrs. Poremba refers to the toy dinosaurs that will serve as models.

"There's my *Brontosaurus*," says Freddy, who had brought his toy to school for the dinosaur unit.

"Some people call them *Apatosaurus*," says Mrs. Poremba. "That's another name for *Brontosaurus*." Yesterday, Jason and Mrs. Poremba had learned from Jason's book, *Dinosaurs: An A-Z Guide* (Benton 1988), about this alternate name (see chapter 7).

"That's mine," repeats Freddy.

"And we put the dinosaurs out near the center so you could look at it. Why we put the dinosaurs out is so you could look at them closely to see what kinds of things you see on their bodies, because the dinosaur cutouts don't have anything on them. They're just either plain brown or plain green. And when I look at this *Apatosaurus* or this *Brontosaurus*, Erin, I notice things on his head."

"Eyes," suggests a kindergartner.

"You need to add some eyes—"

"Nostrils," adds the same kindergartner.

"Could I go to the *Pterodactyl* center?" asks Nicole.

"You know, Nicole, I'm going to let you choose where you can work today."

"Yes!" says a kindergartner.

"Because I like *Pterodactyls*," explains Nicole.

"I think you should be able to work on the dinosaur that you really want to work on. What we'll do, though, we'll hopefully spread it out so there's about four people at each dinosaur."

Mrs. Poremba suggests ways to decorate with chalk and paper and with more unusual objects. "We have macaroni, we have some egg shells, lots of tissue paper, yarn, little styrofoam squigglies. If you need more things for decorating, you can find more things back in the writing center."

"And one more thing—" says Kaitlynn. "Tissue paper."

"Yes, there is tissue paper," says Mrs. Poremba.

They discuss ways to use tissue paper, and then Mrs. Poremba explains the last decorating step. "The *last* thing you do is your paint. If we did our paint first, our dinosaurs would be wet with paint, and that way when you went to use crayons and chalk and other things, it would get all sticky in the paint. So we'll save the paint for last."

THIS IS BLOOD, YOU GUYS!

When kindergartners go to the stations of their favorite dinosaurs, there are two groups of five, two groups of three, and one group of four. "Jason, and Elise, and Lauren, can you work on *Brontosaurus* all by yourself?" asks Mrs. Poremba. "Can you three handle *Brontosaurus*? Make sure you get both sides done? Can you handle that?"

Jason suggests a division of labor with his working exclusively on one half of the dinosaur.

"Actually, you can work on both," says Mrs. Poremba. "You can work on both sides, because they're going to be put together to make one dinosaur. You might want to talk to Lauren about—or you know what you could do is all three of you work on one side and then move to the next side."

But this group of three rejects Mrs. Poremba's suggestion. Lauren and Elise are chalking the feet black. Jason has drawn an eye and a smiling mouth and is now lying on his stomach, painstakingly chalking his entire half of *Brontosaurus* gray.

The room quickly becomes a busy studio, buzzing with the creativity and industry of twenty kindergarten artists. On the gold carpet, another group of three, Steven, Erin, and Alyssa, have chalked large areas of both halves of their green *Triceratops* blue and red. Steven is kneeling over one half carefully applying glue from a glue stick. At the white and blue tables, Freddy and Jeff on one half of their green *Tyrannosaurus* and Eric C., Nathan, and Zack on the other, have chalked brown stripes in key areas, such as around the shoulders. Now, Freddy and Eric are applying glue from glue sticks along one edge of their cutouts, Zack is cutting from a piece of brown scrap paper, Nathan is chalking a staccato of dots, and Jeff is carefully gluing black paper scraps to the dinosaur's feet. Ian, Sarah, and Meagan are on one side of the green and yellow tables, and Nicole and Tara G. are across from them, working on just one half of their green *Pterodactyl*. Ian glues gold and black paper scraps to its tail. Tara carefully measures and cuts a white strip of scrap paper to fit across its upright wing. Nicole is drawing with crayon. Others have applied cotton balls in various places. Kaitlynn and Elizabeth on one side of the orange and red tables, and Tara J. and Mayra on the other, are taking a similar approach to decorating their brown *Stegosaurus*—concentrating on just one of the cut out halves. Mostly, they have so far applied small pieces of white and red tissue paper, but Kaitlynn has chalked one of *Stegosaurus*'s spikes blue, and Elizabeth is making markings with a pencil on another spike.

Now Jason is joined by Elise in his project of chalking his entire half of *Brontosaurus* gray. Jason is still lying on his stomach as he works *Brontosaurus*'s long neck. He notices that the right sleeve of his yellow sweat suit is gray from dragging his unprotected arms through the chalked parts of *Brontosaurus*. (His paint shirt has no sleeves.) "Ooops!" he says, and gets up to a kneeling position. He examines both sleeves, each tinged gray now, and displays them to Elise. "Oh, that's okay," he says. Elise laughs, and Jason pulls his sleeves up to his elbows and settles back down on his stomach to chalk more of *Brontosaurus*'s neck.

Lauren begins chalking her half red and brown. Then she glues small yellow squares of crinkled tissue paper from its front foot, up the neck, around the head, down the neck, across the back, and up the tail. It is the most unified, completely executed scheme in the whole room. "Mrs. Poremba, look at mine," she says.

Mrs. Poremba comes from across the room. "Lauren, that is absolutely beautiful." She crouches down between the two halves and once again tries to foster some communication and cooperation among the *Brontosaurus* team. "That's quite a dinosaur. That will look nice when we put it together with that side." She points to Jason's and Elise's half. "Do you have some ideas for this side, Lauren?" And she asks Jason and Elise, as she points to Lauren's half, "Do you have some ideas for this side?" Jason is not taken by Lauren's idea, but he and Elise do enlist her to help them with the graying of their half of *Brontosaurus*.

"This is blood!" says Zack at the *Tyrannosaurus* center.

"Hey, this is blood," echoes Eric. "This is blood, you guys."

"We're going to make it like Godzilla," declares Jeff.

"Make your own dinosaur, how you like it," says Nicole.

"Nathan! You're making that like Godzilla?" Ian calls across to the *Tyrannosaurus rex* group, his voice showing appreciation and delight.

"—look at 'em," says Zack about the *Tyrannosaurus rex* toys at his center.

"Yeah, you can look at them to get your ideas," says Mrs. Poremba.

"Wc'rc making blood!" says Jeff.

"Someone had a—that's where the claw, someone bit his claw there," says Nathan about one of the toy *Tyrannosauruses*. Then he speaks for one of the toy characters, "'I don't understand—Ooohhh!'"

"You know what? It's fun working together," says Jeff. He and Freddy have settled at one half of the *Tyrannosaurus*, and Zack, Nathan, and Eric are at the other.

"We can make blood," says Eric.

A bit later, Jeff declares, "Somebody shot him!"

"Is this something like the real dinosaurs?" asks Eric.

"No, this is decoration!" says Freddy.

"Somebody shot him," repeats Jeff. "Look at all the blood!"

"Oh, Zachary," says Mrs. Poremba, "I'm anxious to hear what you're going to do with those triangles you're cutting out! Look at Zack."

"Did you know that Godzilla is more powerful than King Kong?" asks Jeff. He has been calling *Tyrannosaurus rex* Godzilla.

"Hey, look at this!" says Freddy.

"'Cause he has a tail, he can go Poosh! Poosh!" continues Jeff. Then he addresses a classmate in a dead serious note: "You know that could go in your eye?"

"That's a very good idea you have there, Zack," observes Mrs. Poremba.

"Freddy, somebody shot him," says Jeff.

"Did you see what Zack's doing?" asks Mrs. Poremba. "He cut out triangles, and now he's tracing them on the *Tyrannosaurus*."

"Somebody shot him," repeats Jeff.

"Godzilla—Godzilla's dead," asserts Eric.

"We know that!" says Freddy. "It's a *Tyrannosaurus rex*!"

"Every dinosaur's dead," says Nathan.

Later, Mrs. Poremba comes by. "Your triangles turned out really nice, Zack." And still later, to the kindergartners at the green and yellow tables, she says, "That's the fanciest *Pterodactyl* I've ever seen! Doilies and hearts!"

Eric claims the same distinction for his tablemates: "That's going to be the fanciest *Tyrannosaurus*."

"That is one very fancy *Tyrannosaurus*," agrees Mrs. Poremba.

Finally Zack says to Freddy and Jeff on the other half of *Tyrannosaurus*, "Hey guys, we're done."

"You are?" asks Jeff.

Freddy brings up the matter of paint: "Are we gonna paint? Jeff, are we gonna paint?"

"Yeah."

Then there is a chorus of thoughts about paint from both sides of the *Tyrannosaurus* center: "I'm not." "I am." "You can't paint." "You can't?" "Do you want to paint?"

Soon, all five groups are using paint. With the small square sponges attached to clothespin handles, most groups dab paint over the entire surface of their dinosaur cutouts. This has a unifying effect on what so far have been very disparate decorating motifs. And the paint colors create some almost kaleidoscopic effects. *Triceratops*, for example, has dramatic, vertical, pointillistic bands of contrasting colors, from its front shoulders and legs across its back to its back legs and tail. The *Tyrannosaurus* team has given their dinosaur a similar paint treatment. Jason and Elise paint two dark blue stripes on their now gray half of *Brontosaurus* and then dab dark blue spots over the rest of its expanse. Jason gets blue paint on the legs of his yellow sweat suit.

Meagan urges total paint dab coverage of the *Pterodactyl*. She says to Ian, "You need to put some on the wings."

When they finish decorating their dinosaurs, the kindergartners wash up. Jason, Kaitlynn, and Mayra are waiting behind Elise at the sink. They take liquid soap from the dispenser on the wall and rub it between their hands, relishing the feel and the look. They face each other in a small triangular group, smiling and rubbing their hands together and comparing results as the soap mixes with the paint and chalk in their hands to form a colorful goo. Mayra's is a lavender that almost matches the pants she wears today. They gleefully dispense more soap onto their extended palms, not minding at all that Elise is taking a long time with her washing up.

SIGN MAKING

Next, each group makes a sign identifying their dinosaur and listing their names. Jeff, Nathan, and Freddy are in the big wooden crate in the Reading Center. Jeff has Jason's *Dinosaurs: An A-Z Guide* in his lap; Freddy is sitting cross-legged next to him; and Nathan is behind them looking over their shoulders. They are looking for the spelling of *Tyrannosaurus*.

"See, now we need page *C*," says Freddy.

"You guys making a sign for yours?" I ask.

"Yeah," says Jeff.

"Yeah," echoes Freddy.

"Whatcha looking for?" I ask.

"*Tyrannosaurus rex* and Godzilla," answers Freddy.

"So how you gonna find *Tyrannosaurus rex*?"

"There's not Godzilla in any book," says Nathan. "He's pretend, I think."

"We, we need, how do you, what's *Tyrannosaurus rex* start with?" asks Freddy.

"I can read," says Jeff.

"It starts with *t-t-Tyrannosaurus*," I say.

"*T*," says Nathan.

"You're right, Nathan, it's *T*."

"I can almost, I can almost read," repeats Jeff.

"You *can* read, Jeff," I say. "I've seen you read."

"I can almost."

"I just heard Nathan say *T*, so you could look for the pages that start with *T*," I suggest.

"We're in *D*," says Freddy.

"You're in *D* right now," I confirm. "So are you close or do you have quite a ways to go yet?"

"*T*, *T*, *T*," says Freddy.

Nathan and Freddy decide to sing the *ABC* song: "*A-B-C-D . . . Q-R-S—Teee-T*!"

"*T*! You've got a ways to go to get to *T*, don't you?" I observe. "That's a good way to think about it."

The boys page forward in their book, singing the names of the letters as they proceed.

After a bit, Zack and Eric C. join them, each with a book, completing the group that worked at the *Tyrannosaurus rex* station. Eric and Nathan lie on the cushions behind Jeff and Freddy. They page through the photo-illustrated *Jurasic Park: The Movie Storybook* (Mason, Koepp, and Chrichton 1993).

"Guys, we're all grouped," notes one of them.

"*Tyrannosaurus rex*!" exclaims Freddy. "Eric found it!"

Jeff defends Freddy's and his resource, *Dinosaurs: An A-Z Guide*: "We're gonna look at it in here—there's bigger words."

"Oh, I'll show you a part about him!" says Nathan, showing a page from *Jurassic Park*. "Look, here's a part about him!"

"Yeah," says Eric.

"I know, but that—we're looking for *T*," says Freddy. "Just go like this—" As they near the end, Freddy says, "—*T-U-V*, *W-X*—Guys, we're almost to the end. If they don't have any *Tyrannosaurus rex*, we're dead meat!"

"We're not dead meat!" objects Jeff.

"There's tons of *Tyrannosaurus rex* books," says Zack. "I'm going to see if I can find another—"

"Look for that one." "That one is much harder—" "Nooo, that one," say the boys.

"The big books, only use the big books," directs Freddy from his place still next to Jeff. "They're—the little books are no help 'cause they're not true." Freddy refers to the mostly fictional books in the nearby collection of small books for checking out to read at home.

One of the boys disagrees: "Yes, the little books *are* true."

"Hey! We're on page *T*!" says Freddy.

"We're on page *T*!" says Jeff.

"Page *T*! Yes!"

"Huh?" asks Nathan.

"We're on page *T*! We're on page *T* already!" says Freddy.

"Come on! Get back in here!" Jeff directs his groupmates who had gone to the book display adjacent to the crate.

"Are you getting close?" asks Mrs. Poremba.

"Does that say *Tyrannosaurus rex*?" asks Jeff.

"No, that doesn't *look* like *Tyrannosaurus rex*," replies Freddy.

The boys look at more of the *T* entries. After I help them eliminate two *T* dinosaur names because they do not end with *X*, I look ahead to the correct entry. "Okay, now this one, actually, it doesn't say *Tyrannosaurus rex*, but it does say 'ty-ran-uh-saur-us.'" I explain, "It just doesn't have the *rex* part."

Copying from the book, the boys write TyrANNOSAUrUS

"Freddy," I ask, "what does *rrrex* start with?"

"*T*!" Freddy answers.

"*Rrrrr-ex*?" I ask. "What does the *rrrex* start with?"

"*X*," answers Freddy.

"It ends with *X*," I acknowledge. "You could add the *X* yourself."

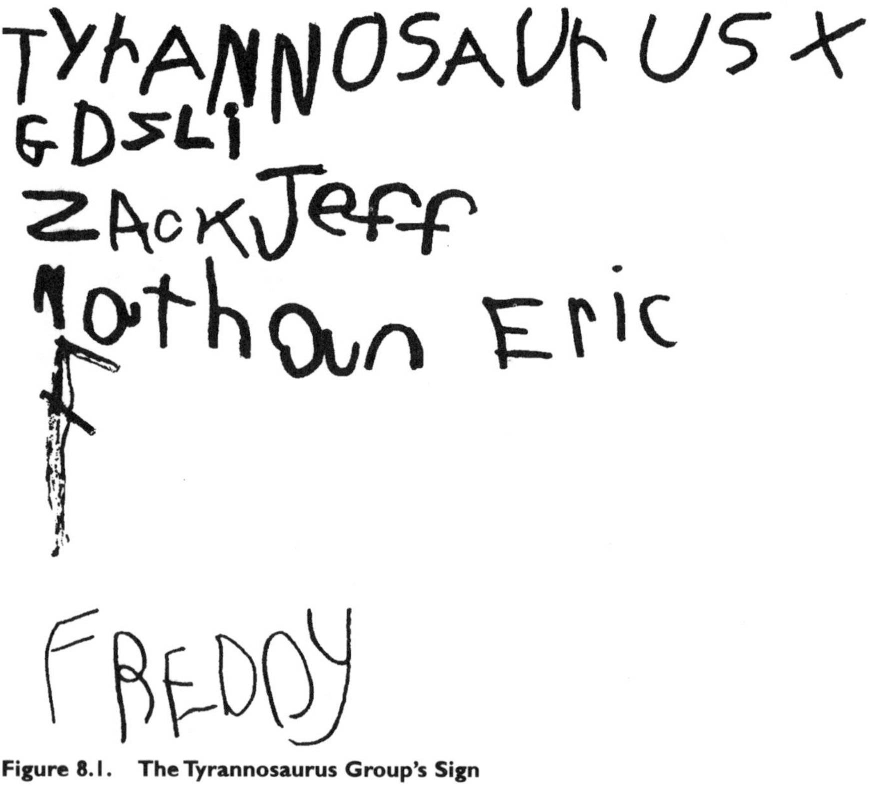

Figure 8.1. The Tyrannosaurus Group's Sign

"So we just have to put an *X* here," says Freddy.

"That would be a way to do it, yes."

They add X (see figure 8.1).

Meanwhile, Zack has found *Tyrannosaurus* in a picture book. "I got Tyranna!" he shouts. "I found it! I found Tyranna!"

"We've got it!" says Jeff.

"—that's the same word as the one that we found!" says Freddy .

"Let me see," says Jeff.

"It's on the same, it's the same word. It doesn't say *Tyrannosaurus REX*," says Freddy.

Jeff extends his left hand and snaps his fingers at Zack. "Gimme it." Zack holds the open book closer to Jeff.

"It's the same one we found," agrees Jeff. "Except it didn't have a *X* at the end."

Freddy leans over Zack to make sure about his find: "That one doesn't have an *X* at the end?"

Nathan reaches for Jeff's marker, but Jeff pulls it back and says, "Hey, wait for Godzilla." He also wants to write *Godzilla*, the name they were using as they decorated their *Tyrannosaurus*.

"How do you spell *Godzilla*?" asks Freddy.

"I'll use a brown for *Godzilla*," says Jeff.

Eventually they ask for Mrs. Poremba's help. "You could use your kindergarten spelling for *Godzilla*," she suggests.

"Ohhh!" moans Jeff.

"*GodZILla*! *GodZILla*! *GodZILla*!" says Freddy trying to emphasize the big sounds in *Godzilla*. "*A*," he decides. "*A*, it starts with an *A*. Jeff, it—Jeff, look, *GodZILla*, *A*."

Jeff is not impressed. "Nathan might know how to spell *Godzilla*, 'cause he has his dinosaur."

"My dad knows," says Nathan, "but I don't. I have two Godzillas."

After the distraction of Eric's too-late announcement that now he, too, has found *Tyrannosaurus* in his book, the boys ask for my help.

"That's going to be like the nickname of your dinosaur?" I ask. Jeff holds up his sign, on which he's already written TyrANNOSAUrUS X. I observe, "That's the scientific name—"

"There's two names, there's two names," says Jeff.

"—and you're also going to have a nickname? Okay."

Jeff gets on his knees and holds his paper against the interior wall of the crate, ready to write.

"Anyway, Jeff, what do you hear at the beginning of *guh-godzilla-guh*?"

"*G*?"

"*G*, mmm hmm."

Jeff writes G. Zack, who's kneeling next to Jeff and leaning his back on the same wall of the crate that Jeff is writing on, turns and watches Jeff's work.

Then Zack and Jeff turn to me, expecting the next letter. "Then *God-duh-duh*," I say.

"*D*," says Jeff and turns to write.

"*D*," I confirm.

Zack turns to me, "Just like *God*," he notes.

"Mmm hmm," I agree. "Then *zzzz*—"

"Z!" says Zack.

"—*Godzzzilla*," I continue.

"Z!" says Jeff and writes.

"Mmm hmm," I confirm as Zack claps his hands, bows, and wags his clasped hands beside his head. "And then *zilllll*—" I continue.

"*-il*," says Zack.

"*L*," says Jeff and writes.

"*L*, mmm hmm," I confirm.

"Where's that fish?" asks Zack, getting up and heading toward the book display.

"*Godzilluh—uh*," I say.

"*I*," says Jeff and writes. He ends up with GDZLi, with a backwards Z (see figure 8.1).

"*I* would be a good way to do that," I say. "Very good, Jeff. Now, what else do you guys have to put on your sign?"

Zack and Freddy are arguing over a book. "Give me that back," says Freddy.

"That was a short name," observes Jeff.

"Mmm hmm. Well, we just wrote the big sounds, so that's why it's short."

"Well, I had it first," says Freddy.

"So what else do you guys need to write on your sign?"

"Jeff, Zack—" says Jeff.

"All of your names. So you each write your own name on your sign."

GUYS, THIS IS THE *BEST* BOOK!

They write their names, and Jeff leads the group in playing hideout in the crate. Only Eric wants to continue treating the crate as it is designated, as the Reading Center. He has another dinosaur book. "This will help us find *more* dinosaurs! Jeff, Jeff. Jeff, Jeff. Jeff, this book is real cool. I went through it once."

But Jeff only declares, "This is our hideout!"

"Guys, this is the *best* book!" Eric persists.

"Nice scoopy hideout."

"Look-at—look at this. Look at how many buses that takes—" Eric is showing a page that shows the length of a dinosaur in school bus units. "Look at how many school buses that takes to get a—Look! Look-at, guys! This. Look at this."

Meanwhile, Jason comes to the Reading Center looking for a resource. "What do you guys need?" I ask.

"*Brontosaurus*," answers Jason.

I show Jason his *Dinosaurs: An A-Z Guide*. "Well, Jason, this is your book, right? I'm sure *Brontosaurus* is in here. Do you want to take this back to the Writing Center and work on it back there?"

At the Writing Center, Jason and Lauren copy from the tiny print by the *Apatosaurus* entry, the only source for the alternate name, *Brontosaurus*. I indicate the *Apatosaurus* entry and suggest, "So you could either write that or you could copy here. They wrote down some little writing for the other name for it."

They decide to copy the small but more familiar word (see figure 8.2).

Later, as the children gather to listen to Tara J.—whose week to shine it is—read to them, Mrs. Poremba says, "Jason, make sure that you tell Mom that the paint on your pants is the kind that comes out in the wash with soap and water. Okay?"

At free-choice time, there is a big group at the Housekeeping Center. Tara G. and Meagan are in dress-up dresses, Tara's yellow and Meagan's

Figure 8.2. The Brontosaurus Group's Sign

pink. Erin wears a white, satiny dress, high heels that she clicks on the floor, and long, white gloves, and she carries a drawstring, black-and-white-patterned purse on her right shoulder. Elise, Alyssa, Tara J., and Sarah are also present but just in their school clothes. They play arriving at a dinner party at the house of one of the participants, but completely unremarked in their midst is Kaitlynn. She participates like all the others, but she is again wearing the green and blue dinosaur costume that she delighted in wearing yesterday, too (see chapter 7). Before putting it on today, she had had to devote considerable time, remarkable care, and uncharacteristic patience to turning the costume right side out.

"What kind of dinosaur are you, Kaitlynn?" I ask.

"*Stegosaurus*," she answers without hesitation.

At the wall work area, Jeff, Ian, Eric C., and Nicole are staging dinosaur fights with some of the toy *Brontosauruses* that were out for the *Brontosaurus* group. Nearby, Mrs. Roloff is playing a board game with Zack, Jason, Elizabeth, and Mayra. Lauren, Steven, and Freddy are in the Reading Center, where Steven is washing the chalkboard.

At the end of the day, Jason's mother picks him up. He has gray chalk on his sleeves and blue paint on his face and pants legs, but he can't contain his excitement as he shows his mother the stuffed dinosaurs that he and his classmates have made today. "This was the *best* day!" he declares.

A MESSAGE BOARD

One week later, on Wednesday, March 9, the 116th day of school, the dinosaur unit is finished. Mrs. Roloff has brought a two-by-three-feet plastic message board salvaged from a concession stand. It comes with black plastic letters and numbers that have little prongs that fit in grooves on the board. The letters and numbers were used to tell the foods, drinks, and prices of items for sale at the concession stand. The sign has a permanent red and white logo for a popular cola soft drink. As children arrive at the beginning of the day, it is on the yellow table.

"Boy, that is a neat letter board, isn't it?" I observe.

"I know what these things are," says Jason about broken-off prongs that stayed behind in the grooves when letters had been removed from the board. He becomes obsessed with removing these and doesn't want any letters displayed until all the prongs are removed. And when his classmates want to place letters, he wants them to be careful not to break off any more prongs. "Don't stick 'em in too much. Nicole, don't put them on—See, these come off them." He enlists others in this work, but they are less persistent than he.

"I got one out," says Ian, but he'd rather write with the plastic letters. "How do you spell *dog*, again? I forgot." He repeats, "How do you spell *dog*, again? I forgot."

Jason gives him a quick and confident answer: "*D-O-G*!" And then he removes a prong. "I got another one!"

Later, during free-choice time, Elise and Tara J. are at the concession stand message board. Tara is using a magnifying glass in a three-legged stand to examine numbers as she puts them on the board. Elise is using the letters to write *Girl Scouts*. So far she has GARL S.

"What are you writing, Elise?"

"You'll see." She gets an *O* from the bucket of letters.

"What did you decide to write?" I ask.

"Girl Scouts."

"Girl Scouts. That's a good message. Do you belong to the Girl Scouts?"

"Yeah."

Elise replaces the *O* with a *C* and finishes writing GARL SCOUT.

OH, ELIZABETH, YOU'RE FINDING ALL YOUR LETTERS!

Mrs. Roloff helps Elizabeth to spell her name. "Ooo, here's an *I*. I hope you can find a Z."

"Mrs. Roloff, what is this?" asks a kindergartner about the soft drink logo, and Mrs. Roloff reads it.

When Elizabeth finds an *A*, Mrs. Roloff says, "There's an *A*."

Elizabeth finds and places a *B*.

"Oh, Elizabeth, you're finding all your letters!" says Mrs. Poremba.

"What comes next?" asks Mrs. Roloff. "Tell me what letter."

"*E*," answers Elizabeth.

"*E*! Let's help you find an *E*," replies Mrs. Roloff.

Elizabeth and Mrs. Roloff each find an *E*. "Ope! Here's one, too," says Mrs. Roloff. "Here's two *E*s. Do you need two or just one?"

Elizabeth places one *E* next.

"What comes next, Elizabeth?"

"*H*," answers Elizabeth.

"An *H* comes next? Is there something besides the *H*, before it?"

"*T*," answers Elizabeth.

"A *T*. Do you see a *T*?"

Elizabeth completes ELIZABETH and begins on her last name, with similar prompting from Mrs. Roloff.

Deborah begins writing her name. Tara G. and Alyssa spell their first and last names. And now, Elise writes ELISE above GARL SCOUT DIS. There is much commentary as they proceed: "I need a ___." "I need a ___." "I need another ___."

"There! I'm all done. See?" Alyssa draws out the reading of her first and last names as she points along the letters that spell them.

"Good job!" says Mrs. Roloff.

Elizabeth places a string of numbers in order. "You know what?" asks Mrs. Roloff. "You've got your 6 upside down." After Elizabeth turns over her 6, Mrs. Roloff requests, "Read your numbers out for me, Elizabeth. You know what? There's no 8, but let's just read off our numbers. Okay?"

Elizabeth says, "Zero, zero, one, two, three, four, five, six, seven, eight."

Mrs. Roloff asks, "How many letters in *Elizabeth*?"

"One, two, three, four, five, six, nine, ten, eleven."

"Ooo. I think you miscounted. Let's try it again. Okay? Start at the *E* and start over."

This time Elizabeth correctly counts the letters in both her first and last names. And when Mrs. Roloff asks which name has more letters, Elizabeth correctly answers, "Elizabeth."

NO PUSHING IN TOO HARD

The next day, Thrusday, March 10, during sign-in writing time, Jason and Freddy are at the message board. They have written NO PS. This is the beginning of a small group's playful exploration of writing's possibilities. Jason and Freddy and the boys who will join them are not yet conventional writers, but by March of their kindergarten year, they have learned enough about our alphabetic writing system to enjoy experimenting with what letter combinations can do.

Jason asks me how to write *pushing*.

"You have the *push* part," I tell him. "You just need the *ing* part."

He adds, after a small space, an *E* for the sound of the *I* in *ing*, and I pronounce the *ng* sound for him. He adds an *N*. So he has NO PS EN. Jason is still worried about the prongs on the letters. He doesn't want any more broken off by pushing letters in place too forcefully. Next, he wants to write *these*, so I pronounce the *th* sound at the beginning. Jason tells me that it is spelled *T-H*, but he has difficulty finding a *T* and becomes distracted from spelling *these*.

"I can't find a *T*."

"You're looking for a *T*?" I ask

"Yeah."

"There's so many letters—" I say.

Freddy assesses their progress so far: "We've got the 'No pushing—'" Then he tells what is needed next: "*—in too hard*."

Freddy has recruited Ian, who picks this up: "*—in too*—Okay—*T-O*!" Thus Ian, who was not party to the spelling of *pushing* as PS EN, is the first to read the EN Jason had written for *ing* but displaced by a space from his PS as the word *in*.

"*T-O*," repeats Freddy.

"It's *T-O*," Ian says.

"That's what I said," says Freddy.

"Well, Jason's working on the word *these*," I offer. "He's got 'No pushing,' and now, he wants to write *these*."

Jason, still unable to find a *T*, tries a creative solution.

"You know," I say, "that's a good idea to put those two pieces together to make a *T*, but I don't think those little bars [prongs] will fit that way."

"They don't," says Jason.

"You're looking for a *T*?" I continue.

"Yeah."

"There has to be a *T*. Here's one."

"*T-O*, that's how you spell *too*," says Ian.

"I know, and—" says Freddy.

"Are, are you spelling *two* like in numbers?" asks Ian.

"I think he's spelling *these*," I persist. Ian and Freddy place TO.

"No—" Jason protests. "What does that say?" he asks me.

"Now it says, 'No pushing too,'" I say, reading PS EN as Jason wrote it rather than as Ian later read it (recall, he read it as *pushing in*).

"No, let me think, Freddy," says Jason.

"I think Jason was working on the word *these*," I repeat.

"No, Freddy, I just need something," says Jason, who is still holding his *T*.

"What else did you want with that *T*, Jason?" I ask, thinking that Jason is still working on the *th* sound at the beginning of *these*. Ian and Freddy have left plenty of room between PS EN and TO for *these* if Jason is still thinking that way.

"Dr. Richgels, what is this?" asks Freddy about an & sign he has found in the letter and number bucket.

"That means *and*," I answer. "It's just a short way to write *and*."

"Okay," says Jason, "now what's the next letter? What's the next letter? Dr. Richgels, what's the next letter?"

But Mrs. Poremba makes an announcement reminding the kindergartners to make their number guesses at the 110 chart because wall work will begin soon.

"Finish writing it," says Freddy in an urgent, quiet voice.

I persist in coaching Jason, "Okay, you were writing the *th* part of *these*. What else do you need for that, Jason?"

"I don't know."

Freddy says, "There's tons of lines and I have big—"

"I think you were talking before about an *H* to go with that *T*—"

"How does Freddy want it?" asks Jason.

"—*T-H*." I finish.

"'No—pushing—in—too—*hard*!'" says Freddy, having adopted Ian's reading of PS EN. "See, we need *too*," he adds, justifying his and Ian's placing of TO.

"So, Freddy doesn't think we need the word *these*," I offer. "What do you, how do you feel about that, Jason?"

"Okay," agrees Jason.

"Okay." And I review, "'No pushing too —'" I pause.

"*Hard*," says Freddy.

"What would *hhhhhhard* start with?"

Jason places an *H*.

"*H*. Okay, and now, *harrrrr*—"

"*Duh, D*," says Jason, finishing my prompt instead of spelling my *R* sound.

"*Harrrrrrrrr*," I repeat, continuing the *R* sound even longer.

"*R*?"

"Mmm hmm."

"*R*," Freddy agrees.

"And then what—to finish off *har*d?"

"*D*?" asks Jason.

"*D*, mmm hmm."

"Where's that *D, D, D, D*?" says Freddy.

"Here's one," I say. Now, the boys have written NO PS EN TO HRD. "So it looks like you have your whole message. What does it say?"

"'No pushing in too hard,'" reads Freddy.

"Great job! How do you feel about that, Jason? Is that what—"

Now, of all people, Freddy revives *these*! Perhaps, he wants the message to be *No pushing in too hard these letters* because he interrupts now, saying "*These, these, theeeese*" as if he is not finished but is now working on spelling *these*.

"Are you satisfied with that, Jason?" I ask.

"They look okay. Just only one problem."

"What's that?" I ask.

"Are we gonna leave it on?"

"Are we gonna leave it on—"

"Yes! Yes!" interjects Freddy.

"—that's a good question. I guess it depends on if other people think that's a worthwhile message to leave on there, huh?"

"I'm not. I'm just trying that idea."

Freddy wants to do something with his & sign.

"How about it was Freddy's *and* Jason's idea," suggests Jason.

"Yeah!" agrees Freddy.

Freddy has left the group by the time Jason and Ian have written JASON&IAN&. Jason says, "We need *Freddy*. Do you know the word for *Freddy*?"

"I don't know how to spell his name," says Ian.

"*F-R-D-D-Y*," says Jason.

"Mmm. Okay." Ian begins to place letters for Freddy's name.

"*F*—like for *fff*—*F, R, E, E-D-D-Y*," spells Jason. "I think I know where a *Y* is."

"I just saw one, I think."

"I did, too."

"Here it is!"

When they have written JASON&IAN&FREDDY, Jason reads, "'Jason and Ian—'"

Ian interrupts with his own reading, "'Jason, Jason and—'"

"'Ian and Freddy,'" they finish together.

"Boy, that turned out really nice," I observe.

NOBRRRRRRRR

Ian doesn't want to stop. He suggests, "Let's just put like, how about, *No Talking*." He laughs.

"But, we don't want to put *No Talking* on this sign," says Jason.

Ian continues laughing. "We do!" He gets silly; he suggests, "*P-P*."

More boys are involved now. One suggests a *P* word: "*Punky*." Another says, "*Peachy*."

Then Jason says, "Here, *P-P-P-P-P-P*. Wantta put all the *P*s in a line?"

"No, just *P-P*," says Ian. "No, no, put *P-P*."

"*P-P*?" asks one of the boys.

"Yeah, *P-P*," Ian repeats. "Like," he says in a conspiratorial voice, "like *pee-pee*." He gleefully pursues his potty joke.

Meanwhile, someone has placed a *B*, and then the boys begin a string of *P*s.

"No, *R*s!" says one.

"I changed—" says another.

"I found a *P*! I found a *P*!" says another.

Freddy returns and asks, "What are you guys doing?"

"We're just writin' words," answers Ian innocently.

"One of 'em is *B*, *B-P-P-P-P-P-P*," says Jason.

"Hey, guys, you spelled my name?" notes Freddy.

BPPPPPP reminds Jason of a familiar word. "*Brrrrr*!" he shouts. "*Br-rrrr*! Is it *brrrrr*? Hey, I'm gonna put *brrrrr*."

"Take all the *P*s out," suggests Freddy.

"And put *R*s on it," adds Jason. They begin their revision. "*Brrrrr* has a thousand *R*s in it," Jason suggests.

"Let's make it all the way to here," Freddy proposes.

"Yeah," says Jason.

"How many *R*s does that need?" asks Freddy.

"Another *R*?" asks one of the boys.

"Here's another!" says Jason. After a bit, he asks, "Want to take one out of *Freddy*?"

"No!" protests Freddy. After still more work time, he proposes, "Nathan, let's count how many *R*s. One, two, three, four, five, six." But as two more are added, he ups his count to eight. "Eight *R*s. How about we get up to ten?"

"Fifteen," suggests one of the boys.

Mrs. Poremba rings the bell for wall work.

"Who cares about that?" says Freddy in a low voice as they continue with their project. He counts nine *R*s. "We need one more."

"Now what are you doing?" I ask.

"We're writing *brrrrr*," says Jason.

"Oh, you've got a lot of *brrrrr* there," I observe. But they also have two *N*s before their BRRRRRRRRR. "What are the *N*s for in the *brrrrr*?"

"'No, no brrrrr,'" answers Ian.

"*No, no brrrrr*?" I ask.

"Yeah."

"How about *zoo, zoo, zoo brrrrr*?" asks Jason. "*Zoo brrrrr. Zoo, zoo, zoo.*" Someone has written **ZOOO** (with a cent sign before it) to the right of **NNBRRRRRRRRR**.

"We could put *No brrrrr*," suggests Ian. "Here—do *No brrrrr*! *No brrrrr*!"

"*No brrrrr*?!" asks Jason.

They trade the second *N* for an *O*, so that their final message is **NO-BRRRRRRRRR**.

"Okay, come on over to the carpet now," I direct.

"'No brrr-r-r-r!'" reads Tara G. with a shudder as she passes by.

PIZZA PARLOR

In one section of the folding room-divider-like wall of the Housekeeping Center, separating the center from the rest of the room, is an opening, with a small shelf that folds down into the center. For March 9 and 10, this shelf is the counter of Zack's and his classmates' pizza parlor. Zack sits there on March 9 with a tin cup and clipboard on the counter next to him and his elbows on the counter. Jeff sits behind him, before the stove, a telephone, and a cash register. Jeff grabs for, but Zack defends his possession of, a pair of sunglasses with big, neon green temples. Zack puts them on. "Hurry, hurry, hurry!" he calls to potential customers. Lauren, with a white dress-up dress over her school clothes, and Deborah, with a lavender scarf tied on her head, prepare food in the background.

"Hey, mister!" Zack calls to me. "Mister!"

"Yes, Zack?"

"You hangin' around here?"

"Pardon me?"

Zack shakes his head. "You eat or you go!"

I laugh. "Okay—I'll go."

Jeff calls to me, "He's just kidding, Dr.—He's just kidding, Dr. Richgels."

When I return a bit later, Zack has his sunglasses up on the top of his head, and he is paging through the notepaper tablet clipped to his clip-board. Freddy has taken Jeff's place and is on the phone. Jeff is at the snack table for now. Eric C. is at the cupboard/refrigerator/oven behind Freddy. Ian runs up, leans into the window, and says something into

Zack's ear, causing Zack's glasses to slip back onto his nose. Then Ian runs around the Housekeeping Center wall and joins the boys inside the pizza parlor. Deborah and Lauren have shed their dress-up clothes and are at the overhead projector experimenting with transparent, colored plastic shapes, which project designs onto a screen. Ian grabs a wooden box and stirs its imaginary contents.

Zack takes a drink of whatever imaginary liquid is in his cup. He pulls his glasses off and asks, "You want pizza?"

"Can I order another pizza?" I ask.

Zack replaces his glasses. "Yeah," he says.

"Could I have a large—"

Cup still in his left hand, Zack leans over his clipboard, his mouth set in a firm straight line, and writes on the note paper in his clipboard.

"—thick crust, um, with pepperoni and black olives, please?" Zack writes four wavy lines of mock cursive, one for each element of my order: *large*, *thick crust*, *pepperoni*, *black olives*.

Eric comes up to the counter at Zack's left shoulder. "We've got it all made," he says.

"Already!" I exclaim. Zack knows the drill; he is tearing the notepaper from his clipboard and handing it to Freddy even as I tell Eric, "I think Zack needs to give the order to the kitchen before it will be ready."

Freddy is on the phone. Ian takes the order from him. "Okay, new order."

"Be ready in ten minutes!" Zack says, taking a sip from his cup.

Ian and Eric are busy in the kitchen. Ian is spooning imaginary sauce from a can.

Freddy hangs up the phone. "There's another guy that ordered. Hey, man," he says to Zack, "another guy ordered."

Eric asks, "Did you order drinks, too?"

I order a soft drink.

Zack takes another swig from his cup. "How about tea?" he asks me.

"Tea? That's a good idea."

"Tea!" Zack shouts over his shoulder. "Another cup of tea!"

Eric hands me a cup over Zack's shoulder.

"Thank you!" I say.

Zack has a pencil in his right hand and his cup in his left hand this whole time. He shoves his glasses up on the top of his head again.

"Oh, that was delicious tea," I say. Zack looks at me almost as if questioning that I am still in the play world. He pulls his glasses back to his nose. "What brand is that?" I ask.

Zack's answer is lost as Ian hands me, over Zack's shoulder, the wooden box in which he's prepared my pizza. "There you go!"

"Thank you. Oh, just what I ordered. How much does that cost?"

"Need a fork, mister?" asks Ian.

"Pardon me?"

"Need a fork with that?"

"Yes, that will help."

Ian hands me a yellow plastic fork.

"Thank you."

"I take over my job now!" announces Jeff, back from the snack table. Freddy relinquishes his post with no question.

"That's our messages," says Jeff, grabbing the wooden box. But Zack pulls it back and into my hand; he knows it contains my pizza.

"Thank you. How much do I owe you now?"

"Owe me—five dollars," answers Zack.

Jeff is working the cash register. "No, six dollars!" he says.

"Six dollars," Zack repeats.

"All right." I get out my wallet and count out six pretend bills.

"Ten bucks!" suggests Eric from the kitchen.

"I tell him how much," asserts Jeff. "I tell him how much."

The boys' pizza parlor play continues for fifteen minutes before, and then another fifteen minutes after, gym class. And the next day, March 10, Eric C., Jeff, Ian, Freddy, and Zack are back at their places in the pizza parlor, Zack again wearing his sunglasses. This becomes a popular pretend play option for the rest of the year, with many players, both boys and girls.

MORE SIGN MAKING

On March 11, Mrs. Poremba capitalizes on the kindergartners' interest in sign making. We have already seen the signs students made to identify their stuffed dinosaurs and the messages they wrote on the concession stand message board. Today, Freddy brought to school a sign he made at home (see figure 8.3), inspired by the class's new unit about protecting the environment. Mrs. Poremba introduces a sign-making project. "You know, Freddy," she says, "that sign that you brought reminds me of a really good idea I have for all kindergartners." She reads *The Signmaker's Assistant*, by Tedd Arnold (1992), about an apprentice signmaker who causes trouble by making his own signs when his master is away, in order to take advantage of the power of signs (people usually obey them). Then Mrs. Poremba tells the class, "I want to show you something that I was working on this morning because I decided to make a sign of my own. And I'll show it to you."

"Wow!" say several kindergartners.

"I started thinking about ways we can help our wonderful world. And I started thinking about Freddy's idea about making signs to help people know how to help our wonderful world. And, Freddy, I decided to make a sign. And you know why I did? You gave me the idea! Thank you! Let me show you my sign." She shows a picture she has drawn of someone turning off the lights before leaving a room, and then she models writing *Turn off the lights*. With the kindergartners' help, including their paying attention to the big sounds in *turn* and *lights*, she writes Trn off the lits.

Mrs. Poremba gives directions, and soon the room is buzzing with activity. Some kindergartners consult a chart of ideas they shared and Mrs. Poremba recorded two days ago for how to take care of the environment.

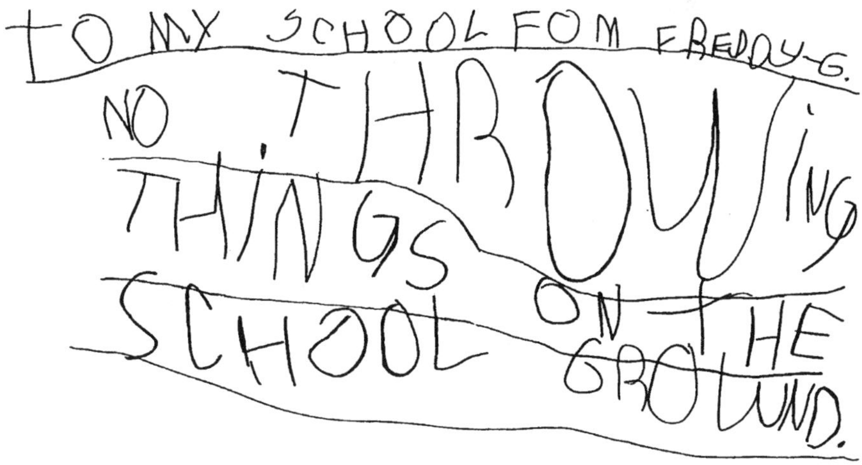

Figure 8.3. Freddy's Sign

Alyssa's item on the chart is *In the summer and winter my mom's going to make a bird feeder.* She points with her pencil to the first three words and reads them as "'Me and my mom —'"

"Mmm hmm."

"'We will throw—'" She stops, her pencil still pointing to *and.*

After a pause, I say, "Something about birds, remember?"

Alyssa finishes, her pencil resting on *winter*: "'—bird feeders out for the birds.'" She diligently copies her idea from the chart on to her sign. She alternates between standing with her clipboard by the easel and leaning over her clipboard at a nearby table. In the end, her sign is In the summ / er And minter / my moms goi / ngto / bird, with a backwards y in my and backwards gs in going. She writes ALYSSA.

Despite Mrs. Poremba's suggesting that kindergartners not use her sign idea, Zack and Tara J. write the same message. Tara's words are arranged vertically on the page, Turn / OFF / THE / LiHys, with a backwards n. Zack's version is TDTD NO EV ITs. He has drawn a picture of a black-cloaked figure with big stick arms and hands, one grasping a huge switch.

Some kindergartners use crayon and markers, some type their messages, some paint their signs. Ian uses the concession stand message board to write DO NAT. He calls to me, "Dr. Richgels?"

"Yes?"

"Did I spell *not* right?"

"*Not*? Well, that would be a good way to do it. I can tell that that's *not*. Do you want it to be the way grown-ups do it, or do you want it to be your own way?"

Ian wants the grown-up way.

"The grown-up way is with an *O* instead of an *A* in the middle: *N-O-T*."

Ian changes an *O* for his *A*. I move on and Ian writes LART so that his message is DO NOT LART.

"Dr. Richgels," he calls to me again.

"Yeah?"

"Look what I said." He underlines his message with his finger.

"And now, read it to me," I suggest.

"First guess," he directs.

"'Do not litter'?" I read.

"Uh huh!"

"Good job!"

Ian adds BY IAN. Later, he makes a paper-and-pencil sign: BKARFL BY IAN / DAN GO ON! ThE / SATT. "Tell me about all this writing now, Ian," I say.

Ian reads, "'Be careful.'"

"I can see that: 'Be careful —'"

"'Do, don't—'"

"'Don't,'" I confirm.

"'—go on the street.'"

"That is a great sign, Ian."

"Thanks."

"And tell me how you figured out all that writing."

"I just listened to the words."

At one of the back-to-back painting easels, Deborah wields a brush with the confidence of a Japanese calligrapher, dipping it in the pot of blue paint for each letter, making graceful movements across the paper. She wears a large, light blue sweatshirt that is spattered with colors from other painting jobs, its cutoff sleeves coming to her wrists, it's waistband to midthigh. She writes NO.

Steven is at the other painting easel. He paints a big, red NO O and below that, PIOE, the PI in blue, the OE in red. His message is *No pollution*. Deborah comes around from her easel and coaches him, "*E-N*. I mean *I-N*, *I-N*. That's how you spell *in*." She hears an *in* in "polooshin."

Steven paints a big vertical line between his NO and O. But when he is finished, a big red blob has overtaken everything to the right of NO, and he has turned the O in PIOE into a smiley face. He writes his name with pencil, STEVEN, with a backwards S.

When Deborah has written NO:Th, she stops to ask me, "Dr. Richgels, how do you spell the rest of *throwing*?" She takes up the brush from the pot of orange paint.

"The rest of *throwing*? Well, what do you hear next in *thrrr*?"

"*R*." She makes the vertical part of *R* with a down-up-down retracing and then the rest in an easy, fluid, continuous movement of her brush. But then, she makes one reverse tracing of the diagonal part.

"And then *throwwww*," I say.

"*O*," says Deborah, immediately beginning to paint that letter, but her brush runs dry before she finishes it. So she dips her brush, repaints the

O, but makes an imperfect tracing, so that in the end, she decides to fill in the center of the *O* with orange paint.

"Okay, that's 'No throw.' Now, you need the *ing* part."

"*Ing*?"

"The *ing* part of *throwing*," I clarify.

"How do you spell *ing*?"

"*Ing* is *I*—"

Deborah starts a new line of print, making the vertical in *I* with a down-up retracing.

"*N*, *I-N*," says Nathan who is standing nearby, waiting for a turn at the easel.

"*I*—" I begin again.

Deborah pauses, brush in air, and turns to Nathan to inform him that I am the giver of spellings here. "Dr. Richgels—"

"Nathan is right," I interject, "*N*. After the *I* is an *N*, and then a *G*."

Deborah adds the horizontals to her I and makes a backwards n.

"How did you know that, Nathan?" I ask matter-of-factly, wanting to convey curiosity but not surprise.

"'Cause I hearded it."

"Yup. Mmm hmm."

"*I*, *N*, binto men, *N*!" Nathan chants to himself and then announces loudly, "*N*-pen!"

"And a *G*," I remind Deborah, and "Mmm hmm," I say to Nathan.

Deborah makes a vertical line and pauses, seeming to have lost her way.

"What letter are you making now?"

Deborah looks up from dipping her brush.

"After the *N* is a *G*," I clarify.

She points to what she has written so far and reads, "'No throwing.'"

"Mmm hmm."

Deborah makes a *G* over the vertical line.

"Okay, now you've got 'No throwing.' Do you think you can make the rest just by listening to the letters? And the sounds?"

Deborah waves the fingers of her left hand over her work. "I'm just going to say that. I'm just going to say—" And now, she points with the pointing finger of her left hand. "—'No throwing.'"

"That's good. Then maybe you could draw a picture or paint a picture of what you're not supposed to throw."

She takes up the pencil hanging by a string from the easel. “I wanna write my name now.”

“Okay, that’s fine.”

“After I write my name, I’ll make a little picture,” Deborah adds. With pencil, she writes BY: and below that, DEBORA, and then below that, H, even though she had plenty of room for the H after the first six letters of her name. Then, true to her plan, she paints with bold, blue strokes a smiling-faced stick figure, it’s left arm touching the first of two parallel, vertical lines, suggesting a person dropping something into a trash can.

Nathan’s painted sign is a big, green NO and a red P, another admonition against polluting.

1 + 1 = 2

The children go to gym class. Afterwards, they have partner reading, and many make up for not getting to the snack table before gym. At the snack table, the children respond to another message on a sign. The snacks are little crackers that allow having more than one, whatever number is described by the sum on the snack table sign. Today, it is 1 + 1 (see figure 8.4).

Some of the snackers begin examining the little cards with other number combinations for using with the snack tray on other days. They state the combinations and then the sums, talking over one another: “One plus eight, nine.” “One plus seven, eight.” “Five plus five, ten.”

“Those are the ones we’re not using,” I observe.

Jeff’s voice is discernable through the others: “One plus four, five; one plus six, seven; one plus seven, eight; one plus eight, nine; five plus five, ten; one plus nine, ten; two plus two, four.”

Zack brings up gym class. “Erin, you weren’t doing real good. Last time when we played kick ball, I got you on my team and you did good! That’s funny! What happened to you?”

“Maybe today’s just my bad day,” Erin answers.

Jeff continues with sums, “Two plus three is—” He hesitates.

“How do you get five?” asks one of the others.

“What?” asks Jeff.

Snack Table Rules
1. Wash your hands.
2. Use a napkin.
3. Take 1 + 1 snacks.
4. Clean up!

Figure 8.4. Snack Table Rules

"How many do we get?" asks Sarah, newly arrived.

"One plus four, five," continues Jeff. "One plus six is seven."

"Yeah, if you want," says a kindergartner about taking more than two crackers.

"But—" says another, referring to the posted limit of *1 + 1.*

"It's one plus one makes two," asserts another.

"Jeff, don't!" says Zack.

"Who said?" says Jeff.

"I'll tell the teacher," warns Zack.

Jeff demonstrates the reader's prerogative of interpretation. He says, "Why not take two more? Take two *more*."

FROM MRS. POREMBA

What would happen if my kindergartners and I were judged by the level of silence in our room? I shudder at the thought! We don't have a quiet classroom. Most often there is a buzz of conversations, deliberations, negotiations, and collaborations going on. I want these to occur. I encourage it with partners, in large and small group work and play, and in formal and informal situations. I have seen over and over that "when two or more are gathered," the potential for learning is magnified.

Literacy is a social experience, and to me this means children roll up their sleeves and do the work of reading, writing, listening, thinking, and speaking as members of a community of learners. One child's question enhances another's thinking. One child's discovery sparks another's questions. One child's thinking stretches another's ideas. Children can be amazing resources and motivators for one another when they are given the opportunity to do so.

9

TODAY, A LOT OF CHICKS HATCHED.

It is Wednesday, May 11, the 156th day of school. For days, the children have been waiting impatiently for chicks to hatch in their classroom incubator. After the kindergartners went home yesterday, several chicks hatched. The new chicks crowd the glass dome of the incubator, bumping into one another and stepping on unhatched eggs.

Immediately upon arriving, children run to the incubator. "This one, right over here, is just about ready to hatch," says Mrs. Roloff. At the outside edge of the circular floor of the incubator, egg number seventeen has a saw-toothed crack around its middle that exposes wet, yellow feathers inside. The feathers move periodically as their owner works mightily for every toehold in its struggle to free itself from the shell.

THIS ONE'S ABOUT READY TO HATCH.

Jeff, Ian, Zack, Tara G., Erin, and Sarah are already watching. "People that are close to the table, can you kneel down?" asks Mrs. Roloff. "Kneel down so we can get more people," says Mrs. Roloff. More people immediately crowd around the small table that holds the incubator.

"Ohhhh," sigh several kindergartners.

"This one's about ready to hatch over here; if you want to come over to this side of the table," Mrs. Poremba suggests.

"Ohhhh," the kindergartners say again, the whole class pressing around the table.

"Oh! Oh!" exclaims Kaitlynn, but in a softer voice than is usual for her, a voice filled with urgency.

"That little guy, that guy right there, he wants to get out," says Ian.

Kneeling with their arms resting on the table are Zack, Ian, Jeff, Kaitlynn, Tara G., Jason, and Sarah. Zack is closest, his face almost touching the incubator, a combination of anxiety and awe keeping him at a half-smile.

"Are they ready to go in the brooder box yet?" asks Ian.

"Can you see him, Eric, right here?" asks Mrs. Poremba, pointing.

Movement in egg seventeen prompts a new chorus of *Ohhhs*.

"Watch, guys! Watch him! Watch him!" exclaims Mrs. Poremba. Freddy arrives late. "Come on, Freddy. Freddy, quick! Come! Come here, Freddy!"

"He's pushing!" observes a kindergartner.

There is more simultaneous talk by many kindergartners.

"We're gonna put them in the brooder box," says Mrs. Poremba. "The fluffy ones."

"Mrs. Poremba! They're so cute!" says Kaitlynn.

One of the fluff balls climbs up on top of egg seventeen, its foot on the wet feathers that are pushing up through the crack. This causes a wave of giggles among the kindergartners until the offending chick steps back and stares through the glass of the incubator as if feeling reprimanded. Its action seems to have widened the crack in egg seventeen, and the hatching chick makes a big heave.

"He pushed the egg open!" notes Jeff.

"Look!" says Kaitlynn in her still-urgent voice.

"Jason, you have to kneel!" complains a kindergartner.

"Jason, you have to kneel, bud," echoes Mrs. Poremba. "People are behind you."

"I can't see!" exclaims a kindergartner.

Two more chicks are crowding, bumping, climbing on the hatching egg.

"He's breathing!" says a kindergartner.

"It's cracking!" says Elizabeth.

"One opened its wings!" shouts Kaitlynn, excitement overcoming urgency now.

"It's getting squishy in there," notes Jeff.

A chick has now settled into a sitting position on egg seventeen, its feet grasping a neighboring egg.

"Why is he sittin' on the egg?" asks a kindergartner.

"That's a crowded incubator this morning," explains Mrs. Poremba.

THE HALFWAY POINT

Another move by chick seventeen seems to mark a halfway point; there's almost as much of the wet, breathing, tucked-in-a-ball chick showing as there is egg shell remaining. Part of the top half of the shell has been pecked away to make the crack the children saw when they arrived today. Little pieces of shell that gave way for the crack are lying around the egg at the bottom of the incubator; and the rest of that top half of the shell is like a little cap. A neighboring chick pecks at the hatching chick.

"I see one that's really wet," says Jeff.

"Oh, I see one that's squished," says Tara G.

"That one that's already hatcht-ed is squished," says Nathan.

"We're gonna put the fluffy ones in the incubator," says Mrs. Poremba, "but there's one that just hatched about a half hour ago—"

"You mean the brooder box," corrects Ian.

"—that's not ready. The brooder box. That's what I meant."

Several kindergartners talk simultaneously about the prospect of chicks in the big, open brooder box.

"Shhh. Tomorrow will be handling day," says Mrs. Poremba. "Today, we won't be handling them."

"You mean you can only look at them when they're out?" asks Jason.

"Right. Today is a looking day and not a touching day. But tomorrow you can go to Chick-Holding School and learn how to hold a chick!"

Kindergartners cheer, "Yay!"

There has been very little movement in the outer zone of the incubator for several minutes. The hatching chick seems to be resting in its half-shell, storing up energy for its next progress. "Come on little chick!" says Mrs. Poremba. "Push! Push! Push!"

"Push! Push!" echoes a kindergartner.

"He gave up," speculates Zack. "He gave up! He gave up!"

The hatched chicks move about and one gives number seventeen a peck.

"Look-at! Now, he's eating—" says a kindergartner.

"He's trying to help," says another.

Number seventeen gives a push. We can see its head, resting on the discarded top part of the egg as if on a pillow. It lies with its face up and its wings over the edge of the bottom half of the egg, the still-in-place half.

The children talk over one another and jockey to see, in verbal and physical imitation of the hatched chicks' continued piling on each other and on number seventeen: "I was hoping they would hatch!" "Another one is starting to crack." "Why is Zack standing up?!" "Kneel down!" "I can't see!" "He's coming out!" "Come on!"

"That guy's resting, that one's resting," says Ian.

"Why don't they go on the other side?" Jason says of the crowd of chicks around and on top of number seventeen.

"I bet they wish they were still in their shells," speculates Zack.

The other chicks step back for a moment and number seventeen reappears, still resting on its back, face up, eyes shut, its wings still over the edge of the bottom half of the shell like a baby's arms lying atop its bed covers. "Don't worry, he's not giving up," counsels Ian. "He's not gonna give up!"

"How do you know?" asks a classmate.

"He wants out!" tells Mrs. Poremba.

COME ON, LITTLE CHICK!

After some squabbling over positions and an admonition from Mrs. Poremba that "we're just gonna have to be polite," the kindergartners settle into a kind of harmony around the drama taking place in front of them. One end of the little table is against the wall so that the incubator's electrical cord can be plugged in. The kindergartners are in two U-shaped rows around the other three sides of the table. The first tier of faces belong to the kneelers: Nicole, Elizabeth, Zack, Deborah, Jeff, Eric C., Jason, Lauren, Sarah, Kaitlynn, Tara J. Behind them, the ring of standers are Erin, Ian, Tara G., Elise, Nathan, Ben, Alyssa, Freddy, Mayra, Meagan, and Steven.

One of the hatched chicks assumes a guardian position over number seventeen, and Nicole speculates, "Hey, look, he's tryin' to help him." Suddenly the guardian moves off number seventeen, who pushes and turns and lifts a wing completely out of the bottom half-shell. Now, it is lying on its side. Neighboring chicks are awake and active now, jostling number seventeen even more. One stands on seventeen's head.

The kindergartners gasp and exclaim in unison. "Oh my gosh!" adds one kindergartner.

Again, comments tumble over one another: "Oh, he just looks small." "That one just got off of it." "Come on, little chick! Come on, chick!" "He's comin' out! He's comin' out!" "Come on chick!"

Kaitlynn can't contain herself. "Oh, I love these little chicks!" she says.

Tara G.'s comment is more practical. "If he just broke the bottom, he would be done," she says.

"Why don't you do it?" Sarah asks Mrs. Poremba.

"Why don't you do it?" a classmate echoes.

"You know what?" asks Mrs. Poremba. "I can't help the chick get out. That's something he or she needs to do all by himself because that's what helps him to build his muscles to help him to be healthy and strong. If we helped the chick out, then he won't have a chance to build his own muscles up, and he won't be as strong."

"I need to ask you a question," says Lauren. "What will we, what will we—"

"That guy's sleeping," observes Jeff.

"—what will we name him?" continues Lauren.

Number seventeen flutters its wings and rolls even more onto its side. The children gasp. Mrs. Poremba, speaking very quickly, answers Lauren: "Lauren, you'll have to think of a good name." Then she exclaims to number seventeen and the whole class, "Come on! He's almost out!"

"He's almost out!" echo several kindergartners. But the difference between almost out and all the way out is several more minutes.

Number seventeen makes several more moves, pushing and twisting, so that now a foot is visible up by its head, but its bottom is still in the bottom half-shell. In time, number seventeen flutters its wings, raises its head, opens its eyes. Its feathers are wet and matted, making it look like a different species from the already hatched chicks. They are yellow fluff balls on sticklike legs; seventeen is a wet, long-necked, big-eyed creature who looks like an alien from a space movie. It rests its head on egg eighteen.

There's cheering. "Yay!" "He did it!"

But seventeen's butt is still in the shell. The kindergartners make many suggestions and observations. Jeff says, "He's tryin' to sleep. He just hatched."

Sarah asks, "Why don't you just pull yourself loose?"

"Push out, little fella," urges Zack in a soft voice. "Just a little bit more! Just a little bit more! Come on, little fella!"

Erin resolves, "I'm gonna make a note for my mom to read."

Now seventeen is raising its head and looking around, making bobbing motions, perhaps novice pecking motions.

"That guy right there, he needs to take pecking school," says Ian. He doesn't think the pecking chick is doing a very hearty job.

Zack picks up on this: "Hey, Mrs. Poremba, he should go to pecking school."

"You know, Zack, teaching a chick to peck is something we don't need to do. They come into this world knowing how to peck."

Number seventeen makes another lunge. "It's coming!" says a kindergartner.

"It's cheeping!" says Erin.

"We know it's cheeping. Every chick is cheeping, Erin," scoffs Jeff.

There is much simultaneous talk.

"You guys, quiet. The chick is trying to sleep," says Zack in a quiet but pleading voice. "The chicks are trying to sleep. Quiet."

Several kindergartners join Zack's campaign by *shhh*ing their classmates. One says, "Quiet. You want the chicks to get their rest? Let the chicks get their rest."

HE'S OUT!

Despite renewed cheering on from Mrs. Poremba and the kindergartners, number seventeen seems content just to rest its head on neighboring egg eighteen and occasionally to raise its head, peck, even lunge, without making much effort to rid itself of the half-shell that's still around its bottom.

"I know you can do it, I know you can do it," a kindergartner chants in a low voice, seemingly more for his own benefit than for number seventeen's.

"We should call the, we should call the farmer and tell her these hatched today," says Kaitlynn.

"Good idea, Kaitlynn," says Mrs. Poremba.

A neighboring chick pecks at number seventeen. "He's pecking it!" says a kindergartner.

"Hey, don't eat him!" says Zack. "Don't eat him! Mrs. Poremba! That chick right there is tryin' to eat him!"

"No, you know what?" asks Mrs. Poremba. "He's probably trying to get to know him. Chicks get to know each other by pecking."

"They can't eat each other!" says Jason.

Now number seventeen swivels around and flails its legs, then pauses and looks out as if to study the sea of kindergartner faces watching it. Number seventeen now rests its head on neighboring egg fifteen, opposite the former pillow, egg eighteen.

The kindergartners decide prematurely to declare victory. "He's out!" they exclaim. "He's out!"

"Is he out of his egg?" asks Mrs. Poremba? "Oh he decided to turn over. Now he's gonna look at Sarah! Ope! Now he's goin' back the other way!"

Number seventeen, kicking and flapping, circles back to where it started and puts its head down momentarily on egg eighteen. But a neighboring chick swipes a wing at seventeen's head, seeming to give seventeen the needed final momentum. For number seventeen now fairly leaps out of the half-shell, leaving it behind against the glass of the dome as it lunges and disappears in the cloud of fluffy, yellow chicks in the center of the incubator.

Everyone cheers, "He's out!" "Yay!" "He did it!" The class applauds.

"Now, he's resting," says Ian, pointing into the center of the incubator.

"He's so tired, Ian," says Mrs. Poremba. "He's exhausted."

But seventeen is not so exhausted that it forgets its adoring audience. It stumbles back to the edge of the incubator and looks out at the kindergartners. Katilynn, Eric C., Sarah, Elizabeth, and Nicole stay, but the rest of the class scatters.

THE BROODER BOX

"Them bringing it. Them bringing the box over here," says Elizabeth, as Mrs. Poremba and the others return with the brooder box and the feeding and watering equipment. Zack, Ian, Meagan, Jason, and Jeff are carrying the box, a two-by-two-by two-feet pasteboard carton with a warming light clamped to one side. They begin to set it up in the open gold-carpet area to the left of the incubator table. Some children wander from the box to the incubator and back wanting to keep track of the chicks but not wanting to miss the brooder box installation.

Mrs. Poremba gives the water bottle to Ben and Alyssa to fill. When a kindergartner asks, "Can we each put a chick in there?" Mrs. Poremba repeats the no-handling policy for today and her Chick-Holding School announcement. "But tomorrow you get to go to Chick-Handling School. And if you can graduate from Chick-Holding School, then tomorrow you get to hold the chicks."

"Yay!" respond several kindergartners.

Erin remembers her earlier resolution to write about this momentous event. She announces, "I'm gonna go get paper so I can make a journal." She goes to the writing center and returns with paper and pencil.

Mrs. Poremba plugs in the warming light, creating a warm glow on the wood chips and sides of the brooder box. Jeff says, "It looks like, it looks like red in there."

"It looks like cheese!" declares Zack.

"It looks like fire!" counters Jeff.

"I wish I was a chick," says Zack.

"I don't!" responds Jeff. "I wouldn't be able to play!"

"When we put the chicks in the brooder box," says Mrs. Poremba, "I need you to help count because I'm not sure how many we have altogether. And then what we'll do is, we'll figure out which one of our chicks hatched, and we'll put a chick next to the egg if it hatched." Mrs. Poremba refers to a poster on the bulletin board above the incubator. On the poster, the Count from Sesame Street peers at eighteen numbered eggs. *Kinder-*

garten Hatch Count is the caption. "Yesterday in the afternoon, number seven hatched, and yesterday evening right after school, number one hatched." Those eggs on the poster have yellow, cut out chicks pinned on them. "But we have a lot more that hatched since then."

"Eighteen hatched," says a kindergartner erroneously.

"Two didn't hatch," says another.

Mrs. Poremba enlists Mrs. Roloff to guard the chicks in the incubator when the dome is removed. "Are we ready?" she asks the class. Some kindergartners want to help transfer the chicks, and Mrs. Poremba again repeats the no-touching policy for today and her announcement about Chick-Holding School. Lauren says that she already knows how to hold chicks, but Mrs. Poremba holds her to the Chick-Holding School graduation requirement.

"I know how, but I want to go to Chick-Holding School," says Eric C.

"I'm sure Nicole knows how," says Jeff. Nicole lives on a farm and brought a grown chicken to school recently for the class to see.

"Okay, help me count chicks," says Mrs. Poremba, as she makes the first transfer.

"One," say the kindergartners together. At the back of the group around the box, Ben has been waiting patiently with a clipboard and sign-in sheet. There has been no signing in today because of the excitement of the hatching, but he has chosen to do this. He has written chick on the first empty line of the sign-in sheet, and now next to that he writes a numeral for each transfer: 1 2 3 4 5 6.

"Two," say the kindergartners with the second transfer. They continue in this manner through six.

"Do we leave two in?" asks Mrs. Roloff

"Yeah, these two we're going to leave in," says Mrs. Poremba, "because they're newly hatched."

"One's tryin' to hatch," observes Zack.

"This is the best day of school—the best!" says Zack.

"Why?" asks a classmate.

"Because the chicks!" answers Zack. "But tomorrow is gonna be even better. We get to hold 'em." This prompts kindergartners' talking about Chick-Holding School.

"Can I ask my mom if she wants to come to Chick-Holding School?" asks Eric C.

"I'm gonna go." "I'm gonna come," say kindergartners.

"It's for kindergartners," answers Mrs. Poremba. "Kindergartners will be the Chick-Holding School experts. These chicks are your chicks. You're the ones to learn how to hold them. You're the ones to learn how to take care of them. They're your chicks."

"Do we get to bring them home?" asks Zack.

"No, Zack, they're gonna stay here at school, and when they get bigger, then they'll go back to the farm where all chicks love to live."

"So they're gonna stay in here until they grow up?" asks Zack.

"Well, they're gonna stay in here until they get bigger and until they get too big for the brooder box. When they're too big for the brooder box, and they start getting too crowded, and they start getting ready to fly out of the brooder box, that's when the farmer comes and takes them to the farm."

ANOTHER HATCHING

Eight kindergartners are kneeling around the brooder box. Jeff, Jason, Tara J., and Tara G. have their backs to me. The four others make a half circle of enchantment: Lauren rests her chin on her folded arms which are draped along the edge of the box, Deborah hooks her chin over the edge, Elise rests her chin on her hands that grasp the edge, and Sarah's nose just touches the edge of the box. I wouldn't have to know what's in the box to guess that it's something very special. These four faces glow with the same reflected warmth that colors the interior of the box orange; their silent gazes reflect the wonder of six new lives in the bottom of the box. Ian stands behind Elise but bent over with his hands on his knees, typical of the next tier of awestruck chick watchers who ring the brooder box: Nathan, Steven, Freddy, Mayra, and Meagan. Zack is there, too, but like Erin, who comes and goes, his interest is divided. Suddenly, he gasps and points to the incubator. He repeats his observation from earlier when Mrs. Poremba was removing empty shells from the incubator, only now much louder and more excited. "One's tryin' to hatch!" he shouts. Ian, Nathan, Steven, Elise, and Sarah stay with the brooder box, but Zack and the others hurry to the incubator, in a near stampede.

This one's a quickie. By the time the kindergartners jockey for positions around the incubator, they are shouting, "It's out! It's out!"

"We've got another hatching, boys and girls!" Mrs. Poremba announces to those who are not at the incubator. "If you want to come over and see a brand new baby chick, he's out."

"There's another chick! It's just a busy day today. There's a busy day!" shouts Zack.

ERIN WRITES ABOUT THE HATCHING.

Erin is sitting all by herself at the white table. On one side of her paper, she has recorded the numbers of the hatched eggs and on the other side, has written Dery moM Today A LAT (see figure 9.1). She says, "*Of. Uh.*" She writes A. She says, "*Uhvvvv.*"

I interrupt her, "What're you writing, Erin? 'Dear Mom, Today a lot of —'"

"*Of chicks hatched.*"

"*Chicks hatched*?" I ask.

"*Of.*"

"*Of* is—you have the beginning of *uhvvvvv*. What do you hear at the end of *uhvvvvv*?"

"V!"

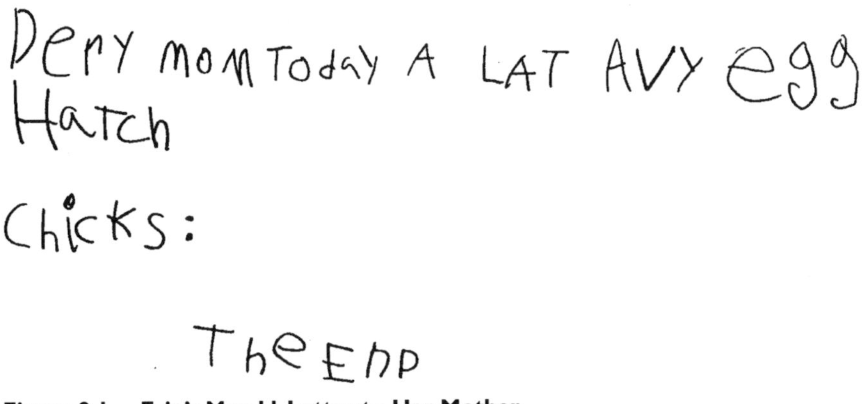
Dery momToday A LAT AVY egg Hatch

Chicks:

The EnD

Figure 9.1. Erin's May 11 Letter to Her Mother

"Yeah! You could write a *V*, and you know how to write *hatch* because it's up there on that poster." I point to the *Kindergarten Hatch Count* poster.

Erin adds a **y** at the end of **AV** for *of*, and then, pointing with her pencil, she reads what she has so far, "'Dear Mom, Today a lot of'" She continues, eventually producing the letter shown in figure 9.1. When she finishes, she shows it to Sarah, who is sitting beside her. "Look, for my mama so she can read it." She gets up and takes it to her mailbox.

Mrs. Poremba suggests that Erin write in her chick journal. Each kindergartner has a five-paged, egg-shaped booklet, each page with a picture space at the top and four lines for writing at the bottom. Already, they have used three pages to draw and write about the incubator and

Figure 9.2. Erin's May 11 Journal Entry

to record observations made by candling eggs on days seven and fourteen of their incubation. On page 4, Erin draws a chick and the two halves of its discarded egg shell (see figure 9.2).

Above her picture, Erin writes Day but doesn't write which day in the incubation process today is (it's day twenty-two). She does write this journal page's number, page 4, and on the lines below the picture, she writes Tes ceiK / TVesciT Aiv Aivv theegg, which she reads as "'The chick hatched out of the egg.'" It seems likely that when she wrote it, she meant the first word to be *this*, because of the s at the end and because she shows in her second-to-last word that she knows how to spell *the*. These two self-directed writing projects are not the last for Erin today. Before the day is over, she also writes in a booklet made of pages cut in the shape of a chick. Again, she writes with no help, inventing spellings of most words, but consulting the calendar for the word *Friday*. I can read that her message is *Dear Mom, Could you come to school on Friday?*, but she takes this piece of writing home with her before I have a chance to photocopy it.

KINDERGARTNERS' JOURNAL WRITING

Erin is not alone in her writing about today's events. Later, Mrs. Poremba asks the class, "Would you like to draw and write in your chick book? Are you ready to do that, Zack? Are you ready, Ben? Okay. Draw a picture of what it looks like when the chick hatches. And you can write 'He's so tired and wet.'" The resulting journal writing (Mulhall 1992; Strickland and Morrow 1990), only a few weeks from the end of the school year, reveals much about the kindergartners' progress as writers. Their abilities vary but these young writers, most of whom came to school in August having to work hard at writing their own names, have come to know much about forms and purposes of written language. They use many composing strategies, including applying knowledge of letter–sound relations, some independently, some with support from their teachers and classmates.

At the white and blue tables with their chick journals are Alyssa, Steven, Sarah, Erin, Meagan, Jeff, Zack, and Ben. At the orange table are Elizabeth, Tara J., Freddy, and Tara G. "Are there any special words you need?" asks Mrs. Poremba.

Nathan asks about the chick journals, "Do we have to do these?"

"Yes," says Mrs. Poremba. "We're, um, you don't have to do it right now, Nathan, but some time today we want you to draw a picture of a brand new chick hatching."

"Okay." Nathan begins his journal picture, sitting with Kaitlynn at the incubator table.

Ben shows Mrs. Poremba his picture, and she says, "Oh, he's got his shell on his bottom still, doesn't he? That happened to one of our chicks." Ben has drawn a chick with a smiling face; it's standing in an L shape with a sawtooth-edged half-shell stuck to its bottom. Beside it is a rectangle, representing the brooder box. Ben writes Wy Pit the cik / In the Bor Box, which he reads, "'We put the chick in the brooder box.'"

Jason, Lauren, and Eric C. have moved to the brooder box, where Ian has been keeping a vigil. "Hey, Mommy," Lauren calls to Mrs. Poremba and then realizes her mistake.

"It's okay," says Mrs. Poremba. "People call me mom all the time. I like that."

Mrs. Poremba points to the way the chicks have grouped themselves in the brooder box. "Four chicks plus two more chicks."

"Makes six," says Lauren.

"Makes six altogether," confirms Mrs. Poremba.

At the incubator, Kaitlynn exclaims, "One's breathing. One's breathin' in its egg! It's number thirteen!" However, there's no revival of interest by the others. Kaitlynn repeats the vowel sound in the word *the* as she writes it: "*Uh, uh, uh.*" Then she asks, "Mrs. Poremba, how do you spell—" She pauses while she recollects what word she needs next. "*—chicks*?"

Mrs. Roloff, who is nearby, answers, "See our yellow sign up there?" She indicates the big, yellow poster of chick facts that is posted across the room on the wall work bulletin board.

"Yeah."

"I think that word is on the yellow sign." Mrs. Roloff goes to the yellow sign, "Can you see it?"

Kaitlynn looks across the room, past the white and blue and orange tables full of writing classmates. She tilts her head one way and then the other. "No, I can't see it from here," she says. Then she kneels on her chair and can see, for she begins writing *chick*. She has drawn a chick's foot and below it, still in the picture space (above the lines for writing), has written IlVTHe. Now, she adds CH to this. Later, she erases all her writing but then rewrites THe. "Are you changing your mind about something?" I ask. "What did you want to write instead?"

"I was gonna write, 'The chicks hatched today and yesterday,'" says Kaitlynn.

Meanwhile, Alyssa asks me, "How do you write 'Our chicks hatcht-ed?'" She has already written Hatch Day, copied from the calendar.

"*Our*? Okay, *our* would be *O-U-R*." Alyssa begins writing. "*R*," I repeat. She has written OUr (with a backwards r). "That's *our*. And you wanted to write *chicks hatched*. *Chick* is up there on, *chicks* is up there on the yellow sign. And, Alyssa, *hatch* is right there where it says 'Hatch Count,'" I say pointing to the *Kindgergarten Hatch Count* poster. "That will help you with that part." Alyssa now adds chck Hatch.

Mrs. Poremba is helping Zack with his writing. He wants to write *A new chick came out of the egg*. She says, "A for *aye*. You use that when you write your name."

Zack writes a, with a thick scribble for the vertical part (see figure 9.3).

"Okay, but when you make your as, just make one line. Okay, aye, now let's try *new* right next to it. *Nnnnew*, *nnnnnnn*. That would be an *N* first. *N* first. Move over at the beginning of a new word. *New*."

Zack writes n.

"Do you hear anything else in *new*, Zack? *Newwwwwwwww*. Do you hear that *ew* on the end? What letter do you want to write for—"

Zack writes o.

"Okay. Now, you can move over here for *chick*. *Ch*. Can you—"

Zack writes c.

"That's right, mmm hmm. *Chi*ck."

"*K*." Zack writes k.

"*K* on the end. Excellent, mmm hmm. 'A new chick.' Now, move down here." Mrs. Poremba directs Zack to the second line in the lined writing space. "'A new, a new chick—' What do you want—"

"Came."

"*Came*. Okay. *Came*. What do you think *came* starts with?"

"*K*." Zack writes k.

"A *K*. Good for you. *Cammmmme*. *Cammmmme*. *Cammmmme*. Do you know that *mmmmm* sound? How do you write that?"

Figure 9.3. Zack's May 11 Journal Entry

"*M*." Zack writes m.

"*M*. That's right, like in *Meagan*. Okay."

"Mrs. Poremba!" says Tara G.

"I'll be right with you, Tara. I can hardly wait to see it." Now, to Zack, "'A new chick came—' Came what? What's the next word?"

"*Out*."

"*Out*? *Out*? *Ow*, *ow*."

Zack writes o.

"Uh huh. *Ou*t."

Zack writes t.

"'Out. A new chick came out—'"

"*Of*."

"*Of*! *Of*. *Uhvvv*."

"V," says Zack.

"A *V*. Okay. Put your *V* down."

Zack writes V. He now has a no ck / km ot V.

"Okay let's see, 'A new chick came—'"

Zack joins Mrs. Poremba's reading of the last two words: "'out of—'"

"—*the*," says Zack.

"*The*? Okay."

"Mrs. Poremba!" calls Jeff.

"I'll be right with you. I'm helping Zack right now."

"Can we get the principal?" Jeff continues.

Mrs. Poremba appoints a delegation of Jeff, Ian, Eric C., and Jason to go to the principal's office. She continues with Zack, "Okay, 'A new chick—' Zack, let's pay attention. What does it say? 'A new chick—' Excuse me. 'A new chick came out of—'"

"—*the*," says Zack.

"*The*. Let's try *the*."

"*T-H-E*!" calls Erin immediately and with rapid-fire delivery from across and two positions down the table.

"That's right, Erin, it's *T-H-E*. That's one of those words that you can just write the whole, all of the letters in, when you learn to write."

"I know, my brother can," Erin tells us.

Mrs. Poremba turns back to Zack. "Okay, 'A new chick came out of the—'"

"*Egg*," says Zack.

"*Egg*. You need to write *egg* right over here. What do you know about *egg*?"

"*E*?"

"Mmm hmm. Do you know what else is in the word *egg*, *guh*? Do you hear the *guh*?"

"*T*?" asks Zack.

"It's not a *T*. *E-gguh*." Mrs. Poremba reminds Zack of a classmate's last name that starts with *guh*. Then, she tells Zack, "It's a *G*, like this." Mrs. Poremba writes gg on her paper as a record and a model. "You need two of them for the word *egg*."

From across the table, Tara G. shows Mrs. Poremba that she, too, wrote *egg* (see figure 9.4).

"Yeah. Did you write *egg* in yours? Oh, you sure did."

"Okay, good job," Mrs. Poremba says to Zack as he finishes (see again figure 9.3). She begins reading, "'A new—'"

Zack takes over, "'—egg—'" He shakes his head. "I mean, '—new chick came out of the egg.'"

"Zack, that is important, and you did a good job with that!"

Zack heads for the brooder box to check on the chicks.

Tara G. is ready to present her work to Mrs. Poremba.

"Can I see it, Tara? Can you read it for me?"

Figure 9.4. Tara G.'s May 11 Journal Entry

Tara reads her entry (see figure 9.4) as, "'This is a chick when a chick is out of a egg. The end.'"

"That's wonderful." And about Tara's picture, Mrs. Poremba says, "That looks exactly like a new baby chick that just hatched. Great!" Mrs. Poremba gets up and walks around the table to monitor the other kindergartners' chick journal writing. As she passes the incubator table, Nathan says, "Mrs. Poremba, I'm ready to write."

"You're ready to write? Okay, Nathan, come on over here. We'll write together over here." She indicates the spot at the blue table where she had helped Zack. When they finish writing together, Nathan's final written message is A chk gst / Hd! As he reads it, he points with his pencil's eraser to the beginning and says, "'Ch-, ch-'"

Mrs. Poremba prompts, "'A—'"

Nathan moves on to chk and points to and reads correctly the rest of his message, "'—chick just hatched.'"

"Nathan, that's wonderful. Excellent job! Good job on your illustration, too."

Elise works all on her own, two chairs down the table from Mrs. Poremba. She draws an oval-bodied, round-headed, stick-legged, three-toed chick in profile, with one little dot eye and a big carrotlike beak, and writes I SAW A BABY Chick CAm / out of the egg.

Meagan also works on her own; her journal entry about Chick-Holding School is shown in figure 9.5. Tara J. writes 9 chicks Hach and today's date followed by an exclamation mark. She writes 11 for the date inside a daisy (as it would have been on today's calendar, though we never did wall work today).

I tell Sarah how to spell *the* and direct her attention to the chick facts and *Kindergarten Hatch Count* posters for *chicks* and *hatched*. She writes The chicks Ha before becoming distracted. She looks down the table at Mrs. Poremba and Nathan, wags her pencil, transfers her pencil to her left hand, and makes big waving motions with her left arm. Then she watches Eric C. at the flannel board, where he is one of a succession of kindergartners today to play with the components of a flannel board version of Eric Carle's *The Very Hungry Caterpillar* (1992) (see chapter 3). She drops her pencil, picks it up from the floor with her right hand, and now watches Ben and Deborah playing in the Housekeeping Center. These distractions fill a

Figure 9.5. Meagan's May 11 Journal Entry

whole two minutes and ten seconds. Then, unprompted, Sarah returns to writing. In twenty seconds, she finishes her writing, looking up to the *Kindergarten Hatch Count* poster, looking down to write another letter, wagging her pencil, looking back to the poster, until she has added Tch to her message. It is now The chicks HaTch, which she reads to Mrs. Poremba: "'The chicks hatched.'"

Freddy writes May 11 / DAy 22 and TeH chicks Teh / EGSOK-DiD. Only the last word is audible as Freddy reads to Mrs. Poremba: "'—exhausted.'" Mrs. Roloff, who was at the same table as Elizabeth, Freddy, and Tara G., later told me that Tara gave Freddy suggestions for the spelling of *exhausted*, but that he didn't give much credence to her input.

"That's a big word, *exhausted*!" says Mrs. Poremba. Later, when Freddy reads his first sentence to me, he decides that he doesn't need the second Teh, and he changes his message to TeH • chick • is / EGSOKDiD. He adds NOW thAt tehchcick / is ReDDy / TO fly / teh eND.

Other kindergartners' journal entries include Jason's NOW tHE • CHICK • / IS COMING / Ot Of tHE EGGS / byJASON (with a backwards y and a backwards J); Ian's HAC DAY / DAy 22; Eric C.'s FInAlly the Shell / breAKSIn two / PIeces Anb the / chICK hAtcNes (with backwards ns, a backwards y, and a backwards d, and with ts that have up-curved tails at the bottom like those in the type font of a book), which he copied from *Inside an Egg* (Johnson 1982); Lauren's There was chicks / HatchinG iN our / CLASS room (with a backwards a in was); Steven's ThE chick HE; and Deborah's There yasz chicks HatchiNG / At [school's name] SSCHOOL Thechicks / r SLepiNG iN The BrOOder / BOX.

Steven reads his entry as "'The chick hatched.'" Mrs. Poremba had helped him with the first sound in *hatched.* As she had walked among the journal writers, she noticed Steven breathing into his hand and saying, "*Huh, huh, huh.*"

"Are you wondering about that *huh* sound?" she asked as she, too, held her hand before her mouth to catch the breath from the *H* sound. "That's an *H*."

Deborah had copied *chick* from the chick facts poster and *hatch* from her neighbor Lauren's writing. I helped her to listen to and decide on spellings for the beginning sound in *there*, the beginning *sl* blend in *sleep*, the end sound in *chicks*, and all the sounds in *was*, *at*, and *are*. I showed Deborah a source stamped inside a reading center book for copying the school's name. She copied BrOOder BOX from the sign on the brooder box. She knew how to write without help *the*, *in*, and *-eep* in *sleep*. I told her how to spell *ere* in *there* and *ing* in *hatching*.

In a hushed voice, because by then Mrs. Poremba was reading a book to the rest of the class, and to the accompaniment of cheeping chicks, Deborah read her entry to me: "'There was chicks hatching at __________School. The chicks are sleeping in the brooder box.'" (Deborah named the school where I have used a blank.)

CHICK-HOLDING SCHOOL

When the kindergartners arrive the next day, there is some disagreement about Chick-Holding School. "We get to, I'm gonna go to Chick School," says Erin.

"We are!" "You are, Erin!" exclaim several kindergartners.

"What?"

"You *are* at the Chick School," says Kaitlynn.

Kindergartners argue: "No, we aren't!" "Yeah, we are!"

"We are not in Chick-Holding School yet!" Sarah says to Kaitlynn, holding her hands out, palms up, and shaking her head.

"We will in this classroom," says Jason.

At the brooder box, Elizabeth asks, "Are you gonna take the sign off?" She refers to two *No touch, yes look* signs—similar to Freddy's for his robin egg (see chapter 3)—that Nicole and Steven had written and posted on the brooder box yesterday.

"No, for today. Not 'til we go to Chick-Holding School," answers Mrs. Roloff.

Jeff has a theory about the chicks: "They probably think we're giants!"

SIGNING UP

Meanwhile, two kindergartners have news: "You have to sign up over there." "You have to write your name over there."

Jason says, "I'm going to ask who wants to and who doesn't want to go to Chick School." He writes his name first at the top of a chick-shaped piece of paper (see figure 9.6). Then, he approaches Elise at the brooder box and taps her on the shoulder, holding his sign-up sheet behind his back. He asks her a question. When she nods yes, he pulls the sign-up sheet from behind his back, explains its purpose, and leads a smiling Elise to the incubator table.

"Put your name on this?" asks Elise, amid the shouting of a math game going at full throttle next to them.

"It'll be who does and who doesn't," explains Jason.

Elise signs about a third of the way down from Jason's signature.

Jason moves on, into the crowd playing the math game at the chalkboard. But they don't look like likely prospects, and so he moves back toward the brooder box where Sarah is kneeling next to Elise. Jason says, "Sarah, you want to go to Chick-Holding School?" She turns away from the chicks. Elise points to Jason's sign-up list. Jason asks, "Sarah, do you want to?"

Sarah indicates that she does.

"Then write your name," says Elise, "right on—"

Figure 9.6. Jason's Chick-Holding School Sign-up Sheet

Jeff has been looking on from his perch on the radiator next to the brooder box. "Do we have to sign our name?" he asks.

"Yes—" Jason answers, as Sarah writes her name about two-thirds of the way down the sheet.

"Come on! Let me write my name!" says Jeff. And Jason has a winner. The rush is on!

"—so we know who wants to go—" Jason is explaining.

"I'm after Jeff!" says a kindergartner.

"I'm after—" says another.

"Okay! It doesn't make a difference—" declares Jason as Zack, Ben, Eric C., and Meagan gather around.

"Then me." "I'll go last." "I'm next!" "I know." "I'm after Zack." "I'm after Meagan."

"Ben, you want to go to Chick-Holding School?" asks Jason.

"Hey, Chick-Holding School!" Jeff announces, and many more kindergartners arrive.

The number of kindergartners playing the math game diminishes as they crowd around Jason for his sign-up. And at the brooder box are those who've already signed. "This clears it so we can see!" exults Zack as he kneels up to the brooder box. And in the sincerest form of flattery, Erin is busy preparing her own sign-up sheet.

As the sign-up proceeds, Mrs. Poremba stops at the incubator table just long enough to say, "Jason, are you handling the sign-up for Chick-Holding School?"

Jason nods, with an eye at the waiting line.

"Thank you," says Mrs. Poremba.

When it's her turn, Elizabeth turns the paper ninety degrees and writes her name along the right side of the right column of names, from bottom to top, EliZABETH (see figure 9.6).

Meanwhile, Erin approaches Jason with her sign-up list. "Jason, sign up!" she says.

"I don't think we need two. I'm not signin' up to yours."

But Jason does sign on Erin's list. After she moves on, he says, "Why is Erin makin' one?" To me, Jason observes, "Elizabeth writed hers sideways."

"Okay," I say.

Elizabeth is still writing. "I *want* to!" she declares, causing Jason to look down at her and cringe at the same time.

"Oh, you want to," he says in a conciliatory voice. With a shrug, a smile, and a look back to me, he says, "That's okay."

At the brooder box, Jeff raises the earlier question, "Where is Chick-Holding School anyway? Where *is* Chick-Holding School?"

"Where is it gonna be? Probably right here around the chicks," answers Mrs. Roloff.

A kindergartner jokes, "People-Holding School! The chicks have to go to People-Holding School!"

In the end, every kindergartner but Tara J. signs Jason's sign-up list, though the four names on the back seem to have been written by one person (see figure 9.6), and everyone signs Erin's. Jason and Erin sign their own and the other's.

CHICK-HANDLING RULES

After wall work, the kindergartners sit in a Headline News Circle, and I solicit ideas about chick holding.

"Not dropping 'em on the floor," suggests Eric C., "or stepping on them."

Zack offers, "Um, if you're gonna hold 'em, don't like squeeze 'em or like, um, let 'em walk anywhere where they'd fall off."

And Deborah says, "You gotta be gentle with chicks."

"Boys and girls," says Mrs. Poremba in a very quiet, serious voice, "you have told us some very important things that you know about chicks. I'm glad that you know that chicks are living things. They are not toys. They are different from your stuffed animals at home. They have to be treated—"

"Very different," says Kaitlynn in a serious voice.

"—with respect and gentle, loving care. And that's something you will learn about today. Let me show you our Chick-Holding School rules" (see figure 9.7). Mrs. Poremba displays the rules on the easel.

After some time "just to look," Kaitlynn announces, "I've read one thing: 'Wash your hands.'"

Mrs. Poremba calls on Zack, who reads as he points one word at a time with a ruler to rule number one: "'Wash your hands.'"

"Zack, thank you so much for reading that. That's the very first thing you need to do."

Zack points and reads again, "'Wash your hands.'"

Chick Holding School
1. Wash your hands.
2. Use 2 hands.
3. Be gentle!
4. Set chick in brooder box.
5. Wash your hands.

Figure 9.7. Chick-Holding School Rules

Mrs. Poremba says, "You need to," and she points with her finger and reads, joined by several kindergartners, "'Wash your hands.'" Mrs. Poremba and the kindergartners continue in this way with the remaining rules.

Mrs. Poremba emphasizes the reminding function of written language: "And if you're not sure what to do, where could you go to look?"

"Up there," say a few kindergartners.

"You could come right up here," agrees Mrs. Poremba, "to our Chick-Holding School rules, and this will tell you exactly what to do."

Mrs. Poremba also demonstrates the recording function of written language. She explains that the kindergartners will be called to practice all the rules. "*And* if you remember, when all of that is finished, to 'Wash your hands' again, you will be presented with—" With a flourish that causes many kindergartners to laugh, Mrs. Poremba holds up a copy of a certificate of Chick-Holding School completion. "That says, 'Kindergartner.' And I'll write your name right here. I'm going to use one of your names here to show you what it would say. I'm going to use Steven's name. It says—" Mrs. Poremba points and reads, "'Certificate!' and boy this is important. 'Kindergartner Steven is a Chick-Holding School graduate.'" She reads the date. "'Signed Mrs. Poremba!' I'm going to be watching you very carefully when you practice."

The kindergartners laugh, but Jeff tries to quiet them.

"Jeff, I'm glad you see this is serious. And if you can do it, if you practice well and follow all the rules—" Mrs. Poremba passes her hand over the rules "—you will be presented with your very own Chick-Holding School—" Mrs. Poremba points to **Certificate** at the top of the sample "'—certificate.'"

"That means you get to hold 'em any time you want?" asks Zack.

"That means that you are a graduate of Chick-Holding School; that means you know how to hold a chick; and you will be able to hold a chick when it's chick-holding time in our classroom."

"Yay!" "Yippee!" shout several kindergartners.

Mrs. Poremba holds up Jason's list. "And Jason, I thank you very much for getting a list of Chick-Holding School people who are interested. I will use your list when I call friends back to Chick-Holding School. Thank you."

"I did it, too," says Erin.

"Erin, do you have a list for me, also?"

Erin nods.

"Could you get it for me, please"

"Well, why do you need two lists?" asks Jason.

"I'll, I think I can use them both. I'll check both lists to make sure everyone's name is on it. And when I, I'll use the lists when I call friends back. Thank you, Erin and Jason." Now, Mrs. Poremba explains how the kindergartners, when they are not in Chick-Holding School, will sequence pages in individual, small booklets that tell the incubation and hatching process for a chick.

During Chick-Holding School sessions with groups of five kindergartners, Mrs. Poremba often refers to the posted rules (see again figure 9.7). She says to a group of Nicole, Tara J., Alyssa, Nathan, and Steven, "The first thing you need to do—can you check the rules to see what you need to do first?"

"'Wash your hands,'" read Nicole and Steven.

"Well, then, I think you need to go wash your hands," directs Mrs. Poremba, and the five chick-holding students go to the sink.

Nathan is the first one back from the sink. He stops before the rules and studies them, pointing with big downward swings of his arm as he reads to himself. Steven joins him.

"We have a few more friends who are washing hands," says Mrs. Poremba. "While we're waiting, could you come up to the rules and read what you need to do next? Rule number two."

She points and Steven reads, "'Use two hands.'"

Everyone practices the chick-holding rules using a pretend chick made of tissue paper, and everyone earns a certificate.

HOLDING THE CHICKS

At free-choice time, Mayra and Kaitlynn are the first to try holding a real chick. Mayra is kneeling at the brooder box and reaching in; Kaitlynn is standing and bending into the box. The box's orange glow illuminates their faces.

"Kaitlynn, you need to get down," directs Mrs. Poremba. Kaitlynn shifts to a kneeling position, still reaching into the box. Mayra edges around the box, following the chick she wants to pick up, while Kaitlynn comes up with a chick in her two hands, just as the kindergartners practiced. The chick is cheeping loudly and regularly. "Sit down on the carpet, Kaitlynn." Kaitlynn sits beside the box, against the radiator, holding the cheeping chick, stroking it with her thumbs. Kaitlynn's torso and head are very still, her face looks very serious. She seems to be holding her breath. For once, she is speechless. Mrs. Poremba continues her cheerleading: "There we go! Beautiful! Oh, Kaitlynn, you're doing beautifully! Oh, Kaitlynn, you're doing so w—"

Meanwhile, Mayra is edging back around the box, still chasing her target chick. Finally, still kneeling over the glowing box, her face in profile, she opens her mouth in a gasp that tells she has picked up her chick. Over the edge of the box come her hands and her chick, its feet extending straight out between her hands. She swings into a sitting position, her eyes and mouth smiling in delight. Then she, too, seems to hold her breath, but she holds her chick closer to her face than Kaitlynn does, examining it at close range.

Now, Kaitlynn swings into a kneeling position and lifts her chick back into the box. She stands, her legs apart, her bottom in the air, as she bends way into the box in order to set the chick all the way down onto the floor of the box. Now, she straightens and breathes and speaks: "I just did it very well! I did it so well!" She holds her hands before her, palms up, as she heads for the sink to wash them. Mayra continues holding her chick, while Lauren comes to the box, shaking her just-washed hands. Lauren barely has a chick out of the box when Kaitlynn returns for a repeat! It's as if she had shortened her first trial in order to get it successfully done and now is confident and ready for more.

Then the crowd descends! Chick-Holding School gives way to chick holding. Each kindergartner makes personal contact with a chick. Kaitlynn is already making adjustments to the standard Chick-Holding School protocol. She shifts her second chick around so that it is facing her in her cupped hands, its feet extended toward her. She rubs under its chin with her index finger. The intimacy thus established is shattered when Kaitlynn's index finger accidently pokes the chick in the eye.

Nicole retreats to the white table where she sits in a chair with her chick and releases it momentarily into her lap. Ian's chick seems supremely relaxed, draped over his bottom hand, its feet extended, while Ian's top hand barely touches the chick. Ian strokes its head with his top thumb. Tara J. holds her chick against her shirt front. An amused smile crosses her face as the chick begins to climb toward her shoulder.

Zack, who has come to school with a self-inflicted haircut that has left a big chunk of hair missing from over his forehead, holds his chick in the prescribed two-handed way while he lifts a forearm up to wipe his eye and nose. "Do we get to hold 'em everyday?" he asks Mrs. Poremba. When she indicates yes, he smiles broadly and says, "Cool, we get to hold 'em everyday!"

"They're so cute!" coos Kaitlynn, as she returns her second chick to the brooder box.

"Aren't they wonderful?" responds Mrs. Poremba.

"Yeah, they're so wonderful!" Kaitlynn echoes, still with her cooing voice.

Zack remarks about Eric C.'s chick's feet. Eric's chick is one of the many whose feet are sticking straight out between the holder's hands, often as if the chick is groping in panic for contact again with the ground.

That would be a fair interpretation in this case, anyway. "Ra, ra! Look at my feet! My stinky feet!" Eric says, swinging his chick from side to side.

"He's scared," says Zack about his own chick. "He doesn't know us."

Deborah has a different notion about her chick: "Mrs. Poremba, mine likes me!"

"Oh, sure it does," Mrs. Poremba responds.

"Jason, you graduated from Chick-Holding School," says Mrs. Poremba. "You're welcome to come and hold a chick."

Jason seems leery. He is kneeling next to the brooder box, and there are two free chicks inside, but he doesn't connect with one. "That one is too jumpy," he says.

"I told you they're jumpy and wiggly, aren't they?" responds Mrs. Poremba.

Steven is sitting on the radiator next to the brooder box. A chick sits calmly in his hands, which are resting on the edge of the box.

"I want this one," says Jason, but Steven isn't ready to give it up. Jason has one later, though, when he's involved in a chick transfer to Jeff.

"Can you take that one from Jason?" Mrs. Poremba asks. "Two hands. Go ahead." The transfer must have been less than perfect, even with usually brave Jeff, for Mrs. Poremba adds, "The first time you do it, it gets a little scary."

Ben is rewarded for being the quietest, stillest chick holder. "Ben," says Mrs. Poremba, "I think your chick is going to fall asleep right in your hand. Oh, Ben! He's so comfortable, isn't it?"

Several kindergartners respond with a claim for the salubrious effects of their own chick-holding techniques. One says, "My chick is comfortable!"

"Quiet!" directs a kindergartner. "They might want to go to sleep!"

"You know, boys and girls," says Mrs. Poremba, "this was the chicks' first time ever being held for very long by a person. You're the first one—"

"The farmer!" protests a kindergartner.

"Well, were they held by the farmer?"

"No, but the egg—" The remainder of this is lost as many kindergartners talk at once.

"Well, the egg was, that's true," concedes Mrs. Poremba.

Nicole is not concerned about confessing a violation of Chick-Holding School rules: "Mrs. Poremba!" she calls. "I'm so proud. One time I put him down on my back, and he laid right there! He liked me so much."

Jeff laughs about his chick: "He likes the new view here! I'm not even stroking him, and he likes it!" Later, he admonishes a classmate: "Don't squeeze him, Mayra!"

"I have a cat!" says one kindergartner, initiating one of those odd, disjointed conversational exchanges that seem to lack sense but are accepted by kindergartners.

"He's a dalmatian chick," responds another kindergartner about the chick she's holding.

"Dalmatian?" asks the first kindergartner, with good reason, for none of the chicks is spotted, much less black and white.

"Yeah, like Goldilocks."

"Little guy, little doll, little doll."

HOW COULD WE READ IT?

Mrs. Poremba tells that it's almost time for the buses to come and that kindergartners holding chicks must return them to the brooder box and wash their hands. As the kindergartners stand in line to go home, she tells about what is in their school–home–school envelopes: "You'll find your Chick-Holding School certificate. You'll also find a list of our Chick-Holding School rules. Please read your rules with mom and dad so they know what the rules are. Also, you have your *How a Chick Hatches* book. Sit down and read it with your mom and dad—"

"I can't read it!" protests Jason. "You didn't read it to us!"

"Jas, could you listen, please?"

"How could we read it?" Jason asks quietly.

"You can read it by looking at the pictures, and you can tell the story of how a chick hatches. You could look at the words, or you could look at the pictures, or look at both to tell the story—"

"'Cause I can't read that book," continues Jason. "It's too hard."

"Well, what could you do then, Jason?"

Jason has no answer.

"Could you look at the pictures to tell the story? Okay? Mom could also read the words for you, or Dad could. Okay? Those are good things to do. You ready, Ian? Your mom's picking you up today?" They sing the

Good-Bye Song, with *Cheep, cheep, cheep! Cheep, cheep, cheep!* at the end instead of *Everyone! Everyone!*

"We could say, *Pet, pet, pet. Pet, pet, pet,*" sings Kaitlynn.

"Well, that would be another good word to use," responds Mrs. Poremba.

"*Hatch, hatch, hatch*!" suggests another kindergartner.

A NEW SIGN

The next day, Friday, May 13, the 158th day of school, a kindergartner reads one of the two *No touch, yes look* signs that are still on the brooder box from before Chick-Holding School: "Oh, man! 'No touch.'" Each sign has **no** with a drawing of hands and **yes** with a drawing of eyes.

"You can touch," asserts another kindergartner.

When Kaitlynn arrives at the box with clean hands, she says, "We should make a new sign: *Yes touch, yes look.*"

Mrs. Poremba looks at Kaitlynn with appreciation. "That would be a good sign to make, Kaitlynn." She nods and smiles, "Why don't you go to the Writing Center and make it for us?"

Kaitlynn springs up and heads immediately to the Writing Center where she makes a sign by writing **yes** twice (with backwards **y**s), one above the other, and **K** (for Kaitlynn?) to the left of the bottom **yes**. Beside the top **yes** is a very primitive drawing of a hand, merely a blob with some bumps on one side for fingers; beside the bottom **yes** are two eyes, circular and with distinct pupils in their centers.

During today's first session of chick holding, Jeff asks, in a quiet voice, "Why are they so afraid? They got picked up yesterday."

"Really," agrees Tara G.

"They probably don't remember us," suggests Sarah.

"Yeah," agrees a kindergartner.

"Because we're wearing different clothes," continues Sarah.

Everyone laughs.

"They can't, chicks are not smart enough," suggests Tara.

"Well, they have a brain," says Jeff.

"Well, they're not as smart enough as us," clarifies Tara.

"I know. They're not in kindergarten," agrees Jeff.

FROM MRS. POREMBA

I have been incubating and hatching chicks for years. The procedures are basically the same every spring, yet I always find the experience incredibly stirring. I am filled with wonder year after year. What is it that inspires, excites, and refreshes me? In a word—children. It is an awesome thing to look into the eyes of a child who is head-over-heels engaged in learning. It is a privilege to support and nurture children as their minds, hands, and hearts converge simultaneously.

Consider the chick-hatching experience. I believe it is significant that in the midst of all that exuberance, children seek out opportunities to read and write. They make protective signs for their chicks, write birth announcements to take home to their mothers, register classmates for Chick-Holding School, and draw and write about the miracles they witnessed. Literacy seeps in, and it is welcomed.

As I reflect on the memorable year recounted in this book, a year spent with amazing children who bloomed where they were planted in kindergarten, I am reminded of how much I learned from them. It was on their watch that I did some blooming of my own. They left an indelible mark on me as a teacher and fellow learner. I thank my kindergartners for being such astute teachers.

10

THE LAST DAY

It's Wednesday, June 8, the 175th and last day of school. At free-choice time at the beginning of the day, some kindergartners are enjoying for the last time their favorite activities. "We'll play with our favorite things," says Jeff. Others are taking advantage of their last chance to explore puzzles and math toys that they have neglected lately or never used all year. Deborah and Nicole are at the Writing Center. Deborah has made a card: TAKi YOU / MSiS / ROLLOFF / FORTETING / Me. She reads it to me, "'Thank you, Mrs. Roloff, for teaching me.'" She makes a stenciled heart on the card.

FAVORITE THINGS

Freddy, Ian, Steven, Tara G., and Ben are at the green table with a balance scale. Ian fills one pan with little, three-dimensional, plastic bears from one of the math tool cart bins. Freddy tries to balance these by filling the other pan with flat, see-through, plastic bears from another bin. These don't weigh enough to tip the scales. Sarah, Elise, Erin, Meagan, Tara J., and Alyssa are at the orange table making designs by filling a tray with multicolored plastic tiles of different geometric shapes. The kindergartners call these *pattern blocks*. Eric and Zack are on the gold carpet with an alphabet puzzle. On the carpet by the wall work bulletin board are several small groups. Mrs. Roloff reads a book to Mayra. Jason, Nathan, and Jeff assemble a structure of interlocking slanted tubes through which marbles roll, taking a circuitous route from the top of the structure to the bottom. Ben joins them.

Elise and Tara G. leave the pattern blocks to play with a magnet kit. Lauren moves from the marble-in-tube group to the balance-scales group. Others stroll from place to place, including Kaitlynn. She is dressed in bright-pink-and-yellow-flowered, bib-fronted, short-panted overalls over a yellow T-shirt. She wears a floppy cloth hat that matches the overalls. She leads Mrs. Poremba to the birthday song displayed with word cards in the pocket chart on the wall work bulletin board. Katilynn jumps up and down as she tells Mrs. Poremba something important. Mrs. Poremba hugs Kaitlynn. Kaitlynn continues talking, smiling in excitement, shifting her weight back and forth from one leg to another, clasping and unclasping her hands. Mrs. Poremba listens intently, bending forward, her hands on her knees. They talk head-to-head about Kaitlynn's important news. Today is Kaitlynn's birthday. She is six years old on the last day of kindergarten.

Ben, Jason, Jeff, Nathan, Ian, and Steven chase a big fly around the room. They swing pasteboard building blocks from the block center at it. Finally they shoo it out the door with the big atlas from the Reading Center.

SOME OF THE SIGNING WE LEARNED THIS YEAR

To bring the kindergartners together for wall work, Mrs. Poremba leads them in singing—and, as they often did during the school year, signing—the Come Sit Down song. This suggests a good last-day activity. "I was thinking about some of the signing we learned this year," she says, "and I was wondering if somebody would like to show us the signs that you learned and shared. Who can remember?"

The kindergartners recall and demonstrate many: Ben, the *Please sit down* sign; Tara J., *Good morning*; Jason, *apple* and *bear* (these were the shapes for the dates of the September calendar, repeated in an A-B pattern—apple, bear, apple, bear, apple, bear); Freddy, *Thank you*; and Ben, *on the ground*. Another kindergartner demonstrates the sign for *I love you*, and Mrs. Poremba leads the kindergartners in signing the days of the week. When she quizzes the class about their special classes, Ian remembers the sign for *art*, Deborah and Steven *music*, Zack *gym*. As Mrs. Poremba says the words, the class continues with signs for *library story*, *yes*, and *no*. Freddy looks in a reference book of signs for the numbers, *one* through *ten*, which Mrs. Poremba then demonstrates.

THE 175TH STRAW

Wall work today is punctuated with lasts. As birthday girl, Kaitlynn puts the last straw in the straw cup. It is the 175th straw. Mrs. Poremba asks, "When you started school, way back in August, when we put up that number *1*, did you ever think we'd get to a hundred and seventy-five?"

"No." "Yeah," answer several kindergartners.

"That's a lot of numbers," observes Mrs. Poremba.

"I thought we were going to get up to a hundred and seventy-seven," says Deborah.

"Well, you were very close," responds Mrs. Poremba. " A hundred and seventy-five would be very close to that."

"I thought it was going to be a million!" "I thought it was going to be a thousand!" "I thought infinity!" shout three kindergartners.

Kaitlynn writes 175 on the number line. As children grow talkative, first one kindergartner and then another try a new version of Mrs. Poremba's quieting routine: "One, two, three: *First-grade* check time!"

CALENDAR

The calendar has two red stars displaying the dates *1* and *2* in the Wednesday and Thursday spots of the first row, two white stars displaying *3* and *4* in the Friday and Saturday spots, two pink stars displaying *5* and *6* in the Sunday and Monday spots of the second row, and one green star with a *7* in the Tuesday spot. "We need to put up the last number of our calendar," announces Mrs. Poremba. Jeff is horsing around with Ben near the back of the group. "Jeffrey, you need your eyes right up here," Mrs. Poremba directs. Then she asks, "Jeff, do you know how to figure out what day of the week it is today?"

Jeff immediately answers, "Wednesday." When Mrs. Poremba asks him how he figured that out, Jeff reveals a different method from what the kindergartners have been doing all year. Since September, they have followed Mrs. Poremba's directions to "take an elevator ride," following the column in which the new date is displayed up to the day-of-the-week card at the top of the column. Jeff uses the row in which today's date will be displayed, not the column. Recall the second row of the calendar has two pink stars and then one green star with *5*, *6*, and *7* in the Sunday, Monday, and Tuesday spots.

"What did you look at?" asks Mrs. Poremba.

"The green right there." Jeff points from his place at the back of the group.

"You looked at this star?" Mrs. Poremba interprets, pointing to the green *7* star in the Tuesday spot.

"Yes."

Mrs. Poremba is leaning toward Jeff with a look of respect and interest. She really wants to know what he was thinking. "How did that help you to know that it was Wednesday?" The other kindergartners are silent and attentive.

Jeff responds, "'Cause there's three stars."

"What?" asks a kindergartner.

"Yeah, okay," says Mrs. Poremba, and she moves her hand to the left, to the pink *5* star in the Sunday slot at the beginning of the row.

"And we started with Sunday, Monday, Tuesday." Jeff wags his pointing finger at the three stars, and Mrs. Poremba keeps up, moving her hand under each.

Mrs. Poremba smiles in recognition of Jeff's solution. "Okay." And she moves her hand to the empty spot for today, Wednesday.

"And the fourth day is Wednesday," Jeff explains in a quiet, steady voice.

Mrs. Poremba nods and says, "Thank you for explaining your thinking to me, Jeff. Thank you ver—"

"What?" asks a kindergartner.

"Jeff did a beautiful job of explaining his thinking," says Mrs. Poremba. And so she transforms the need to remind Jeff about his behavior into an opportunity for him to shine.

Mrs. Poremba had asked Jeff's participation not with the intention of tripping him up for not paying attention but with genuine confidence that he would be able to contribute. Then she stuck with him when his solution was not an obvious one, with further trust that he would be able to explain it to her and to his classmates. The other kindergartners' silent attentiveness demonstrated their sharing Mrs. Poremba's trust in Jeff. Finally, Mrs. Poremba not only accepted a solution different from the one she had trained the kindergartners all year to use, she also celebrated it.

All the children know that the number for today's date will be *8*. When Mrs. Poremba asks what color star the *8* will be on, Tara G. explains her prediction that it will be green: "Well, because red, white, and pink have two, so I figured out if there was green for yesterday, there might be a green for today."

Mrs. Poremba nods and smiles. "Interesting the way you figured that out." She removes a green star with an *8* from the envelope, holds the envelope open and upside down, and says, "Guess what, my envelope is empty!"

Kaitlynn puts the star onto the calendar, and the kindergartners recite today's date as she points to the appropriate parts of the calendar: "Today is Wednesday, June, 8," and they say the year.

Next, Mrs. Poremba asks if anyone has lost a tooth. No one has, so she will not be adding any more names to the tooth graph for June. She points to it and says, "It looks like our June tooth graph is going to stay looking like that." Not every kindergartner lost a tooth during the school year. Those who did received a special felt pouch in which to put their teeth when leaving them under their pillows for the tooth fairy. Mrs. Poremba announces, "Today, I definitely will be asking you if you need a tooth pouch. That means if you haven't been given one already, if you haven't had your name up on our tooth graph—"

Tara G. interrupts with a suggestion that shows she is aware of the important record-keeping function of writing: "If you don't know, you could always look on the tooth graphs."

As the others say the Pledge of Allegiance, Deborah crouches over the tooth graphs from the whole school year, one for each month, held together with a ring. She is following Tara's advice, checking to see whether her name is on any of the graphs.

SHAVING CREAM

After wall work time, I show the kindergartners part of an edited videotape I have made that records activities across the whole school year. Each will take home a copy, a gift from me. This video reminds them of favorite experiences. Mrs. Poremba says, "Some of you saw things on the video that made you think of something you wanted to do."

"Shaving cream!" "Shaving cream!" answer several kindergartners.

"We don't have our paint shirts," says Mrs. Poremba. The kindergartners have already taken those home for the end of the year.

"Ohhh!" "Ohhh!" moan several kindergartners.

"Well, we could do record—those record things," says a kindergartner.

"Record player art," confirms Mrs. Poremba. Record player art is created by holding different colored markers on a piece of paper as it spins on the turntable of a record player. "Well, I could put some paper out for that." And when she does so, Erin, Elise, Kaitlynn, and Lauren enjoy a reprise of that activity.

But the children are still disappointed about not getting to do the shaving cream activity. "I could put shaving cream out," says Mrs. Poremba, "but you have to be very, very careful."

"I will!" "I will!" promise the kindergartners.

"I want to do [math] cubes," Ian had said when he saw on the video the room-long snake of cubes he and several of his classmates had built on January 10. Now, as free-choice time begins, several kindergartners chant, "[Math] cubes! [Math] cubes." They get the bins containing the cubes from the math tool cart. Soon Ian, Eric, Freddy, Jason, Meagan, and Nathan have made a snake that extends almost the length of the room. "We're almost there!" one of them shouts. Jason, Freddy, and Nathan vie to be the one whose added segment will fill the eighteen-inch space before the classroom's end wall. "I've got just the right fit!" shouts Freddy, but Jason scoots in with the finishing piece. No matter. "Make another one!" Ian suggests, and now joined by Tara G., they are soon busy building a second snake beside the first. It, too, will extend the length of the room. Jeff, Zack, and Sarah join the math cube group as they begin a third snake, but it's completion is interrupted by the end of free-choice time.

Meanwhile, Mrs. Poremba squirts dabs of shaving cream on the blue and white tables and the green and yellow tables. Jason, Tara J., Deborah, Elizabeth, Erin, Kaitlynn, Alyssa, Ben, Nathan, Steven, Elise, Tara G., Meagan, Sarah, and Lauren have a ball spreading the shaving cream over the tables and writing and drawing in it with their hands and fingers.

Another remembered favorite activity is color mixing. Mrs. Roloff sets up egg cartons filled with water. To three compartments of each carton she adds a drop of food coloring, red, yellow, and blue. Kindergartners mix colors by transferring water from compartment to compartment with eye droppers. Steven, Mayra, Jeff, Tara G., Elise, Alyssa, and Zack choose this activity.

BEN'S WRITING AND READING

Ben, who has been in Mrs. Poremba's kindergarten only since April 25, seems to be trying to squeeze into today as many experiences as possible. Unlike most of the kindergartners, he is new to many of these experiences. He has a terrific time with the shaving cream, laughing with glee as he first pokes at and then spreads his dab around on the table before him. Then, he is off to the color mixing table. Then, with kindergartners clamoring around him as they build the math cube snakes, he kneels on the floor and leans on his elbows to write a story in one of the dinosaur story folders that were so popular with his classmates in March. He has chosen a folder with a picture of a white-coated scientist in the foreground and a dinosaur skeleton display in the background, a worker kneeling under the arch of the dinosaur's spine and adjusting a leg bone. Ben writes, quickly and purposefully, after *Once upon a time,* Ben / Thr wos a / siyct TisT / sos Biy The / wos a DiN / assr (with backwards ys). He writes By (also with a backwards y) at the end, but he has already written Ben on the top line, so he stops with that. Ben is in a hurry. He barely lingers long enough to read his story to me ("'Once upon a time there was a scientist. Close by there was a dinosaur.'") before heading to the Housekeeping Center for one last episode of playing pizza restaurant.

As free-choice time draws to a close, Ben sits in the blue chair, his right foot dangling fifteen inches above the floor, his left ankle propped on his right knee, a book in his lap. He wants the experience of doing as he has seen several of the kindergartners do in the last month of school, of reading a favorite book to his classmates. He begins reading even before all the kindergartners have settled on the carpet before him. He reads with ease but often forgets to show the pictures.

"Ben, you're supposed to show every picture," Zack advises.

Soon the game of catching and reminding Ben about showing the pictures becomes a disruption. Ben restores order with a "One-two-three. First-grade check time." The story is about littler fishes being eaten by ever bigger fishes, until in the end a really big tuna is eaten by people, in their tuna fish sandwiches. Ben reads, "'People—people eat big, big fish.'"

"That's for sure!" says a kindergartner.

Ben hops down from the blue chair, and his classmates applaud.

"Ben, you did a great job on that!" says Mrs. Poremba.

KAITLYNN'S BIRTHDAY

When there is only half an hour left in the school year, Mrs. Poremba summons the kindergartners to the wall work area, where she directs them to form a Headline News circle. "Kaitlynn," she asks, "would you like to make some introductions for us today?"

"My mom and my dog Joel."

Kaitlynn and her mother attempt to lead their golden retriever through a series of commands: "Sit." "Stay." "Lie down." But ordinary expectations apply as little to Joel as to the kindergartners. All are excited about this final pet visit (a favorite privilege of the kindergartner-of-the-week all year). Joel sometimes obeys, sometimes surprises (once with an accident; "It's the last day of school—that's okay," Mrs. Poremba says), and always produces loud exclamations from and exchanges among the kindergartners. "Oh!" "Whoah!" "Yeah!" "This dog, he's a wild one!" And rambunctious laughter.

Kaitlynn's mother and dog leave. From time to time, kindergartners remember that they have gifts for Mrs. Poremba, or their parents arrive with gifts. Now, Lauren presents a gift, and Mrs. Poremba thanks her. "This is from you? Thank you very much! Thank you!"

"Open it!" "Open it!" urge several kindergartners.

"I'll open it up later. I think we have a few other things to do," says Mrs. Poremba, but she does not miss another opportunity to teach about functions of writing.

As Mrs. Poremba writes on the bag containing Lauren's gift, Elizabeth asks, "What you writing?"

"I just wrote Lauren's name on the bag," answers Mrs. Poremba, "so I would always remember." Then she explains the contents of a Summer Learning Packet, a several-page booklet, including calendars for the summer months, with daily suggestions of things "you could do at home on that day that will help you with your learning and that will be fun for you. Let me show you the July one."

"That's when my birthday is," says Deborah.

"I wrote something you could do every day of July to help you with your learning."

"Can you tell us one?" asks a kindergartner.

For July 6, Mrs. Poremba relates, "It says, 'Go on a number hunt in your house. Write down the numbers you find.'"

Tara G. laughs. "That would be funny!"

"What number?" asks Jason, as usual wanting to be sure he understands a task beforehand and remembering that number hunts at the beginning of kindergarten were for a single featured number, as when he and his classmates went on a 9 hunt on the ninth day of school.

"I'll have my friend come over," a kindergartner plans.

"You can go on a number hunt with your friend," agrees Mrs. Poremba.

"I'll win a game of finding numbers!" exclaims Deborah.

"Hey, Mrs. Poremba," says Nathan. "I know how you could write numbers down. On your license plate."

"That's a good idea. You could find them there."

The Summer Learning Packet also includes blank calendars so kindergartners can continue their daily calendar construction, a number chart so they can remain familiar with numerals from *1* to *110*, and a rhyming-pairs game.

Finally, after many interruptions and digressions, such as the retiring gym teacher's stopping to say good-bye and my distributing presents to the kindergartners, in a day when schedule and routine often elude them, Mrs. Poremba and the kindergartners settle into a favorite routine, honoring the birthday girl. Kaitlynn's mother has returned, having traded Joel for a birthday cake. Kaitlynn is crowned with the traditional hat, a wide, construction paper headband with six cutout candle shapes standing atop it. Up until now, she has worn her floppy yellow and pink cloth hat all day. Earlier Mrs. Poremba had warned, "I think you'll need to take that off. Yeah. You won't have room on your head for your other hat, too."

And the kindergartners had compared ages. "I'm seven." "I know." "How old are you?"

"I'm almost six!" Deborah had said in her distinct voice.

"I *am* six," Tara G. had added.

"I'm five," a kindergartner had said.

"I'll be six next June," another had interjected, meaning this month.

Now Mrs. Poremba announces, "We need to move over to our birthday song." The words of the traditional *Happy Birthday* song are on word cards displayed in a pocket chart on the wall work bulletin board. Over the school year, the kindergartners have become very familiar with this text. For months now, they have vied for the privilege of putting the word cards, including the birthday person's name card, in the chart in the right order, on days when there is a birthday to celebrate. "And we need our birthday girl to come on up." Kaitlynn stands before the group, serious and quiet, her wispy, long, blonde hair winning out against the birthday headband's attempt to rein it in. Below the cutout candles atop the headband, Mrs. Poremba has written Happy Birthday, and Kaitlynn has written KAITLYNN. The letters march in uniform size across the headband, and all face in the right direction, so different from her sketchy signature of nine months ago, with its backwards *N*s. She holds a piece of birthday cake before her. Her arms are extended almost straight out, so that the piece of cake, ablaze with six lighted candles, is even with her face.

"Can we get our voices warmed up?" asks Mrs. Poremba.

The kindergartners know well what this familiar routine demands; they sing, "Mi-mi-mi-mi!"

"And we're going to sing"—Mrs. Poremba points to and reads the song's title in the top pocket of the pocket chart—"the 'Birthday Song.' Can you see the words? Okay, here we go."

Mrs. Poremba points to the words as she and the class sing the birthday song. On the last measure, Kaitlynn blows out the candles, still dead serious, and her classmates clap and cheer.

And so this busy day ends in relative calm as the kindergartners, at their familiar table places, eat birthday cake and settle into casual conversation. I catch snatches of talk: "Mmmm." "Good." "Hey, Zack." and then a motor noise, "Rrrrrrr!" "Hey, you guys don't have any blue table any more—see no *blue*." (The *blue* sign for the blue table had been a casualty of the shaving cream writing there earlier in the morning.)

"Happy birthday to us," sing a group of kindergartners.

This prompts more talk about ages. "Three quarters."

"I'm ten quarters."

"I'm older than you."

"Older than the class."

"But Elizabeth and Mayra are seven, too."

"But they're not seven and a half, so you're bigger." Elizabeth is one of the oldest in the class and one of the littlest.

Cries of "Cheese! Cheese!" echo around the room as Jason's mother takes photographs of Jason with teachers and groups of classmates.

GOOD-BYE

"Is school finished?" asks a kindergartner.

"It is," answers Mrs. Poremba. And then she announces, "As a matter of fact, you may go to your locker, and you may get your jackets and line up at the door."

Twice during the year, the Good-Bye Song has been amended—to end with *Dinosaurs! Dinosaurs!* during the dinosaur unit and with *Cheep, cheep, cheep! Cheep, cheep, cheep!* during the chick-hatching unit. Now, amid the clamor and drama of good-byes, there are more suggested substitutions: Deborah's *No more school! No more school!*, Erin's *Good-bye school! Good-bye school!*, Eric C.'s *We're in first grade! We're in first grade!*, and Nathan's *We're on vacation! We're on vacation!*

"Boys and girls," announces Mrs. Poremba. "at the end of our song, um, one of the great ideas that we got was—are you ready, Eric? We're in first grade—"

Eric joins Mrs. Poremba, "—we're in first grade."

Mrs. Poremba cues the class: "Are you ready?"

They sing together, with spirit, but then they stop in the middle of the phrase that names the next day of school. It's the sudden silence of the group's losing their place. There is no name of a day of the week posted on the Good-Bye Song poster; there is no day when they will again see all their classmates.

As she has so often all year long, Kaitlynn breaks the silence. "School's over," she intones.

Mrs. Poremba picks up with the planned refrain and is immediately joined by the full, loud group, "We're in first grade! We're in first grade!"

"Have a great summer!" says Mrs. Poremba. "And stop by and visit! When you go to your first-grade classroom, come right past our classroom, and come pay a visit. Okay? And remember to keep learning in the summer!"

Jason, one of the least confident of kindergartners in August, now lingers, seeming to envy Mayra, who gets to stay for one more half day of kindergarten this afternoon. She is helping Mrs. Roloff prepare the calendar for the afternoon class. Now, Jason takes pictures of his teachers.

His mother tells Mrs. Poremba, "It was a wonderful year! Take care."

"Can you say good-bye to Jason?" Mrs. Roloff asks Mayra.

"Good-bye, Jason," says Mayra.

Jason's voice is little: "'Bye, Mayra."

"Good-bye, Jason," I say. "You, have a good summer, and be a good first grader. I know you're going to be a terrific first grader!"

Jason is quiet and still doesn't seem ready to go.

"Jason had wonderful time," his mother says. "Good-bye, Mayra."

"Good-bye, Jason," says Mrs. Poremba. "Have a wonderful summer, okay? Good-bye, first grader. Stop by and visit!"

"'Bye, 'bye!" says Mrs. Roloff.

"'Bye!" says Mayra.

"Good-bye," Jason's mother says for him. And he leaves quietly, the last kindergartner to depart—except for Mayra.

"Oh!" says Mrs. Poremba. And to Mayra: "And you get to do this again in the afternoon!"

"Yay!" responds Mayra.

LAST WORDS

Mrs. Poremba has shared her thoughts at the end of chapters 3–9. Now, I am going to take the opportunity to have the last word (though it is tempting to let Mayra have it!). Throughout this story, I have tried to stay out of the way as much as possible, to let the kindergartners' and Mrs. Poremba's words and actions speak for themselves. I only want to add that the year chronicled here was the best learning experience of my professional life. The children and Mrs. Poremba taught me so much.

I hope this book will serve as a resource. I invite others to use the descriptions in this book in order to study responsive teaching, child-centered teaching, successful teaching. I encourage using those descriptions as examples of a not-overly-academic kindergarten curriculum and of possible transformations of usual kindergarten units (e.g., dinosaurs), usual kindergarten centers (e.g., Writing Center, Housekeeping Center), and usual kindergarten routines (e.g., calendar). Mrs. Poremba accomplished those transformations partly by especially effective talk, by facilitating true conversation, even in a large-group setting. She demonstrated what a teacher can elicit from her students by carefully chosen questions, observations, recognition, and—sometimes—silence.

Finally, I hope that I have entertained, that I have managed to communicate some of the fun of kindergarten in Mrs. Poremba's room. When the kindergartners arrived on August 30, they represented a wide range of abilities, knowledge, and skills. All experienced significant growth between then and June 8. And they did it with joy and as collaborators, not competitors. Sharing that joy, witnessing that collaboration, was a daily pleasure. Thank you, Mrs. Poremba, Mrs. Roloff, kindergartners, and parents.

REFERENCES

Arnold, Tedd. 1992. *The Signmaker's Assistant*. New York: Dial Books for Young Readers.

Baratta-Lorton, Mary. 1995. *Mathematics Their Way: An Activity Centered Mathematics Program for Early Childhood Education*. Menlo Park, Calif.: Addison-Wesley.

Benton, Michael. 1988. *Dinosaurs: An A-Z Guide*. New York: Derrydale Books.

Benton, Mike. 1991. *All about Dinosaurs*. Illustrated by Ann Winterbotham. New York: Mallard Press.

Burton, Grace M. 1992. "Using Language Arts to Promote Mathematics Learning." *Mathematics Educator* 3 (2): 6–31.

Carle, Eric. 1992. *The Very Hungry Caterpillar*. London: Mantra.

Clay, Marie. 1975. *What Did I Write?* Auckland, N.Z.: Heinemann.

Clay, Marie M. 1991. *Becoming Literate: The Construction of Inner Control*. Portsmouth, N.H.: Heinemann.

Cobb, Paul. 1991. "Reconstructing Elementary School Mathematics." *Focus on Learning Problems in Mathematics* 13 (2): 3–32.

Cohen, Daniel. 1993. *Dinosaurs*. Illustrated by Jan Zallinger. New York: Dell.

Crews, Donald. 1990. *School Bus*. New York: Scholastic Books.

Cullinan, Bernice E., Marilyn C. Scala, and Virginia C. Schroder. 1995. *Three Voices: An Invitation to Poetry across the Curriculum*. York, Maine: Stenhouse.

Dixon-Krauss, Lisbeth A. 1995. "Partner Reading and Writing: Peer Social Dialogue and the Zone of Proximal Development." *Journal of Reading Behavior* 27: 45–63.

Downing, John, and Peter Oliver. 1973–1974. "The Child's Conception of a Word. *Reading Research Quarterly* 9: 568–82.

Dyson, Anne Haas. 1990. "Symbol Makers, Symbol Weavers: How Children Link Play, Pictures and Print." *Young Children* 45 (2): 50–57.

Eastman, David. 1989. *Story of Dinosaurs*. Illustrated by J. Snyder. Mahwah, N.J.: Troll.

Ehri, Linnea C. 1975. "Word Consciousness in Readers and Prereaders. *Journal of Educational Psychology* 67: 204–12.

Fields, Marjorie V., and Deborah V. Hillstead. 1986. "Reading Begins with Scribbling." *Principal* 65 (5): 24–27.

Fisher, Bobbi. 1991. *Joyful Learning*. Portsmouth, N.H.: Heinemann.

———. 1998. *Joyful Learning in Kindergarten (Revised edition)*. Portsmouth, N.H.: Heinemann.

Harste, Jerome C., Carolyn L. Burke, and Virginia A. Woodward. 1981. *Children, Their Language and World: Initial Encounters with Print* (Final Report NIE-G-79-0132). Bloomington: Indiana University, Language Education Department.

Harste, Jerome C., Virginia A. Woodward, and Carolyn L. Burke. 1984. *Language Stories and Literacy Lessons*. Portsmouth, N.H.: Heinemann.

Hildreth, Gertrude. 1936. "Developmental Sequences in Name Writing." *Child Development* 7: 291–302.

Johnson, Sylvia A. 1982. *Inside an Egg*. Minneapolis: Lerner Publications.

Mason, Jane B., David Koepp, and Michael Chrichton. 1993. *Jurassic Park: The Movie Storybook*. New York: Price, Stern, and Sloan.

McGee, Lea M., and Donald J. Richgels. 2000. *Literacy's Beginnings: Supporting Young Readers and Writers*. 3d ed. Needham Heights, Mass.: Allyn and Bacon.

McLean, Anne. 1989. *The Bus Ride*. Glenview, Ill.: Scott Foresman.

Morris, Darrell. 1983. "Concept of Word and Phoneme Awareness in the Beginning Reader." *Research in the Teaching of English* 17: 359–73.

Mulhall, Monica. 1992. "Kinderjournals." *The Reading Teacher* 45: 738–39.

Ogle, Donna M. 1986. "K-W-L: A Teaching Model That Develops Active Reading of Expository Text. *The Reading Teacher* 39: 564–70.

Paley, Vivian. 1990. *The Boy Who Would Be a Helicopter: The Uses of Storytelling in the Classroom*. Cambridge: Harvard University Press.

Peters, David. 1989. *A Gallery of Dinosaurs and Other Early Reptiles*. New York: A. Knopf.

Rahaniotis, Angela, and Jane Brierley, eds. 1994. *It's a Big, Big World Atlas*. Illustrated by Andre Labrie. Montreal: Tormont.

Richgels, Donald J. 1995. "A Kindergarten Sign-In Procedure: A Routine in Support of Written Language Learning," in *Perspectives on Literacy Research and Practice, Forty-Fourth Yearbook of the National Reading Conference*, eds. Kathleen A. Hinchman, Donald J. Leu, and Charles K. Kinzer, 243–54. Chicago: The National Reading Conference.

Richgels, Donald J. 2002. "Informational Texts in Kindergarten." *The Reading Teacher* 55: 586–95.

Richgels, Donald J., Karla J. Poremba, and Lea M. McGee. 1996. "Kindergartners Talk about Print: Phonemic Awareness in Meaningful Contexts." *The Reading Teacher* 49: 632–42.

Robb, Laura. 1994. *Whole Language, Whole Learners: Creating a Literature-Centered Classroom*. New York: William Morrow.

Roberts, Beth. 1992. "The Evolution of the Young Child's Concept of 'Word' as a Unit of Spoken and Written Language." *Reading Research Quarterly* 27: 124–38.

Roskos, K. 1991. "An Inventory of Literate Behavior in the Pretend Play Episodes of Eight Preschoolers." *Reading Research and Instruction* 30 (3): 39–52.

Ruwe, Mike. 1989. *Ten Little Bears*. Glenview, Ill.: Scott Foresman.

Strickland, Dorothy S., and Lesley Mandel Morrow. 1990. "The Daily Journal: Using Language Experience Strategies in an Emergent Literacy Curriculum." *The Reading Teacher* 43: 422–23.

Templeton, Shane. 1980. "Young Children Invent Words: Developing Concepts of 'Wordness.'" *The Reading Teacher* 33: 454–59.

Tompkins, Gail E. 2000. *Teaching Writing: Balancing Process and Product*. Upper Saddle River, N.J.: Prentice-Hall.

Uhry, Joanna K. 1999. "Invented Spelling in Kindergarten: The Relationship with Finger-Point Reading." *Reading and Writing: An Interdisciplinary Journal* 11: 441–64.

Wells, Gordon, and Gen Ling Chang-Wells. 1992. *Constructing Knowledge Together: Classrooms as Centers of Inquiry and Literacy*. Portsmouth, N.H.: Heinemann.

ABOUT THE AUTHOR

Donald J. Richgels is a Professor in the Department of Literacy Education at Northern Illinois University, where he teaches undergraduate and graduate courses in language arts, reading, and language development. He is the coauthor, with Lea McGee, of *Literacy's Beginnings: Supporting Young Readers and Writers*. His work has appeared in *Language and Speech, Reading Research Quarterly, Journal of Reading Behavior, The Reading Teacher, Journal of Educational Research,* and *Early Childhood Research Quarterly*. His current research interests are preschool and kindergarten classroom practice and the relationship between spoken language acquisition and literacy development.